CEAC

D1218919

# THE BOBCAT
# OF NORTH AMERICA

The Northwest Bobcat is recognized as the most beautifully marked of the bobcats. It is often known as the bobcat of Lewis and Clark, who found it in the winter of 1805-06 near Ft. Clatsop, Oregon, at the mouth of the Columbia River. Reproduced from a painting by HAROLD CRAMER SMITH.

# The Bobcat of North America

Its History, Life Habits, Economic Status
and Control, with List of Currently
Recognized Subspecies

**STANLEY P. YOUNG**

## STACKPOLE BOOKS

*Lanham • Boulder • New York • London*

*with the*

WILDLIFE MANAGEMENT INSTITUTE
*Washington, D.C.*

Published by Stackpole Books
An imprint of The Rowman & Littlefield Publishing Group, Inc.
4501 Forbes Boulevard, Suite 200, Lanham, Maryland 20706
www.rowman.com

Unit A, Whitacre Mews, 26-34 Stannary Street, London SE11 4AB

Distributed by NATIONAL BOOK NETWORK

Copyright © 1958 by The Wildlife Management Institute
Reissued Stackpole Books cloth edition 2017

*All rights reserved.* No part of this book may be reproduced in any form or by any electronic or mechanical means, including information storage and retrieval systems, without written permission from the publisher, except by a reviewer who may quote passages in a review.

ISBN 978-0-8117-3721-0 (cloth : alk. paper)
ISBN 978-0-8117-6673-9 (electronic)

♾️ᵀᴹ The paper used in this publication meets the minimum requirements of American National Standard for Information Sciences—Permanence of Paper for Printed Library Materials, ANSI/NISO Z39.48-1992.

Printed in the United States of America

# DEDICATION

This book, the fourth and final on our larger North American predators, is dedicated to my wife, Nydia Marie, my son, Acker Ellsworth, and my daughter, Alice-Christine Yeager, whose devotion and loyalty surmounted all the trials and tribulations attendant with sharing the life of an impatient and, at times, misunderstanding naturalist.

# FOREWORD

In this book, the fourth concerned with North America's larger predators, I have attempted to bring together the scattered worthwhile literature on the bobcat from America's earliest colonial times to the present. As with the wolf, puma, and coyote, this has entailed a review of thousands of published records, and personal interviews with many hunters, trappers, sportsmen, stockmen, and poultrymen.

Outlined here are the results of half a century of field and faunal studies taken from the files of the U. S. Fish and Wildlife Service, including the former U. S. Biological Survey; field observations of the last forty years gathered in connection with the predator control operations; and my own field work in Canada, the United States, and Northern Mexico during more than a quarter of a century.

I hope that this volume will afford a substantial foundation for the use of future workers in furnishing a more comprehensive knowledge of that interesting North American, *Lynx rufus*.

STANLEY P. YOUNG

Washington, D. C.
July 1, 1958

# ACKNOWLEDGMENTS

My sincere thanks are extended to the large number of individuals who so kindly cooperated with me in the preparation of this monograph. Most helpful were: Dr. Remington Kellogg, Dr. David Johnson, and Dr. Henry Setzer of the U. S. National Museum; Dr. I. McT. Cowan, University of British Columbia, Vancouver, British Columbia; Dr. R. L. Peterson and S. C. Downing, of the Royal Ontario Museum, Toronto, Canada; T. Winston Mair, Chief, Canadian Wildlife Service, Ottawa, Canada; Dr. George H. Lowery, Jr., Louisiana State University, Baton Rouge, Louisiana; Dr. Kenneth L. Duke, Duke University, Durham, North Carolina; E. V. Komarek, Birdsong Plantation, Thomasville, Georgia; Wilbur M. Cramer, Pennsylvania Game Commission, Harrisburg, Pennsylvania; Valgene W. Lehmann, King Ranch, Kingsville, Texas; and the artists Paul Bransom, Dick Grossenheider, E. R. Kalmbach, Harold P. Smith, and Mrs. Bess O'M. MacMaugh for the colored plates and other illustrations.

Donald R. Progulske, while working on his Master of Science thesis on the bobcat at Virginia Polytechnic Institute, extended hearty cooperation, as did E. M. Pollack, working similarly at the University of Massachusetts.

Dr. Vincent Schultz furnished valued information on the status of the bobcat in Tennessee.

Practically all of the personnel connected with the Branch of Predator and Rodent Control of the Fish and Wildlife Service, including its Chief, Dorr D. Green, were unstinting in their help whenever it was solicited. Especially so were E. M. Mercer, Arizona; C. R. Landon, Texas; Noble E. Buell, South Dakota; Alvin E. Gray, Oklahoma; G. Hammond Hansen, Oregon; and Owen W. Morris, Utah.

W. Leslie Robinette and Weldon Robinson of the Branch

of Wildlife Research were most helpful in their critical review of the manuscript.

Regional Director Leo L. Laythe, and Assistant Paul T. Quick, Region I, of the Fish and Wildlife Service, were also most cooperative in those field studies that the writer conducted in the Pacific Northwest.

Deep appreciation is also extended to Mrs. Blanche W. Mahlman and George W. Coffey for their meticulous copy work, and to Emma M. Charters for her work on the bibliography and proof-reading the entire manuscript.

# TABLE OF CONTENTS

# LIST OF PLATES

# LIST OF FIGURES

# GRAPHS

---CHAPTER ONE---

# INTRODUCTION

THE fact that the bobcat has long been a part of North America's fauna is attested to by the fact that bone remains have been obtained from Indian ruins dating from late B.C. times to the historic. The Pecos, Jemez Cave, Pueblo Bonito, Alkali Ridge, and Mogollon Cave located in the southwestern United States have yielded numerous bone specimens.

Bobcat is the name by which the wild cats of the species *Lynx rufus* are known in most of the United States, particularly the warmer parts—West and Southwest. Though related to the puma or mountain lion, the bobcat (Plate 2) is much smaller and of somewhat different habits, especially in the choice of food. Its larger cousin, the Canada lynx (Plate 3), often called lucivee (loup-cervier), with which it is often confused, is found in the northern, more forested parts of the United States and in Canada.

During earlier pioneer days, the term catamount or cat-of-the-mountain was often applied to both the puma, (or, as it is often called, panther, or mountain lion) and the bobcat. "Catamount" may have been derived from the Spanish *gato-*

1

*monte,* meaning woods or forest cat. The economic relations of the bobcat and the Canada lynx are similar, except as forest-dwelling habits are modified by the bobcat's environment of plains and deserts in the Southwest. The bobcat is known also by such names as wild cat, bay lynx, barred bobcat, pallid bobcat, and in certain parts of Canada as *lynx bai, chat sauvage,* and *chat sauvage de la nouvelle-e cosae.* Sometimes such names as the Florida bobcat, or Bailey's bobcat are used when designating a specific race or distinguishable geographic segment of the bobcat population. The Mexicans refer to it as *gato monte,* and among the early colonial Swedes along the Delaware it was known as *katta lo* or cat lynx.

John Lawson (1718), the historian, gave one of the best colonial descriptions of the animal, stating: "This Cat is quite different from those in Europe; being more nimble and fierce, and larger; his Tail does not exceed four inches. He makes a very odd sort of Cry in the Woods, in the Night. He is spotted as the Leopard is, tho some of them are not, (which may happen, when their Furs are out of Season) he climbs a Tree very dexterously, and preys as the Panther does. . . . He takes most of his Prey by Surprize, getting up the Trees which they pass by or under, and thence leaping directly upon them. Thus he takes Deer (which he cannot catch by running) and fastens his Teeth into their Shoulders and sucks them. They run with him, till they fall down for want of strength, and become a Prey to the Enemy. Hares, Birds, and all he meets, that can conquer, he destroys. . . . They [the fur] are . . . used to line Muffs, and Coats withal, in cold Climates."

There are numerous differences between the bobcat and the Canada lynx. The Canada lynx is much larger, has longer legs (Plate 4), and much larger feet, often the size of a man's hand, and covered with woolly hair, similar to the foot of a snowshoe rabbit. In contrast, the bobcat's foot is bare, like that of the domestic cat. The lynx has a shorter tail with *black* tip, while the bobcat has a longer tail on the end of which is a black bar on its upper side. The outer edges are tipped with white hairs. This latter feature invariably holds and is most readily recognizable in identifying the animal (Fig. 1). Ears of the Canada lynx are gray with tips of black hair, while those of the bobcat are grayish white on the back and not tipped so prominently with black.

The bobcat has keen eyesight and hearing, and a good sense of smell, though the latter is not so acute as in the wolf[1] or the coyote.[2] Most of its hunting is done at night, and the

## Bobcat          Lynx

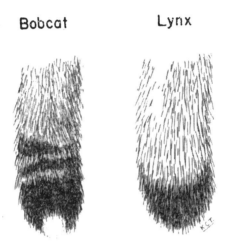

Fig. 1.   Differences in the tail markings, bobcat and Canada lynx.

animal is aided by sight and hearing rather than by scent. The advance of civilization and the use of the bobcat's former ranges for stock raising have not crowded this predator back so much as it has given it a new and satisfying provender—the young of the flocks and herds of stockmen and poultry of the farmer. Control at times becomes necessary to man's economic welfare.

It may be recalled that in pioneer days the acme of virile

---

[1] The Wolves of North America, by Stanley P. Young and Edward A. Goldman. 1944. American Wildlife Institute, Washington, D. C.

[2] The Clever Coyote, by Stanley P. Young and Hartley H. T. Jackson. 1951. The Stackpole Co., Harrisburg, Penna., and Wildlife Management Institute, Washington, D. C.

hardihood was expressed in the saying that a man "could whip his weight in wildcats." The actual performance of these small carnivores among game animals and livestock indicates that no man could survive such an ordeal should these cats use team-work.

It is recorded: "I'm from the Lightning Forks of Roaring River. I'm all man, save what is wild cat and extra lightning." This is part of the speech of one bellicose river man who was looking for a fight during the early days of the Missouri River boatman.

Similarly, the late Benjamin M. Deitz who died in New Orleans on November 18, 1951, at the reputed age of 103 years, carried the nickname of "Wildcat" from early boyhood. It was reported: "When the Union forces tried to burn his father's flour mill in Huntington, West Virginia, during the Civil War, Mr. Deitz, though a youngster, 'whipped' a half-dozen men and saved the mill. . . ." (Anonymous, Associated Press, Washington, D. C. *Evening Star,* November 19, 1951.)

Duncan Aikman (1927) in his "Calamity Jane and The Lady Wildcats" used some of the following picturesque frontier women in synonomy with the bobcat: Cattle Kate, Belle Starr, Lola Montez, Pearl Hart, Poker Alice and Kitty the Schemer. Thus through the years neither sex of the genus Homo have at times escaped being likened to the animal. What can be more expressive than "looking meaner than a cotton sack full of wildcats?" Or that "a really efficient camp cook with a disposition somewhat more amiable than a wild-cat is a treasure indeed."

The Katzenjammer Kids of cartoon fame have long been associated with this animal, and these cats have at times tended to grip the imagination of youngsters as has no other animal.

The famous peaks west of the Hudson, the Catskills, were so named by Henry Hudson, the explorer, who applied the name Kaatskill (Wildcat Creek) Mountains.

As will be discussed later, bobcats are capable of capturing and killing full-grown sheep, goats, and such game animals as deer and antelope, as well as turkeys and other domestic fowl and all game birds.

With the early settlement of North America, many European superstitions associated with the Old World lynx were brought over by the colonists and became associated with its North American cousin. As was the case with the lynx in Europe, and other animals in early Mexico, such as the puma,[1] coyote, and the wolf, the bobcat figured in pharmacopeia. For instance, certain parts of the bobcat flesh, such as the tenderloin, were eaten to cure headaches. The testes of the bobcat when held against the stomach were supposed to ease pregnancy troubles of early Guatemalans. The paws of the bobcat were presumed to aid in the suppression of abdominal cramps. Bits of bobcat fur were used as a poultice for open cuts or wounds, and its dung when smeared on certain skin eruptions such as pimples, boils, or carbuncles was presumed to cause the subsidence of these eruptions, or to hasten their secretions and eventual disappearance. Also, the fur was worn as a "stomacher, for weak and cold stomachs" (Lawson, John, 1718). It was believed by some that the urine of bobcats turned to a precious stone, and that was the reason the animal always covered the spot so no human could find it. A Mexican peon with whom I talked as late as the spring of 1917, near the Mexican border in Santa Cruz County, Arizona, told me of this. He believed the excreta of the puma (Leon) did likewise. The bobcat was presumed by some to have such keen eyesight that it could see through blocks of wood, trees, stone, or boulders, all of which aided it in hunting the rabbit and other natural prey.

The term or name "wild catting," generally associated with an unsound undertaking or one involving a certain amount of chance, brings the researcher to query: How did it originate? The story behind its coinage seems to revolve around the bank notes of an early day bank in a midwestern state which contained a picture of a "wildcat." As these notes were issued with

---

[1] The Puma, Mysterious American Cat, by Stanley P. Young and Edward A. Goldman. 1946. North American Wildlife Institute, Washington, D. C.

practically no financial backing, "wild catting" became associated with any venture or unsound enterprise involving a risk. Before the passage of the National Bank Act of 1863, many western banks also issued bank notes of little value, and hereto was appended the term "wildcat" bank. The term in later years has also been applied to oil drilling, especially in unproven oil fields, where such undertakings involve a certain amount of chance.

Lately, there has come into our shooting parlance the term "wildcat" cartridges, because the rifles "to shoot them have to be made up special by private custom riflesmiths." These are shooting arms favored for killing woodchucks and for precision target shooting (Travis, C. E., Jr., 1952: 25).

While the name "bobcat" is generally associated with the animal's abbreviated tail, its bodily motion while running also is linked to the name. When in full flight it has a bobbing motion not unlike that of a rabbit. It does not, therefore, run as smoothly or as softly as does a fox, coyote, or wolf.

———————— CHAPTER TWO ————————

## DISTRIBUTION

THE bobcat occurs in southern Canada, with the exception of Vancouver Island, British Columbia; throughout the entire United States, and southward to the Rio Mescale, Mexico, just below the 18th parallel (Fig. 2).

### Mexican Distribution

Goldman (1951) in his comprehensive biological survey of Mexico, records this mammal in the Cape region of Baja California, of the Cape Biotic District; northern and central Sonora, of the Yaqui Biotic District; northwestern Sonora, of the Yuma Desert Biotic District; southern Sonora, of the Mayo Biotic District; Coahuila, Tamaulipas, of the Chihuahua-

7

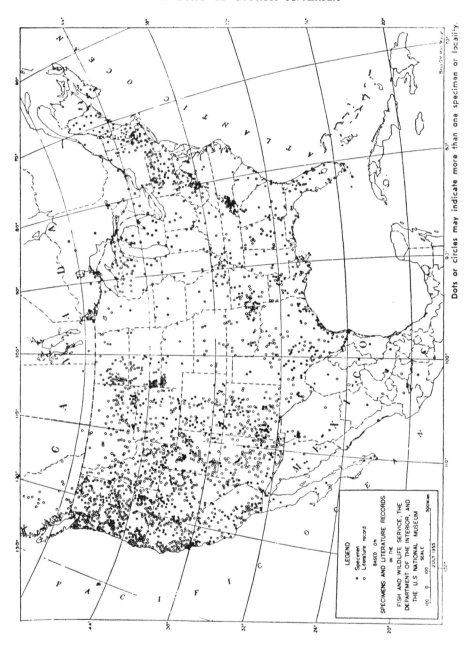

LEGEND
• Specimen
○ Literature record

BASED ON
SPECIMENS AND LITERATURE RECORDS
IN THE
FISH AND WILDLIFE SERVICE, THE
DEPARTMENT OF THE INTERIOR, AND
THE U.S. NATIONAL MUSEUM

SCALE
100    0    100    500 Miles

JULY 1955

Dots or circles may indicate more than one specimen or locality.

Coahuila Biotic District (also in Tableland Biotic District); Coahuila, Tamaulipas, of the Sierra Del Carmen Biotic District; Nuevo Leon, Tamaulipas, of the Tamaulipas Biotic Province; and Sinaloa of the Sinaloa Biotic Province.

Much of the knowledge of bobcat distribution in Mexico was based on the field work of E. A. Goldman and E. W. Nelson, conducted in all parts of that country from January 1892 to February 1906. In the course of their work 49 bobcat specimens were collected in 12 Mexican states.

## Canadian Distribution

With the notable exceptions of British Columbia and Alberta, the bobcat distribution extends northward but a short distance beyond the 50th parallel. Distribution extends farther north in the mountainous areas of the two mentioned far western provinces, but the northern portion of the treeless Canadian prairies seems to be an obstacle to the bobcat's northward penetration in the Dominion. Here the open terrain does not contain habitat to the bobcat's liking.

*British Columbia.*—Much of this province is north of the range of the bobcat, but occasionally one is recorded above the 50th parallel where the breaks of the Canadian Rockies provide suitable habitat. Records known are: One trapped by John Pauli near Strathnaver in 1942-1943; one taken by a trapper named Boyd near Alexandria in 1943-1944 (these places are on the Fraser River, the first north, the second south of Quesnel). A third was trapped 10 miles east of Quesnel during the winter of 1944-1945. A short distance to the south in the Cariboo Parklands Biotic Area the species is common,

FIG. 2. Distribution of the North American Bobcat. Dots represent 1,891 specimens in the Fish and Wildlife Service collection from 1885 (the beginning of the Biological Survey) to April 1955, from 39 states, 3 Canadian provinces, and Mexico, and 154 specimens in the National Museum collection from 30 states, 1 Canadian province, and Mexico. Circles represent 3,843 literature records in the Fish and Wildlife Service files from 1885 (many records were taken from literature previous to that date) to April 1955, from 47 states, the District of Columbia, 8 Canadian provinces, and Mexico. Dots or circles may indicate more than one specimen or locality.

and hides frequently are sold at Williams Lake (Munro, 1947).

In a communication to the author dated May 8, 1950, the Supervisor of Predator Control, W. Winston Mair, of the British Columbia Game Department, who is now chief of the Canadian Wildlife Service, states:

"Inspector W. A. H. Gill, who is the Officer Commanding 'D' Game Division, headquarters at Prince George, tells me that in January of 1949 he saw bobcat tracks twelve miles north of Prince George. He is positive of his identification. He states, however, that he has found no tracks since that time, although he looked a number of times as he hoped to put a dog onto the bobcat.

"I heard another report from our Game Warden at Quesnel. Apparently the report is genuine enough but I haven't been able to contact the trapper personally as yet so as to get an exact date. I hope that I may get more definite data this month. However, for what it is worth, in either 1944 or 1945, one Joe Gerwein killed a bobcat two miles south of 9 mile lake, or Milburn lake as it is sometimes called. This point is approximately straight west of Quesnel."

*Manitoba.*—Soper (1946) states: "It is evidently this form of bobcat *(L. r. rufus)* that was occasionally met with in southern Manitoba. I have no recent records of its occurrence. Seton (1925: 218-219) states that in 1914 it was found at Pembina, and LaRiviere, in Pembina Hills, and he also gives a record for Whitewood, Saskatchewan. Criddle (1929: 157) says that his only record for the Aweme district is based on an individual that was shot there in a tamarack swamp in 1908."

Also he continues, "In 1927 ranchers reported that a few of these animals haunted the wooded sections of Milk River and tributary coulees between Writingonstone and Police Coulee. It was said that, a few years before, two had been shot in the latter locality. Howard Taylor, of Eagle Butte, informed me that an occasional bobcat was taken in the heavy woods of Cypress Hills [Saskatchewan]. In recent years I have not succeeded in securing any further information regarding its presence in that region, nor whether it occasionally wanders north across the 49th parallel on the Missouri watershed of extreme southern Saskatchewan."

L. T. S. Norris-Elye (1951) records a subadult female taken near a creek leading out of Mud Lake (Section 35-2-15 E. P. M.) on March 16, 1951. This area is believed to contain a few more, which are reported to have come into this area within the past eight years.

Norman Criddle (1929) in his Memoirs of the Eighties, states that for the period 1883-1890, the bobcat was rare in the Aweme area of Manitoba. By 1928, he believed the animal to be extinct in this province.

S. Criddle (1929) considered the bobcat in Manitoba extremely rare, and one trapped in the northwest larch swamp in the winter of 1908 constituted his only record. This probably is referable to *uinta* Merriam.

*Ontario.*—Cross and Dymond (1929) say that the bobcat, *Lynx rufus rufus*, at one time ranged over southern Ontario as far north as Georgian Bay. It is still found in parts of its former range where habitat remains suitable. Apparently its range has shrunk with advancing civilization in southern Ontario.

In the National Museum of Canada is a 24-pound adult male taken near Baxter in Simcoe County.

*New Brunswick.*—Morris (1948) says the bobcat, or wildcat, is moderately common throughout New Brunswick. Royalties are collected on 500 to 1,000 pelts annually. From a summary of the earlier literature, Squires (1946) concluded: "It seems probable that during the last hundred years the positions of the two lynxes in our fauna have been reversed; that the Canada lynx was formerly so much the more common that it was the only one that came to the attention of many of the writers, whereas in late years it has become almost extinct in the Province while the wildcat is now abundant."

Also concerning Nova Scotia and *L. gigas*, "This larger bobcat was described from Nova Scotia and is reported to occupy parts of eastern New Brunswick. Some writers are not satisfied as to the specific identity of *L. gigas* and believe it is more liable to be a subspecies of *L. rufus* (Smith, 1940). More specimens are required before its taxonomic position or range in New Brunswick can be determined."

On February 8, 1950, Doctor Harrison Lewis, then Chief, Dominion Wildlife Service, Ottawa, told me that the bobcat was very common in New Brunswick.

In the Forks River District, Huntz County, a male adult bobcat was killed on February 11, 1935, by Victor E. Gould. This specimen, in the National Museum of Canada collection, has a length of 37½" = 953 mm.; tail length 6.5" = 165 mm.; and a hind foot (over-all leg) length of 8" = 203 mm. Also in the National Museum of Canada is a male specimen weighing 28 pounds, collected near Scotch Lake, New Brunswick, believed to be typical *L. r. gigas.*

## Habitats

The distribution and abundance of the bobcat changes with land use. To a certain extent some agricultural practices have tended to aid the animal in its survival. Certain logging operations, debrushing, and opening up of by-paths have created habitat to its liking. Thus it is found in our higher mountainous sections that are interspersed with broken canyons, open fields, and baldy ridges.

Western bobcats prefer a canyon habitat containing such trees and shrubs as pinyon, juniper, mountain-mahogany, sagebrush, and manzanita.

In the South (as in Florida) the bobcat is found in so-called Magnolia Climax Forest, a deciduous forest with weed-grown areas, and swamp areas with grassy borders. It is also very fond of the habitat created by the southern canebrakes, and to a certain extent, hummocky swamps, such as the Dismal Swamp in Virginia, and Okefenokee in Georgia; however, it is not subdued by our arid desert sections of the Southwest where suitable cover exists. Thus the bobcat may be said to inhabit a wide sweep of varying terrain.

## Altitudinal Distribution

Bobcats occur only occasionally above 6,000 feet and there

are no records above 12,000 feet. Apparently the boreal conditions of the high mountains are not suitable.

The late E. W. Nelson, while riding at the head of the Blue River in Arizona, during early fall in October, 1890, saw tracks of more than 20 bobcats while traveling through 10 miles of pine forests on the divide. Some of this area was over 9,000 feet in elevation.

David Lantz recorded an intermingling of Canada lynx and bobcat near Jefferson, in South Park, Colorado, during the summer of 1911. This area is approximately 9,000 feet above sea level.

Merritt Cary recorded bobcat tracks at an elevation of 10,500 feet on Mt. McLellan, Colorado, during June, 1915. In the same month he also found them at 7,300 feet elevation a few miles southwest of Golden, Colorado.

The writer found tracks and other signs near Canelo Pass, Arizona, at 5,300 feet; near Cimarron, New Mexico, above 7,800 feet; and near Kent, northwest Texas, at elevations varying from 4,000 to 8,200 feet. The latter elevation was in that section known as "The Bowl" in the Gaudalupe Mountains (Fig. 3.)

In the foregoing observations it is of interest to note that the terrain at those altitudes consists of broken woods, steep slopes and cliffs, and even, in Nelson's observation, the cienega or swamp, of the southwest, all of which are much preferred by the bobcat.

Paraphrasing the saying "the puma goes with the deer," it might be said "the bobcat goes with the rabbit," which is one of its favorite foods (Plates 5, 6, 7, and 8).

It is of interest to note that for the past several years there has been a tremendous increase in the bobcat population throughout most of its range. For instance, the catch in Wyoming for the fiscal year 1954 by state-federal hunters totaled 1,499 bobcats. This is the greatest number recorded for any year in the 39 years of cooperative predator control work in that State.

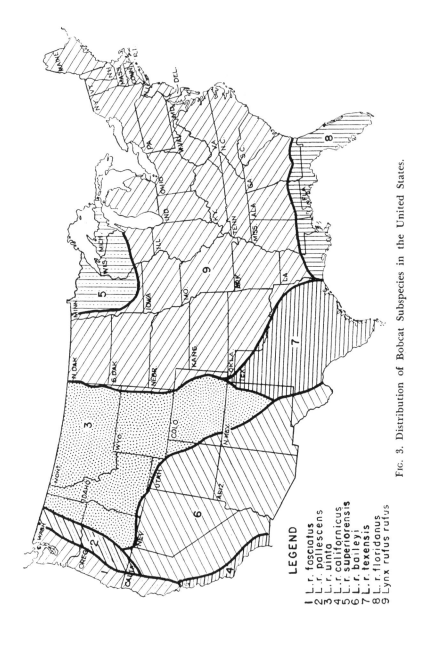

LEGEND

1 L. r. fasciatus
2 L. r. pallescens
3 L. r. uinta
4 L. r. californicus
5 L. r. superiorensis
6 L. r. baileyi
7 L. r. texensis
8 L. r. floridanus
9 Lynx rufus rufus

Fig. 3. Distribution of Bobcat Subspecies in the United States.

---CHAPTER THREE---

# HABITS AND CHARACTERISTICS

### Size and Weight

WHEN farmers, outdoorsmen, sportsmen, and conservationists meet, particularly those individuals prone to gather around the hot barrel stove of the country crossroads store, where the sign on the wall reads "Smokers and Chewers will please spit on each other and not on the stove or floor," very often the size or weight of various denizens of the wild forms the main topic of conversation. These arguments occasionally lead to betting, and if the encyclopedia does not suffice to determine the winner, then recourse is had to a State or Federal agency to settle the dispute.

Jim Hayes, of Pittsburgh, Pennsylvania, gives a bit on the lighter side of such argument in reporting in the *Pennsylvania*

*Game News* for May, 1953, from Clinton County, Pennsylvania, as follows:

"The little town of Renovo has long been famous for its wildcats—both gas well variety and the varmints with green eyes and short tempers. Lately it's been all agog over the latter kind. Seems like a report reached Jack Smythe, editor of the *Renovo Daily Record*, that a huge wildcat—varmint type—had been shot in the Trout Run area. Rumor went that the 'cat weighed 47 pounds, which would make it the biggest wildcat ever killed in those hills and maybe in all Pennsylvania.

"So, Jack had a picture taken, which he ran on page one. The caption read: 'The monster actually weighs 47 pounds (and) measures 51 inches.' This was noted by District Game Protector Charles (Chuck) Keiper, who took the critter to Cross Fork and put it on the Post Office scales. It weighed a miserable 23 pounds. 'And then,' commented Editor Smythe, 'people wonder why newspaper people become unbelieving and cynical!'

"A few days later some fellows dropped into the *Daily Record* office and the talk got around to wildcats. One of the visitors claimed the biggest wildcat ever bagged in those parts had been shot several years back by a pal of his. What's more, he'd call his pal to prove it. Another visitor supplied the 'phone number and the call was put in.

"It turned out to be a 'wrong number,' however, and a voice answered, saying, 'Saint Joseph's Convent.' Somewhat confused by this greeting, all the caller could think to say was, 'Have you killed any wildcats lately, Sister?' "

The weights of the largest bobcats known to the author are contained in Table 1.

Additional recorded weights of bobcats are as follows:

*California.*—Forty-three male California bobcats (of which the heaviest was 31 lbs.) averaged 16.4 lbs., while 36 females (of which the heaviest was 19 lbs.) averaged 11.57 lbs.

*Kentucky.*—Three male bobcats from Kentucky Woodland Refuge near Golden Pond, Kentucky, weighed 28, 23, and

Bobcat

PLATE 2. Bobcat.

Canadian Lynx

PLATE 3. Canada Lynx.

PLATE 4. Canada Lynx, shot 3 miles east of Red Rock Lakes Refuge boundary, Monida, Montana. Killed by U. S. mail carrier, Lincoln Miller.

PLATE 5. Bobcat habitat. North Dakota Bad Lands, near Medora. (Courtesy W. L. Brown, U. S. National Museum).

PLATE 6. Bobcat at bay in canebrakes of Louisiana. (Photos courtesy of Major James Brown, formerly with Department of Wildlife and Fisheries, Louisiana).

Plate 7. Typical desert bobcat habitat. Arizona, near Skull Valley.

Plate 8. Type locality of *L. r. fasciatus*, site of Lewis and Clark's Fort Clatsop, Oregon.

Plate 9. Bobcat killed on Iron Mountain, Maryland, weighing 43 lbs. and measuring 53 inches tip to tip. (Courtesy (Maryland Department of Game and Fish).

TABLE 1.

WEIGHTS OF LARGEST BOBCATS KNOWN TO AUTHOR

| State and locality | Sex | Weight (pounds) | Date killed |
|---|---|---|---|
| Arizona: 7 mi. W. of Fort Huachuca | ♂ | 44-5/16 | . . . . . . . |
| Colorado: Near Meeker | . . | 39 | Jan.-Feb. 1901 |
| Colorado: Walsenburg | ♂ | 69 | Late 1951 |
| Idaho: Deep Creek area | ♂ | 40 | Winter 1958 |
| Illinois: Sterling | . . | 40 | Spring 1950 |
| *Maryland: Iron Mt., 5 mi. E. of Cumberland | . . | 43 | Sept. 1949 |
| Nevada: Chas. Sheldon Antelope Refuge | ♂ | 59 | 1954 |
| Nevada: Churchill County | ♂ | 58½ | 1954 |
| New Hampshire: Pittsburg, Coos Co. | . . | 55 | 1925 |
| New Mexico: Hidalgo County | ♂ | 50½ | August 1943 |
| New Mexico: Hidalgo County | ♀ | 36 | August 1943 |
| New Mexico: Hidalgo County | ♂ | 56 | 1944 |
| New York: East Hill, Keene | . . | 37 | 1946 |
| Ohio: Lake County | . . | 55 | 1949 |
| West Virginia: Mill Point, Pocahontas County | . . | 35 | . . . . . . . |

* See Plate 9.

22 lbs. respectively, while two females weighed 21 and 19 lbs.

*Massachusetts.*—Pollack (1949) found the average weight of 14 adult male bobcats taken in Massachusetts to be 21 lbs.: Total length, 843.5 millimeters, tail length, 148.1; right hind foot, 172.9. Eighteen adult females averaged 13.9 lbs.: Total length, 783.9 millimeters; tail length, 137.4; right hind foot, 158.3.

*Montana.*—During the winter of 1953 the weight of 50 female bobcats killed in Montana averaged 14.6 lbs., while a like number of males averaged 19.4 lbs. The smallest female weighed 7 lbs., and the largest 20 lbs. The smallest male weighed 12 lbs., and the largest 30 lbs.

*Nebraska.*—Two male bobcats shot during January 1954, in the northwestern part of Dawes County, Nebraska, weighed 29 and 25¾ lbs., respectively.

*New Hampshire.*—In New Hampshire, Pollack found 47 male adult bobcats to average 21.2 lbs. The average measurements in millimeters were: Total length, 864.6; tail length, 155.3; right hind foot, 177.4. Thirty-four adult females averaged 15.2 lbs., and their average measurements were: Total length, 804.5; tail length, 145.2; right hind foot, 164.8. In this group the largest cat, a male, weighed 35 lbs.

*New Mexico.*—Seventy-eight male bobcats taken from all sections of New Mexico averaged 21.6 lbs. Fifty-nine females taken from the same areas averaged 20.4 lbs. The largest male weighed 26.2 lbs., and the largest female, 27.4 lbs.

*West Virginia.*—A male bobcat trapped during the winter of 1949 on Cooper's Rock State Forest, West Virginia, weighed 25 pounds. Using a deer carcass as bait, C. T. Music, resident wildlife manager, caught a 32-lb. male bobcat at Dagway on the Forks, in the same State, during the winter of 1949.

The average weight for the mature bobcat is between 18 and 25 pounds, with the male weighing the heavier. However, male bobcats weighing 30 to 35 pounds are not uncommon.

Sizes and weights for some of the other eastern and some southern states, as well as Oklahoma, are shown in Table 2.

TABLE 2.

MEASUREMENTS AND WEIGHTS OF BOBCATS

| Locality | Sex | Total length In. | Tail In. | Hind foot In. | Height of ear In. | Weight |
|---|---|---|---|---|---|---|
| Arkansas: | | | | | | |
| 10 mi. from Malvern | ♂ | 43 | 7 | 2½ | 3 | 25 lb. |
| 5 mi. from Helena | ♀ | 41 | 7 | 2½ | 3 | 20 |
| Huntsville | ♂ | 41 | 7 | 2½ | 3 | 20 |
| Huntsville | ♂ | 46 | 7 | 2½ | 3½ | 30 |
| Georgia: | | | | | | |
| Piedmont Refuge | ♂ | 33¾ | 5 | 6½ | 2¾ | 18 lb., 12 oz. |
| Piedmont Refuge | ♂ | 32 | 6 | 6¼ | 3 | 16 lb., 5 oz. |
| Piedmont Refuge | ♂ | 34 | 6½ | 6¾ | 2¾ | 17 lb., 14 oz. |
| Piedmont Refuge | ♂ | 33½ | 6 | 6½ | 2⅞ | 19 lb., 10 oz. |
| Piedmont Refuge | ♂ | 33¼ | 5 | 6¼ | 2½ | 17 lb., 6 oz. |
| Louisiana: | | | | | | |
| Gorum, Natchitoches Parish | ♂ | 33 | 7 | 2 | 2½ | 20 lb. |
| Gorum, Natchitoches Parish | ♀ | 31½ | 6½ | 1⅝ | 1⅞ | 15 |
| Gorum, Natchitoches Parish | ♀ | 30 | 6 | 1¾ | 2 | 14½ |
| Ward 7, Natchitoches Parish | ♀ | 32 | 5½ | 1⅞ | 2 | .. |
| Ward 7, Natchitoches Parish | ♀ | 25½ | 3½ | 1¾ | 1¾ | .. |
| Ward 3, Catahoula Parish | ♀ | 32 | 5 | 1¾ | 2¼ | .. |
| Ward 3, Catahoula Parish | ♀ | 31 | 5 | 1¾ | 2¼ | .. |
| Winn Parish | ♂ | 35 | 6 | 2¾ | 2¼ | .. |
| Caldwell Parish | ♂ | 37 | 7 | 2 | 2¼ | .. |
| Caldwell Parish | ♂ | 36 | 7 | 2 | 2 | .. |

TABLE 2—MEASUREMENTS AND WEIGHTS OF BOBCATS—Continued

| Locality | Sex | Total length In. | Tail In. | Hind foot In. | Height of ear In. | Weight |
|---|---|---|---|---|---|---|
| **Mississippi:** | | | | | | |
| Noxubee Refuge | ♀ | 29 | 5.8 | 2 | 2¼ | 18 lb. |
| Noxubee Refuge | ♂ | 36 | 5½ | 2½ | 2¼ | 19 |
| Noxubee Refuge | ♀ | 35 | 4¼ | 2¼ | 2½ | 17 |
| Noxubee Refuge | ♀ | 34 | 4½ | 2¼ | 2¾ | 20 |
| Noxubee Refuge | ♀ | 34 | 4 | 2 | 2½ | 17 |
| Noxubee Refuge | ♂ | 33½ | 5⅝ | 6½ | ... | 20 |
| Noxubee Refuge | ♀ | 32¾ | 4¼ | 6 | ... | 17 (Estimated) |
| Noxubee Refuge | ♂ | 33½ | ... | ... | ... | 12½ |
| **North Carolina:** | | | | | | |
| Holly Shelter Game Refuge | ♂ | 36 | 6 | 2⅜ | 2½ | 22 |
| Holly Shelter Game Refuge | ♂ | 37 | 5½ | 2⅜ | 2½ | 25 |
| Holly Shelter Game Refuge | ♂ | 38 | 6 | 2½ | 3 | 23 |
| Holly Shelter Game Refuge | ♂ | 36 | 5½ | 2½ | 2⅞ | 27 |
| Holly Shelter Game Refuge | ♂ | 34 | 5 | 2½ | 2⅞ | 16 |
| Holly Shelter Game Refuge | ♀ | 32 | 5 | 2½ | 2¼ | 13 |
| Holly Shelter Game Refuge | ♀ | 31 | 5 | 1⅞ | 2¼ | 12 |
| Holly Shelter Game Refuge | ♂ | 40 | 6 | 3 | 2½ | 25 |
| Holly Shelter Game Refuge | ♂ | 29½ | 5½ | 2 | 2½ | 16 |
| Sandhills Wildlife Area | ♀ | 34 | 5¾ | 2⅞ | 3 | 23 |
| Santeetlah Refuge | ♀ | 31 | 5½ | 2 | 2½ | 14 |
| Santeetlah Refuge | ♀ | 31 | 4½ | 2½ | 2½ | 12½ |
| Wayah Bald, Wayah Mgt. Area | ♀ | 34 | 5½ | 2¼ | 2¼ | 16 |
| Trimont Ridge, Wayah Mgt. Area | ♂ | 35 | 6 | 2¼ | 2¼ | 15 |
| Nantahala R., Standing Indian Mgt. Area | ♀ | 29 | 5½ | 2¼ | 2¾ | 12½ |
| Nantahala R., Standing Indian Mgt. Area | ♀ | 27 | 4½ | 2 | 1¾ | 9 |
| Seniard Ridge, Sherwood Area | ♀ | 27 | 4½ | 6¼ | 1½ | 14¼ |
| Seniard Ridge, Sherwood Area | ♂ | 29½ | 5¾ | 6½ | 1¾ | 26½ |
| Seniard Ridge, Sherwood Area | ♀ | 26 | 5 | 6½ | 1¾ | 11½ |
| End of Parkway W., Sherwood Area | ♀ | 26½ | 4¾ | 6¼ | 1¾ | 17¾ |
| Big Bald, Sherwood Area | ♀ | 25½ | 4¾ | 6¼ | 1¾ | 9¼ |
| Thompson Cr. Trail, Sherwood Mgt. Area | ♀ | 24 | 4¾ | 6 | 1½ | 8¼ |
| Thompson Cr. Trail, Sherwood Mgt. Area | ♀ | 25½ | 5½ | 6 | 1¾ | 12½ |
| Pisgah Ridge Trail, Sherwood Mgt. Area | ♀ | 25 | 4¼ | 5½ | 1½ | 10¾ |
| Pisgah Ridge Trail, Sherwood Mgt. Area | ♂ | 25½ | 4½ | 5½ | 1½ | 10½ |
| Big Bald, Sherwood Mgt. Area | ♀ | 27½ | 5¾ | 6 | 1¾ | 13½ |
| Silver Mine Bald, Sherwood Mgt. Area | ♀ | 32 | 5½ | 5 | 1¼ | 11 lb., 10 oz. |
| Silver Mine Bald, Sherwood Mgt. Area | ♀ | 28½ | 4½ | 6 | 1½ | 12¾ lb. |
| Silver Mine Bald, Sherwood Mgt. Area | ♂ | 35 | 6¾ | 7 | 2 | 23 lb., 2 oz. |

TABLE 2—MEASUREMENTS AND WEIGHTS OF BOBCATS—Continued

| Locality | Sex | Total length In. | Tail In. | Hind foot In. | Height of ear In. | Weight |
|---|---|---|---|---|---|---|
| North Carolina—Continued | | | | | | |
| Fork Mtn., Sherwood Mgt. Area | ♂ | 36 | 6 | 6½ | 2 | 19½ lb. |
| Silver Mine Bald, Sherwood Mgt. Area | ♂ | 33 | 5 | 6 | 2 | 17 lb., 5 oz. |
| Fork Mtn., Sherwood Mgt. Area | ♀ | 31 | 5 | 5¾ | 1¾ | 12½ lb. |
| Bennett Gap, Pisgah Game Preserve | ♀ | 32½ | 5 | 2¼ | 2½ | 18½ lb. |
| Chestnut Mtn., Pisgah Game Preserve | ♂ | 33½ | 5 | 2¼ | 2½ | 23½ |
| Cedar Rock Mtn., Pisgah Game Preserve | ♀ | 32½ | 5¾ | 1¾ | 2 | 12½ |
| Seniard Ridge, Pisgah Game Preserve | ♀ | 30½ | 5 | 2 | 2¼ | 15¼ |
| Bennett Gap, Pisgah Game Preserve | ♀ | 30 | 5½ | 2 | 2½ | 12 |
| Bradley Cr., Pisgah Game Preserve | ♀ | 34 | 5 | 5¾ | 1¾ | 14 lb., 8 oz. |
| Laurel Mt., Pisgah Game Preserve | ♂ | 43 | 6½ | 7½ | 3 | 25 lb., 4 oz. |
| Thompson Cr., Pisgah Game Preserve | ♂ | 34 | 5¼ | 6 | 1¾ | 18½ lb. |
| Mt. Mitchell, Mt. Mitchell Area | ♂ | 30 | 5 | 6 | 1¾ | 18 |
| Green Knob, Mt. Mitchell Area | ♀ | 29 | ... | 6 | 2 | 14 |
| Little Mtn., Mt. Mitchell Area | ♀ | 30 | 6½ | 6 | 1¾ | 14 |
| Green Knob, Mt. Mitchell Area | ♀ | 29 | 5 | 6 | 2 | 14 |
| Little Mtn., Mt. Mitchell Area | ♀ | 28 | 5 | 5¾ | 2 | 13 |
| Curtis Creek, Mt. Mitchell Area | ♂ | 34 | 5½ | 6 | 2¼ | 23 |
| Curtis Creek, Mt. Mitchell Area | ♂ | 32 | 6 | 6 | 2 | 19 |
| Holly Shelter Game Refuge | ♂ | 34 | 4½ | 2¼ | 2½ | 16 |
| Holly Shelter Game Refuge | ♂ | 36 | 5½ | 2½ | 2½ | 18 |
| Holly Shelter Game Refuge | ♀ | 33 | 4½ | 2⅜ | 2¼ | 12 |
| Oklahoma: | | | | | | |
| 7½ mi. S.W. McAlester | ♂ | 34 | 6¾ | 5½ | 2¼ | 18 lb. |
| 3 mi. E. of Page, on Big Cr. | ♂ | 33 | 5½ | 1¾ | 2¼ | ... |
| 3 mi. E. of Page, on Big Cr. | ♀ | 30½ | 4¾ | 2 | 2 | ... |
| 3 mi. E. of Wesley, Ataka County | ♂ | 36 | 6½ | 2 | 2 | ... |
| 3 mi. E. of Wesley, Ataka County | ♀ | 33 | 6 | 1¾ | 2 | ... |
| 4 mi. N. Blocker, Pittsburg County | ♀ | 28¾ | 5¼ | 2½ | 2¼ | ... |
| Tennessee: | | | | | | |
| Tennessee Natl. Wildlife Refuge, Henry County | ♂ | 36 | ... | ... | ... | 23 |
| Texas: | | | | | | |
| Kingsville | ♂ | 28½ | 6½ | 2¾ | 2¼ | 19½ |
| Kingsville | ♀ | 27¼ | 5¼ | 2½ | 2¼ | 18½ |
| Kingsville | ♂ | 25 | 6½ | 2¼ | 2 | 13 |
| Kingsville | ♂ | 33½ | 6½ | 2½ | 2¾ | 32¼ |

## COLORATION

The color of bobcat pelts varies considerably. In general it is a mixture of brown and buff, interspersed with gray, with a darker gray along the back. Black and brownish black are the prominent head colors with ears light black on the exterior with black hairs becoming slightly elongated and bringing the ears to a point at the tip. The body fur at times may be spotted or dotted with black and gray. This serves as a camouflage.

Definite trends in coloration are noticeable in different races correlated with the climate and prevailing habitat. Buff color will often dominate in warm, arid country, while black and gray coloration will be more apparent in mountainous, forested areas. Seasonal variation also causes some fading and predominance of gray, especially during winter months. Bobcat fur is very soft, when in prime condition. This is particularly characteristic of *Lynx r. fasciatus*, which is the most richly colored of all our bobcats (Plate 10). The fact that it ranges the exceptionally humid Pacific rain-forest area west of the Cascade Mountains, from Oregon and northwestern California north to southern British Columbia, may be an underlying cause of this. Lewis and Clark obtained what was probably the first specimen ever collected (December 13, 1805) establishing its type locality on the Lewis and Clark River, near the mouth of the Columbia River. This was the boyhood home of the author, and consequently this handsome race of bobcat is of particular interest to him.

There has been much conjecture regarding the spears of hair which occur on the bobcat's ears (Plate 11). Experiments seem to show that these hairs are an aid to the animal's hearing, acting as a sort of antenna in catching sound impulses. A cat with the spears of hair clipped from each ear does not seem to respond to sounds as readily as does one with the spears retained. Experiments made with a number of animals held in captivity certainly showed that those having the spears clipped at the tip of the ears did not respond to sound effects as did those with hair spears intact.

Albinism occurs occasionally among bobcats at it does with all animals. In the Zoological Gardens, Houston, Texas, I saw an albino female (Plate 12) that had been in captivity for 8 years. It had been roped by a cowboy near Edna in Jackson County, Texas, where it had been seen occasionally for 4 years, making this cat approximately 12 years old at the time I saw it in its cage on February 16, 1948. By comparison with other bobcats I have weighed, I estimated it would weigh between 20 and 25 lbs.

Melanism is also found in this species. Hamilton (1941) reports a pair of black bobcats trapped in February 1940 between Clewiston and Belle Glade, Palm Beach County, Florida. The fur on these specimens is dark brown, shading to black speckled with white hairs on the back. The characteristic spots on these bobcats are only visible from a certain angle.

A male specimen showing a coat with a mahogany tint, which in certain light appeared black, was for a short time resident in the Philadelphia Zoological Gardens (Ulmer, 1941). This animal was captured in Martin County, Florida, 14 miles above the mouth of the Loxahatchee River. (Plate 13).

## LONGEVITY

Little is known about the life span of bobcats in the wild. The specimens listed in Table 3 were acquired from 14 states and Mexico, and were kept in the National Zoological Park, Washington, D. C. The Table gives the life span during captivity.

As is often the case with old pumas, the bobcat also tends to lose its teeth, generally the canine teeth, as it approaches old age. An example of this is reported by Sickels (1949), and concerned a 37-lb. bobcat killed during 1946 in the Adirondacks of New York, near Keene.

Experienced observers believe that these predators, in the wild, may attain ages of 10 to 14 years. One old male bobcat, identifiable because of a cropped ear, was known to range for 10 years over a part of the lands mined by the Butte & Arizona

TABLE 3.

LONGEVITY RECORDS OF 24 BOBCATS KEPT IN CAPTIVITY AT NATIONAL ZOOLOGICAL
PARK, WASHINGTON, D. C.

| Acquired | Died | Period of confinement Years | Months |
|---|---|---|---|
| Feb. 19, 1909 | Dec. 20, 1924 | 15 | 10 |
| Sept. 3, 1907 | Dec. 20, 1922 | 15 | 3 |
| .... .... 1932 | Feb. 19, 1947 | 15 | |
| Jan. 15, 1912 | Jan. 28, 1927 | 15 (old age) | |
| Mar. 19, 1926 | Sept. 4, 1939 | 13 | 5½ |
| Feb. 4, 1902 | Jan. 29, 1915 | 13 | |
| Nov. 17, 1925 | Feb. 27, 1937 | 11 | 9 |
| Sept. 3, 1907 | Jan. 12, 1919 | 11 | 4½ |
| Jan. 15, 1912 | Oct. 28, 1923 | 11 | 2½ (old age) |
| July 9, 1914 | July 6, 1925 (Sent to Wellington, New Zealand Zoo) | 11 | |
| Apr. 23, 1891 | Apr. 28, 1901 | 10 (old age) | |
| Mar. 14, 1895 | June 20, 1903 | 8 | 3  (old age) |
| Mar. 14, 1895 | Jan. 1, 1903 | 7 | 10  (old age) |
| Sept. 16, 1901 | Jan. 12, 1909 | 7 | 4 |
| May 3, 1902 | Mar. 6, 1909 | 6 | 10 |
| Feb. 7, 1910 | Nov. 7, 1916 | 6 | 9 |
| May 3, 1902 | Mar. 14, 1908 | 5 | 10 |
| Feb. 9, 1924 | Oct. 18, 1929 | 5 | 8 |
| Oct. 19, 1905 | Sept. 23, 1909 | 3 | 11 |
| Oct. 18, 1893 | June 24, 1897 | 3 | 8 |
| Dec. 6, 1902 | Sept. 7, 1905 | 2 | 9 |
| Nov. 20, 1913 | Jan. 2, 1916 | 2 | 1½ |
| Mar. 3, 1898 | Apr. 1, 1898 | .. | 1 |

Copper Company, at the head of Ramsey Canyon in the Huachuca Mountains of Southeastern Arizona. When finally caught in a fox trap, its desert coloration had faded to that grayishness typical of a gray fox.

Carter (1955) records a 30½ lb. male bobcat as being over 25 years old at the time of its death. It had been a captive in a private zoo since the fall of 1928.

## STRENGTH

At times bobcats will attack and kill antelope, as well as full-grown deer. A large buck antelope was no match for the bobcat which killed it one winter day of early 1930 on the Wind Cave Game Preserve in South Dakota.

While evidence exists that a coyote can kill a bobcat that is at a disadvantage in a trap, the opinion is held that the coyote would come out second best in a fair fight. I have never seen any domestic dog match a full-grown bobcat in a fair fight. The razor-edged claws of the cat, plus the great power of its legs give it four instruments for terrific ripping and tearing. When used on the belly of any animal, the victim seldom recovers. Attempting to remove a live adult bobcat from a trap is a never-to-be-forgotten experience.

Like the puma or mountain lion, the bobcat is a silent prowler, obtaining most of its food by stalking its prey. When within pouncing distance it hurls itself onto its victim, generally on the head and neck. Whenever it can secure a hold on such a spot it quickly bites deeply into the victim's neck just below the back of the skull. This is a favorite killing hold, particularly on lambs and young deer. Once this hold is securely obtained, it is seldom that the victim can shake the bobcat loose (Plate 14).

Sometimes, in killing deer, as with domestic calves, it will ride the animal's neck and shoulders while scratching and biting the eyes and face.

The late E. W. Nelson recorded an observation at about 8,500 feet elevation in the Sierra Guadalupe of Coahuila, Mexico, where a bobcat had torn off a large piece of fat meat from a bear carcass and carried it a long distance down into a canyon. It buried part of this in the middle of the trail, and hid another fragment under a rocky projection nearby.

While coursed with dogs, bobcats have been seen carrying rabbits in their mouths. The cats refused to drop their prey even after a long chase, and then only when treed.

## SWIMMING ABILITY

The bobcat will take to water if necessary, particularly when crowded by dogs.

Amundson (1943) observed one swimming a 150-foot canal, 21 miles north of Yuma, Arizona.

It swims remarkably well, and will often outdistance dogs by its ability to leap out of deep water in bounding jumps similar to the bounding leaps of a deer. Here we have the so-called bobbing motion mentioned previously. Cat hunters in the areas contiguous to swamps in the South attest to the fact that often a cat crowded by hounds will take to water in a swamp. With dogs still pursuing, the cat will at times about-face in the water, and with bounding leaps of as much as 12 feet run unharmed through a pack of dogs. This trait has often been observed in Okefenokee Swamp of southeastern Georgia. However, when not molested, the bobcat will invariably cross a stream at some natural bridge, such as a fallen log. Spots where it hops upon a log, or where it leaves the log after crossing make ideal trap-setting places for its capture.

## TRACKS

When made in soft earth, sand, or mud, the bobcat track is approximately two inches in diameter. In many respects the track of this creature made when fully grown is not unlike that of a large, ordinary domestic tomcat, though close scrutiny will show it to be more like a miniature edition of its much larger cousin, the puma (Fig. 4). One distinguishable dif-

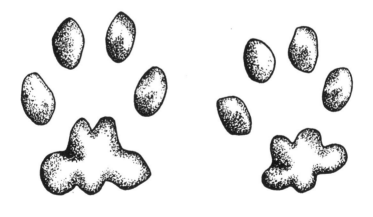

Fore Foot                    Hind Foot

FIG. 4. Bobcat track made when walking. (Note peculiar form of heel pads.)

ference, other than size, is the shape of the heel pad impression. In good tracking ground, the bobcat heel pad will be found to have three blunt, prong-like impressions, with one on each side of the imprint made by the heel part of the foot. The four front toe imprints resemble an impression similar to that made by one's index finger when pressed obliquely in any soft material such as modeler's clay, window putty, or fine wet mud.

In snow-covered mountain regions, lines of bobcat tracks often appear staggered. The individual prints are round and spaced 10 to 12 inches apart. No claw marks show, but fur marks often appear.

## TRAVEL

As a general rule bobcats frequent rocky washes around the points of rough hills, and often in thickets of river bottoms, swamps, dry arroyas or washes, or brushy draws. Little sign is left, in most instances, as an indication of a bobcat travelway or hunting route. The animal travels on rocks, and its range is much more restricted than that of the puma. It is seldom seen or observed in the wild, being of a secretive nature. This permits of its living close to agricultural areas when habitat is suitable.

It is prone to follow an established route rather closely. In Wyoming, during an interval of 90 days, 39 bobcats were trapped in one location with diluted oil of catnip that had been placed near the trap set along the top of a rough canyon wall.

The bobcat, along its travel route, chooses favorite spots for defecating and expelling its urine. The latter is often scratched over as in the case of the puma. Female bobcats will often assume an upright position when urinating, and in this posture expell the urine in a fine jet-like stream against a small shrub or side of a boulder, the expulsion being very similar to that of the skunk when eliminating its world-renowned scent. Coverage of dung and urine is done when the bobcat assumes another posture, i.e. that of squatting to relieve itself, and then completes the function by scratching a small mound up over the deposit. This latter is often referred to as a "scrape" or "rake" in the parlance of the outdoorsman.

The distance the animal wanders in its search for food, or what might be termed its home range, varies greatly. It can be as small in diameter as 5 miles, or as much as 50 miles. The available prey and the extent to which it is subjected to hunting pressure are two of the most important factors that determine the home range.

A. E. Gray, veteran employee of the Fish and Wildlife Service in New Mexico and Oklahoma, and long familiar with the creature, opines the bobcat's range is generally localized (Fig. 5). Some, however, have ranged 25 to 30 miles in Oklahoma. When the animal is trailed by dogs it attempts to escape by running in a large circle, often treeing near the point where first jumped. The old tom bobcat seems to be a greater wanderer than the female. The latter is, in Mr. Gray's opinion, more apt to stay close to a suitable food supply, if possible.

The Fish and Wildlife Service, Branch of Wildlife Research, is directing studies in Montana, which are expected to pro-

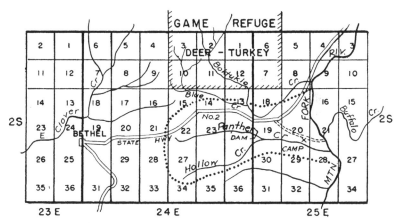

Hunter Melvin Phillips took nine Bobcats with Dogpack within the area outlined in dots in 45 days. April-May 1939

SCALE 1/2" = 1 MILE

Fig. 5. Bobcat concentration, Panther Creek Area, McCurtain County, Oklahoma.

duce much new information. The object of these studies is to accumulate data on the daily range and seasonal movements of the animal. A plan of ear tagging and releasing trapped bobcats is being conducted by nine Montana hunters.

As with the puma, the bobcat in its travelway will scratch on trees as a means of stretching itself, as well as sharpening its claws.

When hard pressed, the bobcat seems to approach the speed of a coyote in full flight, but, unlike the coyote, assumes a hopping motion as it travels full speed ahead.

The late C. Hart Merriam, when approaching Wabuska, Nevada, remarked upon the peculiar gait of a bobcat frightened into full speed getaway by an oncoming train. The animal loped in a rocking-horse sort of way, throwing his rear end high in the air each time and seeming actually to bend up the hinder part of the back as well as lifting his rear end bodily from the ground.

The animal may seek its prey either in daylight or night, for it possesses eyesight seemingly as sharp as that of a crow, and at night comparable to that of an owl.

## VOICE

The voice of the animal is in many respects comparable to that of the house tabby. The most common sounds to be heard, especially when it is being held in a trap or snare, are spits, growls, puffs, and hisses. In a quieter mood it purrs and mews exactly as the domestic house cat, only louder at times. This is particularly true of those raised as pets.

Caterwauling in the wilds, particularly during mating periods, is considerably louder than that made by the domestic tomcat, and in some instances the bobcat sound has been recorded as reaching a distance of a mile. Bachman (1851, vol. 1, p. 13), the 19th century naturalist, is one authority for this distance. Those large male bobcats approaching weights of 35 pounds or more can caterwaul as loudly as the puma. It would be difficult to distinguish these two species if unseen in the forest or other dense habitat.

A number of federal and state predatory animal hunters

have become quite adept in calling up bobcats within shooting distance. Foremost among these is E. G. Pope of Lubbock, Texas. Regarding his success with bobcat calls, Pope states:

"Very few people appreciate the effect of sound on their daily lives. So it is with the wild creatures of the universe. Certain sounds to them mean danger, future existence, while others may mean food. Certain sounds in wide open spaces have some meaning to all wild creatures and they react accordingly whether it is the mating call of a bird or the distress squealing of a rabbit caught in the talons of a hawk.

"The decoying of mammals with imitating sounds is not modern or new. Some Indians were proficient in the use of sound to decoy game within range. Ancient man used it in his time when his weapons were spears or clubs. In recent years many hunters have learned to use sounds to call in carnivorous animals, particularly predatory animals.

"Not too many years in the past most of these sounds were made by mouth. These are yet the most effective but hard to produce. However, in the last few years mechanical devices have been brought into the picture very successfully. With these mechanical devices, there are many imitating sounds that can be produced which will interest carnivorous animals, and particularly the cat family. The most common used for the cat family is the distress rabbit cry, either coarse or fine pitch, or the chirp of a bird, turkey, etc. and sometimes the fighting squall of the tomcat.

"The bobcat is very susceptible to distress calls of animals or birds which it is in the habit of feeding on. Now just because you have a predator calling device, it does not mean you are going to call up a bobcat any more than if you have a duck call that the ducks are going to fly direct into the call. If you don't know how, where and when to use one of these calling devices, it is likely to be worthless.

"The first prerequisite to bobcat calling is a good knowledge of hunting and habits of the animal to be hunted. The hunter should be a good observer, calm, and with patience that won't wear out, and a good marksman. He must know where to hunt

and take advantage of weather and wind as well as terrain of
the area hunted. He should be clad in suitable clothing to
blend with the landscape of the area and he should wear some
kind of soft-soled shoes. Most wild animals are alert and sensi-
tive to ground vibrations or sounds caused by hoofed animals
or the walking of man with hard soled shoes. On the other
hand, cloven-footed animals or man with soft shoe sole may
walk in a hunting area without disturbing the bobcat. The
cat will at least remain in hearing distance of the call. The
best results are obtained by taking the advantage of the wind,
and getting into the cat habitat without the animal knowing
you are around. Many animals can smell man more than one
quarter of a mile distant. Quite a few species have a super-
sonic ear, and can hear sounds not audible to the human ear.

"Once you are successfully in the area of the bobcat, you
must find a suitable location to take a stand before you start
calling. The type of stand you take is very important. Experience has taught that it is much better to take the stand in
front of a well foliaged bush, a rock, a tree, or bluff than to
get behind it and try to look around. Pick a place as near as
possible so as to avoid animals approaching from behind and
where you will have a good view of the terrain out in front.
Once you have settled in a desirable stand, start your calling
with four or five blasts from your call when using the distress
rabbit call. After a pause of from 20 to 30 seconds, repeat the
call again, but not too loud. This procedure should be continued for 30 minutes to one hour for bobcats, gradually taking
more time between calls, waiting at the end of the hour as
long as 5 to 10 minutes between calls. Bobcats generally come
in very slowly, sneaking along from bush to bush, moving a
short distance and stopping to look and listen. However, this
is not always the case as sometimes one will come bouncing
right in on a dead run. When a cat is seen approaching and is
not in a suitable place for a shot, very low short calls should
be made to walk the cat into a desirable location.

"Avoid any movement, especially any fast or jerky movements. Movement is very noticeable to all wild animals and

spoils many chances of a good shot. The animals often see this false movement long before you can see them. Don't forget suitable clothing to blend with the landscape. For example, in a heavy snow, a solid white garment works wonderfully well. If unable to take advantage of wind and weather conditions, a freshly killed jackrabbit placed some fifty yards in front of your stand as a decoy often helps. A second hunter, if experienced, is often a help as two can watch the area better and have a decided advantage. Many times a cat will come in and leave without the hunter seeing it.

"The early morning and late afternoon hours are the best time for calling, although at times animals may be called at all times of the day. The action of hawks, raven, magpies, or other birds often serve as a warning of the approach of a bobcat.

"The calling of bobcats opens a new field of work for the trained and experienced hunter. Also furnishes employment during bad weather when impossible to get over trap line."

## IN CAPTIVITY

Bobcats stand confinement fairly well, and in some zoological gardens, private homes, etc., have lived a normal length of life (Plates 15, 16 and 16a).

Efforts to domesticate this animal are generally unsuccessful, even when taken as exceedingly young kittens. A few attempts have been successful when the young about to be born have been taken by Caesarean operation, and fed by suckling a female house cat already nursing her own young. In these instances the young mature into docile creatures, and castration of the males has also been found to be helpful in bringing about this condition.

It has been aptly said that to tame a bobcat requires the patience of a Job and the gentleness of a St. Francis, and a "little insurance on the fingers might be in order."

One of the earliest instances of a tame bobcat having the run of a building was described by Dr. Jared Kirkland, famed naturalist in the Cleveland, Ohio, region. In part of a letter

Kirkland wrote to Louis Agassiz on September 25, 1851, it was stated: "A young wildcat (Lynx rufus) . . . is running at liberty about the Medical College [Cleveland] and amuses itself playing with the students, disciplining the neighbors dogs and capturing rats. When in a good natured mood it manifests it by a loud purring—about as loud and as musical as the sound of a spooling-wheel when in rapid motion."

Collins (1954) records the use of three bobcats, raised from babyhood, that developed into first-rate hunting animals for quail in the Sulphur Springs Valley, near Wilcox, Arizona. The terrain over which these bobcats were used singly to flush quail was in heavy grass "that worked its way up the slopes of the mountains and flowed on down into the fertile but unculti-vated valleys below." The owner let these cats hunt by instinct as they would in the wild, never trying to break them from eating a bird or so in the course of the hunt. Trained to ride with their owner on the back seat of a buckboard to the hunt-ing grounds, these cats would not leave the seat when the hunt was to begin until told to do so. One of these cats, dubbed Mike, would work all through a morning's hunt "with the tire-less enthusiasm of the born hunter. His sense of where the birds would be seemed uncanny, for although he covered the ground thoroughly, he never seemed to take a direction which did not produce birds. And once down on a 'point,' the birds always were found directly in front of him, although he often began his stalk 50 to 75 feet from the covey."

Even while sharing birds with Mike, the hunters working with him had no trouble in getting goodly quail bags. When the hunt was completed, the owner would call Mike, and he would return to the buckboard and perch on the rear seat ready to return to his master's home.

Hazel E. Wolkenhauer (1949) records interesting experi-ences when she writes:

"It is an interesting life—living with lynxes. We had always wanted such house-guests, but most available bobcats were trapped as adults, and, we feel, all grown wild animals belong in the wild. Finally, however, we heard of a pair of bobcats

PLATE 10. *L. r. fasciatus* in juniper tree. (Photo courtesy Joe Van Wormer, Bend, Oregon).

PLATE 11. Profile showing ear tufts or spears which serve as a sort of antenna for catching sound.

PLATE 12. Albinistic female bobcat *(L. r. texensis)* roped alive by a cowboy near Edna, Texas.

PLATE 13. Melanistic male bobcat *(L. r. floridanus)*. Martin County, Florida. (Courtesy Zoological Society of Philadelphia).

PLATE 14. Bobcat killing a long yearling deer. Reproduced from a painting by Paul Bransom.

PLATE 15. Pet bobcat, mascot of New Mexico Game Department, Albuquerque office. (Courtesy New Mexico Game and Fish Department.)

PLATE 16. Pet bobcat, 10 months old, poised on a boulder near Blackfoot, Idaho.

(32c)

PLATE 16a. Pet female bobcat, one of a litter of four, at the age of 14 months, weighing 13 lbs., Rock Candy Mountains, Utah (Photo courtesy of L. Robinette).

PLATE 16b. Newly born bobcats, approximately 3 days old, with eyes still closed. (Photos courtesy of L. Robinette).

that had been hand raised after their mother had been killed, and we bought them, sight unseen.

"We have done our best to give our guests as natural an existence as possible. They receive nothing to eat except assorted raw forms of meat, chicken, and rabbit. We cannot get them to accept fish. They are given the full run of the house, without even a collar. For fresh air and sunshine they have a large outdoor runway, in which we have improvised trees. Also, they have ramps to and from which to leap.

"The kittens were four months old when we acquired them, but still young enough to accept new owners. They were still kittens then, brother and sister. We have had them for nearly two years, and by the end of that time they had reached a weight of twenty-six pounds each, although the male remained for a long time about two pounds lighter than his sister. We keep a flash camera loaded and ready to record the activities of our pets, and the pictures on these pages are some items in such a record.

"In a sense, a lynx is not a pet for small children. Because of its active nature, it is at times extremely rough while at play. It is a common event for the Wolkenhauers' lynxes to scramble up the nearest door while in the midst of a game of 'chase-me,' balancing with ease. Thus, the rooms of their home all bear claw prints, which would make a lynx an undesirable pet for a fastidious housekeeper.

"A bay-lynx is a beautiful cat, and, if obtained very young, can become a most interesting house pet. It is especially fascinating to observe the comparison between a lynx and its common house-cat cousin. It goes without saying that both species are extremely curious about everything that goes on in the home, and this bobcat is investigating the subject of a watched pot boiling.

"Though more active than a common cat, a lynx also takes time out for cat-naps. There is no favorite spot, for these lynx pets have been found napping atop the kitchen stove, high above cupboards, under beds, and even in empty laundry trays.

This makes their owners wonder if the lynx does not roam constantly in the wild, rather than maintain a permanent site for a home, except, of course, when a mother lynx has a litter of youngsters to care for.

"The lynx seems to be more alert than its house-cat cousin. The Wolkenhauer pets will run to the door when either the phone or door bell rings, and all outside noises are immediately investigated by peeking from the nearest window. On the other hand, house cats will ignore all such noises. The lynx seems to take a great interest in life, and is far less lazy. The female lynx learned several clever tricks. She will roll over at the command of 'Dead Cat!', and has never failed to do so, even once. She will eat from the table, while seated on a chair, but more often than not will end up with both front paws on the table. She plays a grand game of hide-and-seek, and will actually run to hide when she finds one of the family in a hiding spot. Her brother, however, refuses to as much as try to learn a trick, and is content to be just an observer."

For a considerable period a yearling female bobcat (Anon., 1951) has had the freedom of the Albuquerque, New Mexico office of the State Game and Fish Department. Here she has been admired by daily visitors, and the recipient of many a friendly pat from the policeman on the beat and all the youngsters.

At New Bern, North Carolina a bobcat and a raccoon were living amicably in the same cage.

From Kingsville, Texas comes an account stating:

"A big search is on in these parts for John Thomas, a beer-drinking bobcat.

"He is grown, dark gray, and weighs 18 pounds. Besides beer, he like to drink water, right out of a water cooler. He does not like wine. He drank it once and it made him ill.

"John Thomas was the mascot of Seeligson Oil Camp, 14 miles southwest of here, and the personal property of Lew Kinsey who found the bobcat when it was just a bob-kitten on the King Ranch.

" 'I think John Thomas was enticed into a passing automobile,' Kinsey said, 'He loved to ride in cars.'

"John Thomas also liked to ride in airplanes, but did not care for the take-offs. Only liked airplanes when they were up in the air. Then he would look out the window and enjoy the sights.

"When Kinsey found the baby bobcat he took it back to the Seeligson Camp and fed it milk out of a bottle. Pretty soon John Thomas was old enough to eat meat, and from then on Kinsey fed him two hearty meals a day.

"When his appetite was satisfied he played gently with children and amused the personnel at the oil camp by whipping all dogs that were unlucky enough to stray within striking distance.

"John Thomas preferred to drink water out of a water cooler, but someone had to press the spigot for him. He spent a lot of time around the water cooler, waiting for someone to press the spigot.

"About the beer drinking—John Thomas drank beer from ash trays in night clubs."

W. Leslie Robinette adds to the record with the following observations of his experience with bobcat young:

"A litter of 3 kittens was found by Ross Campbell of the Colorado Game and Fish Commission, April 28, 1954, near Meeker, Colorado, in the experimental deer pastures at Little Hills. The den consisted of a hole about 3 feet in depth running down at a 45° angle under a sandstone ledge. The lower end of the den was enlarged to above 16 inches in diameter. There was no nest material except a few dry leaves which could have blown in. Campbell was within 10 feet of the den before the mother came out and fled with Campbell's small dog in close pursuit. The mother showed no inclination to fight. The kittens were barely able to crawl and their eyes were still closed. (Plate 16b). I took two of the kittens to Salt Lake City, Utah with me and the third one was turned over to Paul Gilbert of the Colorado Game and Fish Commission. The two which I took home (both males as determined later) weighed 12.00 and 10.75 ounces April 29 and each had a forehead-rump measurement of 8.0 inches. (Weights for succeeding weeks are listed in Table 3a.) The smaller kitten developed slit eye openings May 2 but it was not until May 4 that its eyes were fully open. The larger one, however, showed slit openings May 5, small circular openings in the lower corner of each eye, May 6, and eyes fully open on May 7. Thus it appears that some variation may occur in the time required for the eyes to open— 3 days in this instance.

"During the first few days the kittens seemed to have more strength in their front legs than in the hind ones. They could walk upright on their front legs but their hind ones were spread out and essentially useless. A week after their capture they could pull themselves out of a cardboard box having 8 inch sides.

"By May 9 the cubs were using their hind legs some al-

### TABLE 3A.

WEIGHTS OF 2 MALE BOBCAT KITTENS CAPTURED APRIL 28, 1954 WHEN ABOUT THREE DAYS OLD.

| Date | Robinette's lbs. | oz. | Wasatch Enterprises' lbs. | oz. | Date | Robinette's lbs. | oz. | Wasatch Enterprises' lbs. | oz. |
|---|---|---|---|---|---|---|---|---|---|
| 4/29/54 | .. | 12 | .. | 10.75 | 9/9 | .. | .. | 7 | 12 |
| 5/6 | .. | 15.5 | .. | 13.5 | 9/16 | .. | .. | 8 | 0 |
| 5/13 | 1 | 4 | .. | 14.0 | 9/23 | .. | .. | 8 | 11 |
| 5/20 | 1 | 9 | 1 | 4 | 9/30 | .. | .. | 9 | 8 |
| 5/27 | 1 | 12 | 1 | 6 | 10/7 | .. | .. | 10 | 4 |
| 6/3 | 2 | 1 | 2 | 2 | 10/14 | .. | .. | 10 | 11 |
| 6/12 | 2 | 7 | 1 | 8 | 10/22 | .. | .. | 11 | 6 |
| 6/17 | 2 | 12 | 1 | 1.5 | 10/29 | .. | .. | 12 | 0 |
| 6/24 | 3 | 6.5 | 2 | 4 | 11/4 | .. | .. | 12 | 6 |
| 7/1 | 3 | 15.5 | 2 | 13 | 11/12 | .. | .. | 13 | 8 |
| 7/8 | 4 | 10 | 3 | 0 | 11/19 | .. | .. | 14 | 2 |
| 7/15 | 5 | 6 | 3 | 2 | 11/26 | .. | .. | 14 | 14 |
| 7/22 | 5 | 14 | 4 | 0 | 12/2 | .. | .. | 15 | 4 |
| 7/31 | 6 | 14 | 4 | 14 | 12/9 | .. | .. | 15 | 1 |
| 8/5 | 7 | 8 | 4 | 2 | 12/16 | .. | .. | 16 | 7 |
| 8/12 | .. | .. | 5 | 1 | 12/23 | .. | .. | 17 | 0 |
| 8/19 | .. | .. | 5 | 12 | 12/30 | .. | .. | 17 | 10 |
| 8/26 | .. | .. | 6 | 9 | 1/6/55 | .. | .. | 18 | 6 |
| 9/2 | .. | .. | 7 | 1 | | | | | |

though it was even a week later before they could use them well.

"On May 8, I noticed that the front teeth (canines and incisors) were coming through the gums.

"On May 8, I took the smaller cub to The Wasatch Enterprises, Murray, Utah where a Disney wildlife film was being filmed.

"The kitten which I retained first showed signs of play. May 15. He would paw the air, bite his feet, and also started to clean the dried milk from his fur at about this time.

"Along about May 22, the kitten showed evidence of being able to see—could distinguish movements and would avoid running into objects.

We fed the kitten nothing but milk until May 27, when we started giving it pablum, in addition. June 20 was the first that it ate meat with relish. Thereafter it took more meat and less milk. It started losing its juvenile hair around the end of June and had lost all of it except on the head by July 16. It also became increasingly playful during this period (Plate 16c). The kitten started filling out and making better growth on the meat diet (Plate 16d). It completely ate a pocket gopher, which I fed it July 5, except for the stomach and intestines.

"We would frequently tether the kitten on the lawn and one day when he was about two months old we saw him wading in a pan of water (about 3 inches deep) which had been placed out for him to drink from. Shortly later we noticed him defecating while standing in the water. In days that followed this event was repeated several times. Hence it was no great surprise when we saw him one day defecating in the toilet bowl of our bathroom. He attempted to balance himself on the edge of the toilet seat but the perch was too precarious and he fell into the water. From then on he would get down inside the bowl with feet braced around the sides and only his head visible above the seat.

"Often when he was in a playful mood, which was usually in the mornings or evenings, he would try and stalk a member of the family or our springer spaniel. In doing so he would rarely make a long straight dash, rather he would take a devious course, sneaking along on his belly and taking advantage of objects to hide behind.

"The kitten died August 11 after an illness of only two days from feline enteritis.

"This kitten and the one taken to the Wasatch Enterprises were weighed weekly until August 5 for mine and January 6 for the other one, at which time the latter developed a nervous disorder and failed to make normal growth gains thereafter. It also failed to make regular gains at two earlier periods because of diarrhea and intestinal worms.

"The Wasatch Enterprises' cat has been raised and kept at the home of Darrel Hendricks, Salt Lake City, most of the time. Hendricks reports that the cat has gotten out of the house on occasions and when only about 7 months of age killed two house cats with some close misses on others. Yet the bobcat is so gentle that a person can hold him up by his tail."

And finally, a Palm Springs, California physician recorded that "three pretty cats" wandered into his hillside yard. The family fed and housed the homeless strays. Shortly after their appearance the physician leaned down to pet one of them. He was clawed severely. A fellow physician, summoned to treat the scratches, saw the animals and remarked:

"Heck, those aren't kittens. They're wildcats."

## ENEMIES

Adult bobcats have few enemies. Young bobcats fall prey at times to foxes and horned owls. Fish and Wildlife Service hunters have found that a puma, which can move more swiftly than a bobcat, may kill its smaller relative when these two meet. This is particularly true in mountainous areas of heavy snow fall (Plate 17). This might be called a case of "cat eat cat."

With respect to the enmity between a bobcat and a puma, Robinette says:

"On December 12, 1949 Tony Sutich of the Nevada Fish and

Game, found the remains of a bobcat which had been killed by a cougar [puma] in the Duck Creek area of eastern Nevada. The bobcat had been covered over almost completely by snow which the cougar had raked over it after eating his fill. I visited the place the following day and found that the entire mid-section of the bobcat, including the backbone had been eaten except the stomach, intestines and some hide connecting the front and hind quarters. The uneaten portions of the male bobcat weighed 17 pounds. Upon skinning the neck region of the bobcat I found toothmarks and blood clotted areas on top of the neck just in front of the shoulders and in the throat region (Plates 17a and b).

"Seventy feet away I found the remains of a mule deer fawn (6 months old) carcass. Further examination revealed deer flesh and hair in the bobcat's stomach. It appeared that the bobcat had been feeding on the deer when he was surprised by the cougar.

"In addition to the foregoing I have analyzed one cougar stomach that contained bobcat remains. The cougar was an adult male killed by federal hunter, Willis Butolph in Cedar Canyon, Iron County, Utah, July 27, 1950. There was one pound one ounce of bobcat remains in the stomach."

Bruce Wright (1948), in his discussion of puma occurrence in New Brunswick, describes the following bobcat-panther relationship:

"About March 1, 1941, Jack MacLean, teamster, reported meeting a panther sitting in the road while driving his logging team. It was about twenty-five yards from him and showed no fear. It finally walked off the road with a slinking gait that reminded him of 'a pacing horse.' He estimated its head was about four feet from the ground when sitting down, and when standing up it appeared to be two and one-half feet high and three and one-half feet long, excluding the tail. The tail was long and carried like that of a house cat. The coat was a mixture of yellow-gray and reddish and the length of the hair was such as to make the neck appear to be thicker than the head.

The tracks were three to four inches across and were quite common in the district. He further reported that a friend, Fidel Hachey, trailed the panther and found where it had chased a bobcat up a tree, tore it to pieces, and ate it in the tree. He brought pieces of the bobcat, including the tail, back with him to prove his story. These pieces were seen by the writer and the Chief Game Warden of New Brunswick. Hachey has tried to trap the panther without success. (Personal interview)"

Occasionally coyotes have been observed to tree bobcats in a manner similar to the domestic dog. Of interest is that recorded by Burr (1948). Says he: "One morning while a wolf trapper was riding his trap-line located in northeastern New Mexico he heard two coyotes barking vigorously in a canyon. The occurrence was so unusual in daytime that he dismounted and carefully stalked the hunters. He beheld an animated scene, around a low pinon tree standing in a canyon bed with wild rye grass growing around it about two feet high. The coyotes had treed a bobcat, who was just out of their reach on a slender limb. They were barking just like dogs and leaping high, trying to reach the cat and pull him out. The coyotes were so engrossed in the attack that they lost their usual caution and Mr. Gimson observed them for several minutes before finally shooting them and the cat.

"Here is presented a rare lesson in natural history. What was the intention of the two coyotes? Did they want this cat for food? One thing was sure—they were doing their best to pull him out of the tree and the two would have been more than a match for the cat."

A paradox to the foregoing (Plate 17c) concerns a situation when a bobcat and coyote were captured in a double trap set on the Malheur Wildlife Refuge, located in southeastern Oregon. They both remained alive until they were dispatched by a hunter while visiting his trap-lines. In this instance, apparently, all feeling of enmity had disappeared, a case of misery likes company, for neither animal had in any way attempted to attack the other in spite of the fact they could easily have done so because of their proximity.

A full resumé of the effect of bobcats on certain of our deer populations is discussed later. It seems appropriate to mention here that doe deer with fawns are known to chase bobcats. If caught, the predator is apt to receive a thorough mauling from all four feet of the doe. Riney (1951) witnessed a part of such a performance on Jawbone Ridge in the central Sierra Nevada of California between Yosemite National Park and the Sonora Pass Road. Here a doe chased a bobcat out of a clearing "a distance of another hundred yards."

Robinette made an observation June 21, 1955 in the Oak Creek area, Millard County, Utah of a doe chasing a bobcat up a tree. He noticed the doe dash up the slope and around a juniper tree and then saw the bobcat in the top of the tree. After a few minutes the doe started on a fast walk down the slope, contacted her young fawn and with it hurried away from the scene.

P. W. Martin, Regional Game Biologist for the British Columbia Game Department, sends an account of a doe and bobcat feud, at Okanagan Lake in the Summerland District in British Columbia, on January 17, 1952 at 2 p. m.:

"The weather was fine with a slight south wind, and the temperature was in the vicinity of 10 degrees above zero. Snowfall had been heavy and about 30 inches of light fluffy snow lay on the flat and exposed areas.

"Upon approaching an open burn with a scattering of ponderosa pine and clumps of willow four deer were observed on a hillside across a little draw about three hundred yards distant. These animals had their attention riveted on some object close by and were unaware of our presence. Almost immediately a bobcat was seen to emerge from behind a willow bush and start up the hill. The smallest of the deer, a doe, immediately approached to within six feet of the cat and snorted loudly, retreating when the cat turned to face her. The cat then took up a position at the base of a snag. The doe approached the cat three times while it was in this position. The cat left the shelter of the snag and started up the hill, the small doe circled above the cat on a dead run and attacked it from above striking it with its forefeet; as the two animals closed the cat appeared to roll and reach up and clasp the deer about the shoulders, the doe rolled over in the snow dislodging the cat and immediately regained her feet and bounded away. At the instant the doe struck, the cat yowled with pain or rage and immediately moved into the shelter of a clump of willows. The small doe again rushed the cat but stopped short as the cat assumed the position of defense, with its back arched, and the doe retreated. One of the larger deer then rushed the cat, stopping short while the smaller doe circled to a position above the cat. Thereafter both deer alternately rushed to within a few feet of the cat but never pressed home their attacks.

"At this time we were winded by four other deer close by, which took flight and the deer harassing the cat followed them.

"The cat climbed the ridge and started to follow the crest; we intercepted it and because of the heavy snow we were able to overtake it and force it to take refuge in a clump of willows, where it was shot. Upon skinning out the carcass a bad bruise was found on the right fore leg and another on the neck obviously caused by the deer's hooves.

"The digestive tract was examined and a small amount of deer hair was found in the colon, the remainder of the tract being empty."

Abnormal situations produced by forest fires or floods will often cause predators and their prey species to associate together with no apparent animosity toward each other. Such a case was witnessed in the heavy floods on the lower Mississippi River in the early '30's. A log floating down the river was seen supporting a bobcat, a rabbit, and a domestic rooster all crouched together in apparent contentment.

## SEX RATIO

For the 12-month period beginning July 1918 to June 30, 1919, a total of 150 bobcats taken in steel traps in New Mexico showed a ratio of 78 males to 72 females.

Sex ratios of 8,703 bobcats recorded by personnel of the Fish and Wildilfe Service in Arizona for the period from July 1, 1919, to June 30, 1944, gave a total of 4,849 males to 3,854 females, representing a percentage total of 55.72 percent males to 44.28 percent females.

Operating a 500-mile trap-line covering about one-third of Malheur County, Oregon, hunter Robert Long, using No. 3 Victor traps and a scent composed of cat urine to which was added a small amount of beaver castor with enough glycerin to give this lure an oily base, took a total of 321 bobcats during the period from July 1 to October 30, 1951. One hundred forty-seven of these were trapped in September, but it was not until the latter part of October when mother cats and their kits began to travel that the females were taken in any numbers. It was found during the 4-month period approximately 75 percent of the bobcats captured were males, old toms; 23 percent old females; and 2 percent kittens. The larger percentage of males in all cases may have been due to a differential in attractiveness of the baits to the two sexes.

## DEVELOPMENT OF YOUNG

The gestation period (determined from field hunting records of the Fish and Wildilfe Service) for the bobcat is from 50 to 60 days. The young are born blind, and remain so for approximately three to nine days. The nursing period is of some two months' duration, after which the young take on a diet of meat. Both parents bring food to the kittens before and after the den is abandoned.

Newly born bobcats weigh between 10 and 12 ounces, the weight of the female being nearer 10 than 12 ounces. By fall of the year in which they are born, they will weigh 8 to 10 pounds.

Table 3a conveys some information on the development of young in the case of two bobcats, one from April 29 to August 5, 1954 and the other from the same date to Jan. 6, 1955. It will be noted that the former gained 6 lbs. 12 oz. in the

4-month period of its life, while the latter gained 17 lbs. 11¼ oz. in approximately eight months.

## DEN SITE

Den sites most commonly observed occur under logs that are concealed by vines, in hollows of decomposing windfalls, in root depressions left by overturned trees, or in small natural rocky caves or recesses such as those found in limestone or eroded sandstone formations. In such locations the bobcat will sometimes bring moss and dried leaves to make a more protective and secure shelter when about to bring forth young.

Instances have been observed where mother bobcats had their litters of young under ranch buildings, such as barns and sheds, in isolated areas. It is possible that the choosing of such sites was influenced by the availablity of food such as young pigs and poultry.

In some places in the South changes in habitat caused by bulldozing and burning of thickets serve to drive out bobcats from local farm woodlots, and in some areas is an effective method of curbing the depredations of these predators.

## BREEDING HABITS

As with the puma there are indications that the young of the bobcat may be born during any month of the year. The most intensive breeding, however, appears to take place in late February, continuing through March, April, and May, and seems to taper off by early summer. Data obtained in Utah indicate that embryos are found from February to June. No record so far (1951) has been found of embryos or young during the months of November or December. Tables 4 and 5, compiled by Jay S. Gashwiler of the Fish and Wildlife Service in Utah, and heretofore unpublished, are of interest in this connection.

There is evidence that the bobcat may at times litter twice in one year. Like the domestic house cat there may be, in the absence of any male, several periods of "heat" in any year.

Beginning in early 1953, a cooperative study of the reproduc-

TABLE 4.

COMBINED BOBCAT REPRODUCTIVE CONDITION DATA, FROM SELECTED UTAH
HUNTERS 1950-51.

| | Males | | | Females | | | | Condition Adult Female | | |
| | Adults | Under 1 yr. | Unclassified | Adults | Under 1 yr. | Unclassified | Nursing | Preg. | Barren | Unclassified |
|---|---|---|---|---|---|---|---|---|---|---|
| July 1950 | 16 | .. | 3 | 8 | 3 | .. | 2 | .. | 6 | .. |
| August | 14 | .. | 8 | 12 | 1 | .. | 1 | .. | 9 | 2 |
| September | 13 | .. | 13 | 19 | 6 | .. | .. | .. | 19 | .. |
| October | 7 | .. | 4 | 7 | 3 | .. | .. | .. | 7 | .. |
| November | 4 | .. | 3 | 4 | 1 | 2 | .. | .. | 4 | .. |
| December | 3 | .. | 4 | 6 | 1 | 4 | .. | .. | 5 | 1 |
| January | 14 | 1 | 2 | 15 | 2 | .. | .. | .. | 15 | .. |
| February | 14 | 4 | 8 | 10 | 4 | .. | .. | 2 | 6 | 2 |
| March | 16 | .. | 6 | 10 | 4 | .. | .. | 1 | 9 | .. |
| April | 10 | .. | 9 | 12 | 5 | .. | 3 | 2 | 7 | .. |
| May | 9 | 1 | 8 | 8 | 3 | .. | 3 | 2 | 3 | .. |
| June 1951 | 5 | 2 | 12 | 13 | 1 | 2 | 5 | 1 | 5 | 2 |
| Total | 125 | 8 | 80 | 124 | 34 | 8 | 14 | 8 | 96 | 7 |

Note: Since this table was compiled a pregnant bobcat was found in August
of 1952 containing 4 unborn young, and one in January, 1954 containing 2
unborn young. William G. Sheldon of the Massachusetts Cooperative Wildlife
Research Unit, at Amherst, reports the killing of 3 young bobcats on October
29, 1957 near Shutesbury, Mass., that were probably born in early August.

TABLE 5.

BOBCAT EMBRYO LITTERS, UTAH

| Month | Year | Hunter | County | Number of embryos per female |
|---|---|---|---|---|
| February | 1951 | James Gray | Beaver | 3 |
| February | 1951 | James B. Lynn | Tooele | 4 |
| March | 1951 | James Gray | Millard | 4 |
| April | 1951 | Royal H. Blake | Washington | 2 |
| April | 1951 | Royal H. Blake | Washington | 2 |
| May | 1951 | James M. Gray | Beaver | 3 |
| May | 1951 | James M. Gray | Millard | 2 |
| June | 1951 | James M. Gray | Beaver | 4 |

tive tracts of some 395 specimens of bobcats obtained from 11
western states, which included Texas and Oklahoma, was conducted with Kenneth L. Duke, Associate Professor of Anatomy at Duke University, North Carolina. On the completion
of the study, tables 6 and 7 and graphs A and B were supplied
by Dr. Duke, with the following explanations:

"In graph B the active group of graph A has been broken
down into four categories.

TABLE 6.

REPRODUCTIVE CONDITION OF FEMALE LYNX RUFUS SPECIMENS

| Month | Number females collected | Pre-ovulatory | Post-ovulatory | Preg-nant | Lactating and/or Postpartum | In-active | Immature |
|---|---|---|---|---|---|---|---|
| January | 42 | 2 | 1 | 0 | 0 | 30 | 9 |
| February | 59 | 4 | 6 | 7 | 0 | 33 | 9 |
| March | 71 | 3 | 8 | 19 | 3 | 29 | 9 |
| April | 57 | 5 | 9 | 15 | 5 | 21 | 2 |
| May | 39 | 5 | 4 | 1 | 5 | 24 | 0 |
| June | 29 | 1 | 1 | 3 | 5 | 19 | 0 |
| July | 12 | 1 | 0 | 0 | 0 | 10 | 1 |
| August | 18 | 0 | 0 | 0 | 5 | 12 | 1 |
| September | 15 | 0 | 0 | 0 | 2 | 13 | 0 |
| October | 19 | 0 | 0 | 2 | 1 | 16 | 0 |
| November | 18 | 0 | 0 | 0 | 0 | 18 | 0 |
| December | 16 | 0 | 0 | 0 | 0 | 13 | 3 |

TABLE 7.

REPRODUCTIVE CONDITION OF FEMALE LYNX RUFUS SPECIMENS

| Month | Number females collected | Pre-ovulatory | Post-ovulatory | Pregnant | Lactating Postpartum | In-active | Immature |
|---|---|---|---|---|---|---|---|
| January | 42 | 5% | 2% | 0 | 0 | 72% | 21% |
| February | 59 | 7 | 10 | 12 | 0 | 56 | 15 |
| March | 71 | 4 | 11 | 27 | 4 | 41 | 13 |
| April | 57 | 9 | 16 | 26 | 9 | 37 | 3 |
| May | 39 | 13 | 10 | 3 | 13 | 61 | 0 |
| June | 29 | 4 | 4 | 10 | 17 | 65 | 0 |
| July | 12 | 8 | 0 | 0 | 0 | 84 | 8 |
| August | 18 | 0 | 0 | 0 | 28 | 67 | 5 |
| September | 15 | 0 | 0 | 0 | 13 | 87 | 0 |
| October | 19 | 0 | 0 | 11 | 5 | 84 | 0 |
| November | 18 | 0 | 0 | 0 | 0 | 100 | 0 |
| December | 16 | 0 | 0 | 0 | 0 | 81 | 19 |

"Graph A, I believe, shows the probable female reproductive pattern in the bobcat. A main breeding season from February to May or June. Females not impregnated during this season may come into heat later on, and perhaps some of the earliest fertile breeders have a second litter too, accounting for late summer and fall cases of reproductive activity.

"From a rather casual observation of testicular size throughout the year, and from looking at histological sections of tests from males collected in January-May, July-August, November and December, it would appear that the males are active year round."

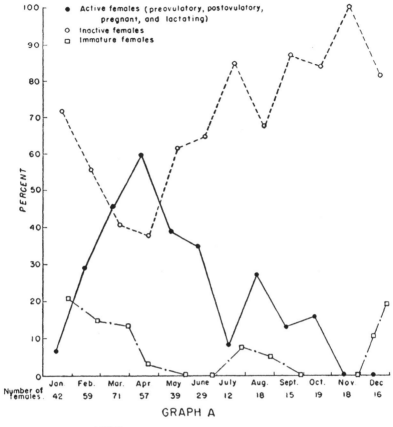

LEGEND

● Active females (preovulatory, postovulatory,
    pregnant, and lactating)
○ Inactive females
□ Immature females

GRAPH A

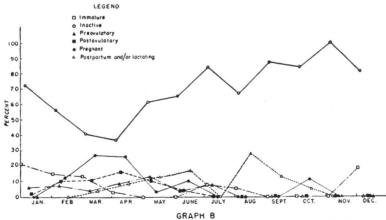

LEGEND

□ Immature
○ Inactive
▲ Preovulatory
◼ Postovulatory
● Pregnant
△ Postpartum and/or lactating

GRAPH B

GRAPHS A. AND B. Summary study of the reproductive tracts of 395 female bobcat specimens.

Unpublished reproductive data on 12 bobcats taken in Marin and Mendocino Counties, California are reported upon by William Longhurst, Assistant Specialist, University of California, College of Agriculture, Hopland Field Station, Hopland, California, in Table 8.

On October 8, 1939, Cecil E. Matteson trapped a female bobcat in Fremont County, Wyoming, which, while held in the trap, gave birth to a male kitten. This is one of the few early fall births of young on record.

TABLE 8.

REPRODUCTIVE CONDITION OF FEMALE BOBCAT SPECIMENS TAKEN IN MARIN COUNTY, CALIFORNIA—COASTAL STRIP SOUTH OF DRAKE'S BAY.

| Age | Lbs. weight | Fetuses | Corpora lutea Right ovary | Left ovary | Coll. date | Lactating |
|---|---|---|---|---|---|---|
| . . . . . . | . . . . | 0 | 1 | 0 | 5/29/51 | Yes |
| Adult | 12 | 2 | 1 | 3 | 5/22/51 | |
| . . . . . . | . . . . | 0 | 1 | 2 | 5/28/51 | Yes |
| Adult | 12¼ | 2 | 2 | 0 | 5/26/51 | |
| Young adult | 12¾ | 2 | 1 | 1 | 5/26/51 | |
| . . . . . . | . . . . | 0 | 1 | 0 | 5/25/51 | Yes |
| Adult | . . . . | 5 | 2 | 3 | 6/ 5/51 | |
| Adult | . . . . | 0 | 2 | 1 | 6/ 5/51 | Yes |
| Adult | 12 | 2 | 0 | 2 | | |
| Hopland Field Station—Mendocino County, California, 4 miles east of Hopland | | | | | | |
| Adult | . . . . | 3 | . . | . . | 3/16/52 | |

According to Duke (1949): "The corpora lutea of the bobcat evidently persist for months and probably years. Corpora lutea were found in the ovaries of all females regardless of the time of year they were trapped. Some ovaries contained only one corpus luteum while others contained as many as 12. Naturally, in the latter case, all the corpora lutea were not necessarily of the same age nor of the same histological make-up (cf. figs. 14, 15, and 16)."

Because of the persistence of corpora lutea it is probable that some of the corpora lutea listed for bobcats in this table did not result from current ovulations; consequently the fertilization success of current ovulations may have been higher than these records would indicate.

## SIZE OF LITTERS

The size of the litter of young will average about two, although three or four to a birth is not uncommon.

The largest number of unborn bobcats on record is as follows: A female killed in Refugio County, Texas, on August 1, 1946 contained six. This cat had killed 65 chickens the

PLATE 16c. Pet bobcat kitten, just over 1½ months old, playing with domestic kitten. (Photo courtesy L. Robinette).

PLATE 16d. At three months, becoming interested in a meat (squirrel) diet. (Photo courtesy L. Robinette).

PLATE 17. Bobcat in snow-drift, California. (Photo courtesy Ralph Anderson through Carl P. Russell, National Park Service.)

PLATE 17a. Male bobcat killed by puma in the Duck Creek area of eastern Nevada. (Photo courtesy of L. Robinette).

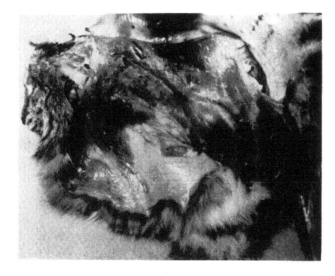

PLATE 17b. Neck region of skinned bobcat to show blood-clotted areas where puma attacked it in making the kill. (Photo courtesy of L. Robinette).

(48b)

PLATE 17c. Caught in double **trap** set, natural enemies seem to have formed a truce.

PLATE 18. Female bobcat and young in Cap Rock country south of Pueblo, Colorado, Reproduced from a painting by E. R. Kalmbach.

PLATE 19. Gordon Delawder, Woodstock, Virginia, after attack by rabid bobcat, winter 1953. (Photos courtesy U. S. Forest Service.)

previous six months on the Amiel Walzel farm, and was exceedingly fat.

Another female, which had killed thirty lambs between April 19 and May 2, 1944, and was finally trapped on the D. Lochlin Ranch in Culberson County, Texas, was found to be suckling five kittens, all of which were captured later.

In Oregon, Hunter Shaver, working in Deschutes County, reports taking, on February 25, 1950, a female bobcat containing 5 unborn young. On the same date another captured female contained only one unborn young. Another Oregon female examined February 28, 1942, had seven embryos as indicated by enlargements along the uterine horns.

In Virginia, two bobcat kittens were taken on September 3, 1951, and when seen in Mount Grove were believed to be approximately 5 weeks old, which put their birth in early August.

Robinette examined a female bobcat caught by Horace Torgerson of Elsinore, Utah, in early March 1954 that had seven unborn young.

One hundred female bobcats taken in Arizona from 1942 to 1946 show an average litter of unborn young of 2.69. The year of greatest food abundance (field mice, ground squirrels, rabbits, etc.) for this interval was 1942, which correspondingly shows the greatest average of unborn litters of 3.13 for 23 litters. This is also reflected by the size of unborn coyote litters which was 5.75 for a total of 95 unborn litters.

In a study of bobcat population vs. coyote population in Arizona it was found over a period of 26 years that the average ratio of bobcats and coyotes taken mainly by trapping by government hunters statewide, and totaling 51,300 coyotes and 9,423 bobcats, is 5.44 coyotes to one bobcat. Comparing this with the birth ratio between the two species in Arizona, an intriguing question arises, i.e.: Why is it that the relative litter size of coyotes and bobcats is approximately 2 to 1 in favor of coyotes, whereas the kill ratio over a period of 26 years is 5.44 to 1? Some Arizona field men conversant with the problem feel that this difference in birth ratio and kill ratio may be due to:

1. Shorter average longevity of the bobcat.
2. Hazards to existence of bobcat greater than coyote.
3. More rapid reproduction of coyote.
4. While there are some indications that bobcats may have their young during any month of the year, their seasonal reproductive periods may not be annual. There is evidence that some bobcats only reproduce every second year.
5. Difference in average number of young per litter.
6. The bobcat's inability to adapt itself to a habitat modified by encroaching civilization, while the coyote seems to thrive on it.
7. Differences in some feeding habits, and the inability of the bobcat to find sustenance in a generally modified habitat.

Although the foregoing points represent the thoughts of some of the Arizona field men, it is probable that their efforts were directed more to the capture of coyotes than bobcats. For the period mentioned, it is likely that the traps were set more in the open country favored by coyotes than in the rougher section where cats are more abundant. Thus, these efforts might be responsible for the indicated 5 to 1 ratio of coyotes over cats in the catch records.

## HYBRIDIZATION

While at San Antonio, Texas on March 21, 1950, W. H. Maclay, of Dallas, Texas reported to me that there is evidence of a successful mating between a male bobcat and a domestic cat at Sandy Creek, Texas during 1949. The offspring were observed by several persons in this area.

Hunter Howard J. Martin, stationed at Beach, North Dakota records the mating of a domestic black female house cat to a wild male bobcat on the ranch of Nick and Pete Melkowski, located six miles west of Belfield, North Dakota in the late spring of 1954. Previously, the domestic female had produced two litters by mating with a domestic tomcat, so she was fully matured.

She was prone to spend most of her time south of the ranch

in the breaks that occurred there. It was here she mated with the bobcat, and in early June brought forth a litter of seven kittens. On June 23 their eyes began to open. The coloration of four of the litter was coal black resembling domestic kittens with the exception that they had larger feet. The remaining three had bob tails, large feet, tufted ears, and were light gray in color with a speckling of black dots on the stomach, legs and sides. The ears were larger and hard and stiff. The tufts on them, made up of eight to ten hairs each, were approximately $\frac{1}{4}$ inch in length. This litter of seven kittens lived until the 27th of June, 1954, when they were killed by a domestic tomcat.

How a domestic house cat may become friendly to the point of living with a bobcat was shown in Oklahoma, when such a combination coming from Antlers was displayed by the Oklahoma Game and Fish Department in their mobile educational exhibit during September of 1952 (Anon. 1952: Feline Felicity).

## FAMILY TIES

There is very strong affection between the female bobcat and her young as there is in the female house cat. This goes even to the extent of fighting off the male should he attempt in any way to interfere with the newly born litter. Near the end of the nursing period, however, the male is tolerated, and, as has been stated, assists in obtaining food for the young. (Plate 18.)

The extent to which a female bobcat will defend her young is aptly described by E. G. Pope, of the Fish and Wildlife Service, when he reported: "Hunter Lewis McDonough, of Motley County, Texas, was on Kingery Ranch hunting pups [coyote] on the morning of June 23, 1949. Near a canyon bluff he decided to make a call for a coyote. He sat down beside a small cedar bush and started his call. Before he had finished making a call a bobcat jumped right in the middle of his back. Needless to say, he came to life. The bobcat bounced off four or five steps and bowed up at him as if to fight it out. He shot the cat with his rifle and on inspection of the area, found some kittens. McDonough was not hurt or scratched."

During the latter part of October 1951, Ernest W. Morton of Valentine, Texas trapped two half-grown bobcat kittens in trap sets about 35 feet apart. When the trap sets were later visited, tracks of a grown bobcat were much in evidence around each trapped kitten, as were numerous bits of rabbit fur. After dispatching the two animals, stomach examinations revealed that the stomach of each was full of undigested rabbit. The traps were reset at the scene of each capture, and that night an old female bobcat was captured in one of the sets. All indications were that this mother bobcat had brought rabbit to the half-grown bobcats while they were held captive in the traps.

E. H. Howell, of Goldsboro, North Carolina, records a female bobcat successfully fighting off a dog in defense of her young on three consecutive encounters, only to be killed by the dog's owner after the third attack [Wildlife in N. C. 16 (6): June, 1952].

─────── CHAPTER FOUR ───────

# PARASITES AND DISEASES

BOBCATS are host to numerous parasites, but much still remains for the parasitologist to complete the picture. The following is a synopsis of present knowledge.

Rollins (1945) reported an examination of the gastro-intestinal tracts of 50 bobcats for helminth parasites, 13 of which were made by Dr. O. W. Olsen and Dr. A. B. Erickson, University of Minnesota. They recorded the following:

| Parasite and location in organs | Bobcats parasitized |
|---|---|
| *Toxocara cati*,[1] intestine | 21 |
| *Toxascaris leonina*, intestine | 2 |
| *Physaloptera praeputialis*, stomach | 1 |
| *Physaloptera* sp., stomach | 2 |
| *Ascarinae*, intestine | 2 |
| *Spirocerca sanguinolenta?*,[1] stomach | 1 |
| *Toxocara* sp., intestine | 1 |
| *Taenia taeniaeformis*, intestine | 7 |
| *Taenia pisiformis*,[1] intestine | 5 |
| *Taenia hydatigena*, intestine | 3 |
| *Taenia rileyi*,[1] intestine | 2 |
| *Taenia monostephanos?*,[1] small intestine | 1 |
| *Taenia krabbei*, small intestine | 1 |
| Unidentified, small intestine | 1 |

[1] Apparently not previously reported for the bobcat in literature but listed in monthly parasitology reports, Division of Entomology and Economic Zoology, University of Minnesota.

"In 36 bobcats (72 percent) there were one or more of 13 different helminth parasites. The nematode *Toxocara cati* was recovered most frequently in 18 (or 36 percent), and in greatest individual infestation, 44 worms from one host. Six other nematodes were recovered.

"Of cestodes, *Taenia taeniaeformis* was most frequent, in 7 (14 percent) and 18 of these worms were taken from one host. *Taenia pisiformis* was recovered from 5 bobcats.

"The bobcat is the definitive host for the parasites reported in this paper. Alternate hosts are known to be deer for *Taenia krabbei* and *Taenia hydatigena,* mice for *Taenia taeniaeformis,* and hares and rabbits for *Taenia pisiformis.* The alternate hosts for *Taenia monostephanos* and *Taenia rileyi* are unknown. It is significant that animals known to be alternate hosts for the cestodes reported were represented in the food analyses above.

"All infestations were relatively light, and it is doubtful that even the heaviest had any serious effect on the host.

"[Thus] thirteen different helminth parasites were recovered from the gastro-intestinal tracts of 50 bobcats, 5 apparently not previously reported from this host."

In Virginia, 9 out of 11 bobcat stomachs contained the following: 1 stomach, 6 *Toxascaris leonina;* 3 stomachs, 30 *Physaloptera praeputialis;* 9 stomachs contained *Toxocara cati; Toxocara* sp. (immature) 4, in 4 stomachs; and *Taenia* sp. in the stomach of 1.

*Trichurus felis,* rarely reported in the bobcat, was found in a Virginia specimen.

The threadworm, *Uncinaria lotoris* has been found in the bobcat intestine.

Pollack (1949) in his thesis on the Ecology of the Bobcat found that most fleas will stay on a bobcat at least as long as five days after the death of the cat. The flea (*Cediopsylla simplex* Baker) was the most common.

The Texas State Department of Health has found the bobcat to be a host for the flea *Pulex irritans.*

Among the internal parasites, the cestode, *Taenia lyncis* Skinker was the most common. In the gastro-intestinal tracts of 100 bobcats, Pollack found only two that showed no parasitic signs.

While not as common in the wildcat family as in the dog family, mange at times infests the bobcat and is carried by the mite *Notoedres cati* (Hering). The effect of the disease is to weaken and greatly emaciate any bobcat young or old. When spread by a suckling female to her young, the kittens seldom survive.

The flea *Juxta pulix porcinus*, occurring on the peccary, has been found on bobcats (*L. r. texensis*) taken on the Norias subdivision of King Ranch, Kingsville, Texas. This flea is rather rare in most of the insect collections of the United States. Only four specimens of this flea are in the immense collections of the U. S. National Museum.

H. J. Van Cleave (1953) in his monumental work on the Acanthocephala of North American Mammals records finding "for the first time a single species of *Oncicola canis* from a lynx [bobcat], all previous records for North America having been from domestic dog and coyote as definite hosts."

He also records five female specimens of *Echinopardalis macrurae* taken from a bobcat living in a zoo. But because of this cat's environment, "the source of the infection is wholly unknown, and the parasite cannot be attributed with certainty to the endemic fauna of North America."

Georgia bobcats were found hosts to the rabbit flea *Cediopsylla simplex* (Baker), *Ixodes* probably *kingi* Bishop (an engorged numph and 4 females), and one eastern wood tick *Dermacentor variabilis* (Say). The rabbit flea probably transferred to the bobcat from a rabbit it had killed recently.

California bobcats taken in Marin and Mendocino Counties have been found hosts to the tapeworms *Hydatigera lyncis* Skinker, 1935, and *H. macrocystis* Giesing, 1950. Voge (1953) records *Mesocestoides variabilis* in a bobcat from the Hastings Reservation, Monterey County.

## TULAREMIA

Up to the time of compiling this manuscript, tularemia has not been reported in the bobcat, but has in the domestic cat (Burroughs, *et al.*, 1945). Because the bobcat so relishes wild rabbits, which are very susceptible to this oft fatal or debilitating disease, it is not beyond the realm of possibility that bobcats do sometimes become infected.

## RABIES

A hunter, while stalking deer on the southern end of the San Isabel National Forest in Colorado during the deer season of 1922, was attacked and badly scratched by a bobcat. The animal jumped on the hunter's shoulders, clawing and biting him on the neck. He killed the animal, took it to Pueblo, and on the advice of a physician sent its brain to the State Board of Health, at Denver, where examination proved positive for rabies. The hunter was given Pasteur treatment. Shortly thereafter, in the winter of 1923, a serious rabies situation developed in the Gardiner area of southern Colorado among bobcats, coyotes, dogs, and livestock. A vigorous rabies control was instituted, and the infestation was brought under control, but not until a similar outbreak occurred on the eastern edge of the San Luis Valley. Evidence indicated that the rabies had been spread by rabid animals in their crossing of the Sangre de Cristo Divide near Mosca Pass (Young, 1950: 26, 30, 42).

On May 22, 1947, A. C. Metherlin, a stockman residing in the vicinity of Ajo, Pima County, Arizona, telephoned the District Office of the Fish and Wildlife Service at Phoenix, Arizona to report that a cowboy at his ranch had been attacked by a rabid bobcat and scratched and bitten on the head. The attack occurred at 5 o'clock in the morning while the cowboy was asleep on a cot in the yard at the Metherlin ranch. By pulling the bed covers over his head, the cowboy in question probably avoided more serious injury. The bobcat bit and scratched the bed covers and tore them badly. Following the attack, the bobcat escaped but apparently returned to the ranch house the next day where it was discovered hiding under a bench. It attacked ranch hands who found it, but was killed before anyone else was injured. The head of the bobcat was sent to a laboratory at Tucson, Arizona where a test revealed that the animal had rabies. Prior to this incident, Mr. Metherlin had noted several dead foxes on his range and two dead coyotes had been removed from nearby water tanks.

From Clarksville, Arkansas comes the report that during April of 1950, a bobcat diagnosed as rabid attacked a farm woman. The attack occurred at the family lumber pile. This lady, who weighed 98 lbs., slightly more than twice as much as the 40-lb. cat, defended herself for the moment with several hard swings at the cat with a club. In the struggle the cat bit the woman severely, then leaped upon a nearby horse which it rode for fully a minute. Then, springing from the animal's back, it fled under a farm building where it was finally shot.

Six rabid bobcats were recorded in Virginia during 1951-1952. In the fall of 1951 sections of Virginia and West Virginia experienced rabies outbreaks of epidemic proportions among dogs and foxes.

Donald R. Progulski (in lit.), while a student at Virginia Polytechnic Institute, Blacksburg, Virginia, on March 5, 1952, authenticated a rabid bobcat attack as follows:

"A week or so ago I came across information about a rabid bobcat here in Virginia and thought you might be interested to know the details of it. It's absolutely true as I have three of the microscope slides showing Niger bodies which the Public Health Laboratory at Luray, Virginia made up on the day the bobcat was killed.

"Mr. Simpson, game warden in Warren County, first told me of the incident as he was the one who took the carcass to the laboratory. On February 21, 1952, the cat entered a yard in Glenn Echo, one mile north of Browntown, Virginia, and jumped two coon hounds tied up or staying in the yard. I don't know what happened to the dogs but the cat then turned toward a woman who was also in the yard. Fortunately she escaped into the house in time. Raymond Rudacille who was in the house at the time shot the cat then turned it over to

Mr. Simpson. As you probably realize, this was right in the area where so many rabid foxes are being collected. Mr. Simpson said the cat's claws were broken and worn like a splintered match stick. Both the front and hind claws were in the same condition. The cat weighed 19 pounds."

And finally, on March 7, 1953, from Harrisonburg, Virginia, comes the report of an attack by a bobcat, undoubtedly rabid, on Gordon Delawder (Plate 19), a timberman of Bird Haven, Shenandoah County. At this time information was obtained from Harrisonburg, Virginia, to the effect that "Gordon Delawder is recovering from the bites of a probably-rabid 20-pound wildcat which he choked to death with his hands after the cat attacked him near here.

"Mr. Delawder, a timberman of Bird Haven in Shenandoah County is wearing bandages on his cheek and right hand and is recovering from the effects of anti-rabies injections.

"Tests on the brain of the dead animal, made at the State laboratory at Luray, showed that it probably was rabid. The carcass was returned to Mr. Delawder as a souvenir.

"It all began a week ago when Mr. Delawder stopped his car, as usual, before the gate at Wilmer Hensberger's home. They were going to Ashby Vansler's woods where they were skidding logs.

"As he started through the gate an animal jumped from somewhere, and landed on his shoulders. Mr. Delawder turned his head quickly and the animal sank its teeth into his left cheek and held on.

" 'I made a grab for it with my right hand,' he said. 'It released its hold on my cheek and bit my hand.'

"He managed to wrestle the animal, still clinging to his hand, to the ground between his knees. He choked it to death with his left hand.

"Mr. Hensberger, hearing the commotion, ran out of his house but by that time the big cat was dead. The two men pried the cat's jaws open.

"They put the dead animal in Mr. Delawder's car and drove to the home of Shenandoah County Game Warden Elon Sheets, who sent the carcass to the laboratory. Mr. Delawder went to a physician for treatment of the two wounds and a precautionary anti-rabies shot."

## CAT SCRATCH FEVER

A fever resembling tularemia, though much milder in its effect on humans, is transmitted at times by the scratch of the domestic cat. The symptoms are weakness, fever, lymph gland enlargement, and some rash. It is believed to be caused by a virus. The scratch of the bobcat may cause this condition, judging by the experience of this writer after scratches were received while removing a presumably dead bobcat from a trap. Some authorities believe this disease is passed on from the cat's mouth.

Infection will often occur when a human is scratched by the bobcat's claws. Such infection is believed to come from a film of rotting meat that gathers on the claws in the course of obtaining its food. The sheaths into which the claws are retracted form ideal pockets for incubation of bacteria.

Both the bobcat and puma are susceptible to feline enteritis. This disease killed the pet bobcat of Leslie Robinette mentioned previously (See Table 3a).

## CHAPTER FIVE

# ECONOMIC STATUS

BEFORE beginning a consideration of the economic problems involved in the presence of predatory species of animals such as wolves, coyotes, pumas and bobcats, I wish to disclaim being actuated by any strictly economic frame of mind. Throughout the years there have been some conscientious people who were opposed to any form of control of injurious mammals. I should like to go on record as being also opposed to the unnecessary destruction of any animal. My personal attitude is that of the naturalist who has studied animals from the depths of the ocean, in the rivers and lakes, on coastal plain, valley, and prairie to the tops of our high mountain ranges. The motivating force has been sheer love of living things and a desire to learn the fundamental laws and forces which activate and control the movements, the development, and the destiny of living creatures. I admit also having strong humanitarian tendencies and being interested in the health, vigor, mentality, education, prosperity, development, and progress of the human beings which populate the Earth and constitute an important factor in the evolution of its fauna and flora. No study of natural factors involved in the evolutionary progress of the animate or inanimate world can be complete without including the dominating, masterful motives and forces of man. These include his primary zoological functions of obtaining food and shelter, and the later social developments. The latter include altruistic considerations for the comfort, convenience, health, and happiness of his family, for the education and business foundations of his children, and the establishment of conditions which make for higher standards of living.

The inquiry which culminated in the monographs on the wolves, puma, coyote, and now *Lynx rufus* therefore has been based upon a recognition of man as a member of nature's community. This involves his primary right in the struggle for existence and in the eternal operation of the principle of survival of the fittest to exert himself in making conditions more favorable for humanity, in extending his range, increasing in numbers and improving the opportunity and the industrial means for gaining not merely a bare existence, but also the comforts, the refinements, and the upward trend which are proper accompaniments of civilized life. These are higher levels of man's evolution and existence and are worthy human objectives everywhere.

Man's evolutionary history indicates that he early came to rely on his agility, skill, and wits in coping with competing animals. As time went on he multiplied his powers of accomplishment through inventive ingenuity, manual dexterity, and skill in utilizing mechanical and chemical means of defense and offense. These are being continued up to the present moment.

With this epitome of man's place and activities in world occupation, it will afford a helpful perspective to review briefly conditions existing at the time America was discovered and the white race began to make a serious effort to gain a foothold.

Without being unmindful of such limited and ancient civilizations as may have existed previous to that time, it will be generally agreed that it was a great land area in which the forces of nature had held free sway. The forests, streams, and forage of plains and mountains, the whole range of animal life from amoeba to the higher vertebrate forms were in the state to which the free operation of natural forces had brought them. The scattered tribes of uncivilized people with their primitive modes of life and relatively limited numbers appear to have disturbed but little the orderly course of the struggle for existence. What a dream world for the modern naturalist if he had only been there!

The coming of the vigorous and progressive white people with their arts of agriculture and animal husbandry introduced new factors into this situation. Let us pass with a mere mention the orgy of slaughter in the havesting of the wealth of peltries, and the pursuit for sport of the natural heritage of big game animals.

The arrival of the white man inaugurated a new biological era. As succulent, nutritious, cultivated crops have been introduced throughout the country various rodents have turned from the scanty fare often provided by native vegetation to feed upon the new source of food and have followed with a vengeance the ancient injunction to be fruitful, to increase, and multiply. In the face of the rodent's ravages, the farmer, the orchardist, and the stockman have been confronted by the dilemma of putting up a defensive and offensive fight, or of leaving the country to the prolific hordes of native vegetarian occupants. The producers of horses, cattle, sheep, swine, poultry, and other domesticated animals essential to civilized existence were similarly confronted by the destructive activities of beasts of prey which, heretofore accustomed to feed upon the fleet or powerful wild species, have found the domesticated forms easy victims. These domesticated animals provided toothsome items in the bill of fare and ready objects to satisfy the cravings of hunger, to gratify their natural instinct to kill, and to supply the means of rearing a numerous and vigorous progeny.

As exploration and settlement advanced it was learned that the timber wolf originally ranged practically throughout the United States. The coyote occupied the Pacific coast, the Great Basin, the Rocky Mountain regions, and the plains country eastward into Illinois, Indiana, Wisconsin, and Michigan. The puma frequented suitable forested areas and made excursions across plains and valleys throughout the land. Various races of bobcats likewise occurred practically from coast to coast while the larger Canada lynx occupied the more northerly sections and its range extended southward in the mountainous regions.

Experience has demonstrated that operation of the laissez faire principle, when applied to rodents and the larger predaceous animals, has not served to afford the farmer, the orchardist, or the stockman satisfactory protection nor has it permitted adequate or profitable utilization of land. As the matter has worked out in practice, the usual forces of nature have permitted both groups to increase inordinately in the face of agricultural and stock raising operations and to cause enormous losses to producers.

The early colonists soon learned that it was necessary to employ active measures to destroy wolves, pumas, and other species which endangered their lives or property. They took steps accordingly. Legislation designed to afford relief was put into effect in Massachusetts in 1630, in Virginia in 1632, and in Pennsylvania in 1683. Ohio and Kentucky in 1795 and Tennessee in 1797 were taking up the fight. The movement spread westward as settlement progressed, until good management plans finally culminated in the employment of government hunters as a more promising method of coping with predators.

In compiling the various predator monographs referred to, I have felt that to do a respectable job one should have as complete knowledge as possible of their history. This means laborious digging into musty literature of historical events, a tedious task, but one that often pays important dividends.

PLATE 20. Lambing range near Carlin, Nevada, where 2 bobcats killed a total of 34 lambs within 48 hours. Some of lamb victims shown in foreground.

PLATE 21. Bobcat, taken near Rowes Well, Arizona, after killing 30 lambs from one band of sheep.

PLATE 22. Bailey's bobcat *(L. r. baileyi)* killing antelope jackrabbit, Arizona. Reproduced from a painting by R. P. Grossenheider.

PLATE 22a. Plateau or Bailey's bobcat, the bobcat of the deserts.

PLATE 23. Bobcat deer kill, South Dakota, showing point of attack, and the 27-lb. cat that made it.

PLATE 24. Bobcat with mourning dove (Texas). (Courtesy Eastman Kodak Co.)

PLATE 25. Top—harvesting catnip. Bottom—distilling catnip oil for use in experiments as a lure for both bobcats and pumas.

What the puma is as an enemy to big game, the bobcat is to small game, and the young of big game. Nature has placed the bobcat's eyes in the front of its face better to see its prey. This is true of most of the predators.

It often runs the coyote a close second as a predator on domestic stock and poultry, particularly sheep when they are lambed in rough, but wide, rocky canyons (Plates 20 and 21). Such lambing sites are often chosen by stockmen because of the protection afforded during stormy, wintry weather.

## AS HUMAN FOOD

Merriam (1886:41) says "I have eaten the flesh of the wild cat, and can pronounce it excellent. It is white and very tender, and suggests veal more than any other meat with which I am familiar."

The author does not agree with the foregoing based on his experience, for bobcat meat was found to be very tough with an extremely nauseating odor while cooking. Hence its palatability was very low. Good bobcat dogs refused to touch it. A young cat might be a more palatable meat.

## USE OF SKIN

During early pioneer days bobcat pelts were used for clothing and the pelts were often listed in early day fur inventory. For instance, Major G. C. Sibley mentions 355 "wildcat" skins in a statement of furs taken in between October 1, 1808 and June 1810 at the U. S. Indian Factory at Fort Osage (Favour, A. L., 1936:42). Of further interest, if for no other point than the spelling, is that of Evan Shelby (1954) recorded on May 20, 1764 to wit:

"Memorandum of What Skins I sent to Mr. John Postlethwaits Waggen

        To 108 pounds of Dear Skins
        To 7 Rackoon skins
        To 5 Fox Dito
        To 3 whiyle Catts Dito"

Among other colonial activities, Evan Shelby was an Indian trader on the then Maryland, Ohio, Kentucky frontier.

Today the common use of prime bobcat skins is making sport jackets, trimming coats, or mounting as rugs.

Bobcat skins were prized by the Indian tribes of the lower Columbia River for making robes. Lewis and Clark reported that four skins were required to make a robe. The race of bobcat *(Lynx rufus fasciatus)* found in this section is beautifully marked, especially the pronounced white belly with black spots. The Plains Indians used the animal's skin for making quivers, often allowing the tail and distended claws to hang intact.

In recent years, the dictates of fashion regulate the use of the skin for modern feminine apparel. Whole coats of the fur become popular for a period, and then wane in popularity. It is not a particularly durable or long-wearing fur because of its brittleness.

## SKINNING OF THE BOBCAT

In skinning the bobcat pelt to be later sold as fur, one should cut the skin around all four feet, approximately 4 inches from the foot. The skin of the front legs should be slit on the inside of the leg to the knee joint, and then pulled loose to the body. The skin of the hind legs should be slit on the inside of each leg to the anus. The tail bone should be drawn using the fingers, a pair of pliers, spikes, or two sticks, after which the skin of the tail should be slit on the under side its entire length. Following this, the carcass should be hung by the hind legs, and the pelt drawn down over the head, pulling the pelt from the body as much as possible. This works easily when the carcass is still warm. Sometimes the feet are skinned out, including the foot pads and claws, particularly when the pelt is to be mounted or used in taxonomic work.

The fleshing of the pelt (removal of meat, fat, and gristle adhering to the pelt) should be done immediately after skinning. Often the separating of the flesh from the pelt with the thumb makes it possible to remove this thin layer in one piece. When done soon after skinning tearing of the skin is more easily avoided than when the skin is allowed to dry. All blood stains on the pelt can be removed by washing in plain, tepid water. Stretcher boards are used in drying the skin. The pelt is stretched on the board, flesh side out, and when almost dry, it is removed, turned fur side out, and placed back on the stretcher. The nose should be rounded over the tip of the stretcher, and the lip tacked so that it will dry thoroughly. Each hind leg should be crossed and tacked at an angle of 45 degrees to the opposite board. Often skins are slightly salted on the flesh side, including the ears, legs, tail and lips. This aids in preventing flies from "blowing" (laying their eggs on) the skin. The skin should be dried slowly in a shady spot, away from artificial heat. The foregoing procedure produces what is called a "cased skin" and is the most acceptable to fur buyers.

## VALUE OF THE FUR

The fur of the bobcat may not interest a lady as the sable or mink does, neither will it wear as well. Nevertheless, it has a distinctive beauty all its own and costs much less.

At first glance bobcat fur resembles lynx, although, as previously mentioned, there is a shorter pencil of hairs on the ear tips. The tail is stubby, and the hair covering is brown, reddish brown, or tan. The sides and belly are spotted, and in some specimens these spots are darker and more numerous than in others. The guard hair and underfur are silky in texture, and the pelts from the north are slightly fuller furred than those from the south. Peltries having the longest guard hairs and darker fur are generally dyed black or bleached and dyed pastel shades, and used for trimmings.

Pelts produced in the south and southwest sections of the United States generally have blacker and more prominent spots. At times American markets prefer these well-marked furs for making sport coats. The flatter furred bobcat pelts with the pronounced spotting are usually sheared before they are made into jackets or trimmings.

The following information concerning bobcat pelt values in recent years, in widely separated geographic parts of this animal's range, may be of interest.

TABLE 9.

NUMBERS OF BOBCAT STOMACHS CONTAINING CERTAIN KINDS OF FOOD.

| Food | Jan. | Feb. | Mar. | Apr. | May | June | July | Aug. | Sept. | Oct. | Nov. | Dec. | Total |
|---|---|---|---|---|---|---|---|---|---|---|---|---|---|
| Beef ............. | 3 | 1 | 2 | 4 | 1 | 2 | 6 | 1 | 2 | 2 | 3 | 6 | 33 |
| Horse ............ | 1 | 3 | 0 | 3 | 2 | 2 | 2 | 0 | 2 | 2 | 3 | 2 | 22 |
| Sheep or goat .... | 41 | 5 | 12 | 20 | 50 | 59 | 60 | 60 | 38 | 61 | 41 | 26 | 473 |
| Pork ............. | 2 | 0 | 1 | 2 | 3 | 0 | 0 | 1 | 0 | 2 | 3 | 3 | 17 |
| Poultry .......... | 5 | 4 | 2 | 2 | 4 | 6 | 9 | 32 | 23 | 10 | 25 | 10 | 132 |
| Grouse ........... | 7 | 7 | 11 | 12 | 5 | 15 | 43 | 29 | 32 | 21 | 14 | 11 | 207 |
| Waterfowl ........ | 0 | 0 | 0 | 0 | 0 | 0 | ... | ... | 1 | 3 | 2 | 0 | 6 |
| Other birds ...... | 40 | 11 | 24 | 15 | 18 | 25 | 47 | 51 | 32 | 43 | 44 | 23 | 373 |
| Deer ............. | 13 | 7 | 5 | 7 | 3 | 5 | 3 | 15 | 9 | 13 | 8 | 6 | 94 |
| Elk .............. | ... | ... | ... | ... | ... | 0 | ... | ... | ... | ... | ... | ... | ... |
| Antelope ......... | 1 | 4 | 2 | 0 | 0 | 0 | ... | ... | ... | ... | ... | ... | 7 |
| Rabbit ........... | 151 | 101 | 106 | 79 | 76 | 71 | 123 | 142 | 160 | 184 | 142 | 127 | 1,462 |
| Ground squirrels .. | 5 | 6 | 11 | 10 | 28 | 31 | 30 | 20 | 20 | 16 | 13 | 5 | 195 |
| Prairie dog ...... | 0 | 0 | 1 | 0 | 1 | 0 | 11 | 3 | 2 | 2 | 3 | 2 | 25 |
| Chipmunk ......... | 1 | 0 | 5 | 0 | 3 | 5 | 6 | 10 | 4 | 6 | 2 | 2 | 44 |
| Groundhog (marmot) .. | 0 | 0 | 2 | 0 | 1 | 2 | 2 | 1 | 0 | 0 | 0 | 0 | 8 |
| Mouse or rat ..... | 22 | 19 | 15 | 20 | 17 | 13 | 29 | 43 | 47 | 33 | 31 | 26 | 315 |
| Bait ............. | 31 | 19 | 47 | 18 | 2 | 13 | 9 | 9 | 24 | 17 | 45 | 37 | 271 |
| Carrion .......... | 3 | 2 | 7 | 1 | 0 | 7 | 7 | 24 | 19 | 3 | 6 | 5 | 84 |
| Insects or worms .. | 0 | 1 | 1 | 1 | 0 | 0 | 16 | 6 | 9 | 1 | 0 | 0 | 35 |
| Fish, frogs, or reptiles ..... | 0 | 0 | 0 | 1 | 0 | 0 | 0 | 3 | 2 | 1 | 0 | 0 | 7 |
| Grass, sticks, or berries ......... | 9 | 7 | 9 | 6 | 7 | 7 | 10 | 35 | 54 | 15 | 15 | 6 | 180 |
| Totals ........... | 335 | 197 | 263 | 201 | 221 | 263 | 413 | 485 | 480 | 435 | 400 | 297 | 3,990 |

For the period 1930-31 to 1941-42, a total of only 25 bobcats were taken in Alberta, Canada. With the exception of the southern part of Alberta, the animal is considered very rare in that province. The value of the skins varied from $1 to $4. For the period July 1, 1943 to June 30, 1944, but 10 bobcats are listed in the provincial take, and the skins of these were valued at an average of $2 each (A. L. Rand, 1948:33, 121-123).

In a summary by Rand (1944), the average annual catch of the bobcat in Nova Scotia for the period 1910-34 was 514. The average annual value of bobcat pelts for the period 1931-40 was $2,065. The usual price per skin fluctuated from $2.50 to $6, with some going as high as $10.63. The bobcat ranked sixth on the list of 11 different marketable furs taken in this province.

The pelts of 137 bobcats taken in Colorado during the season 1947-48 averaged $2.43 per skin. A higher average in Colorado for the period 1946-48 is recorded as $6.90 per pelt. Two hundred sixteen skins sold for the 1949-50 season averaged $1.42 per skin.

Fifteen bobcats taken in North Dakota during that State's fur harvest of 1948-49 averaged $1.40 per pelt.

In the deep South, the bobcat skin is of little fur value. Forty-four pelts taken in Mississippi during 1950-51 averaged 47 cents per pelt.

Specially prepared skins and heads of bobcats are sold as trophies. During 1950 mounted wall-heads, open mouth on panel, were quoted at $17.50 each. Mounted bobcat fur rugs, lined, were quoted at from $15 to $27.50 each, depending on size. Flat rugs without head mounts, but lined for bedside rugs, couch or table covers were quoted at $15 each.

For some years private fur trappers have taken few bobcats, the reason being the low price caused by the lack of demand for short-haired fur except for that which can be sheared.

## FOOD OF THE BOBCAT

### Stomach Analysis—Field

The operations for the control of bobcats have afforded an opportunity to study on a more comprehensive scale the feeding habits of the species. This animal has come into direct conflict with the interests of men engaged in livestock production and game protection. The major charges against it have been based on the reputed destructiveness to livestock and game, and the propensity of the animal to serve as a carrier of rabies and to spread this deadly disease among domestic animals and to man. The studies of food habits have been conducted along two lines which are complementary in character, namely, by examination of material found in the stomachs of animals killed, and by field observation.

The personnel of the Fish and Wildlife Service making the field analysis in those states west of the 94th meridian were versed in bobcat lore and well acquainted with the animal life about them. They were good local naturalists who kept reliable field notes, often making valuable contributions to the animal's natural history.

Compilation of all field data concerning examination of bobcat stomach contents for the years 1918-1922 gives the interesting and significant information in Table 9. In this table it may be noted that of the 3,990 items listed in the stomach examinations reported, 677 were of domesticated animals, 687 were of game mammals, game birds, or other birds, 2,049 were of rodents, and 577 of various miscellaneous materials, most of which consisted of the bait which had been used in the traps. Among domesticated animals, sheep and goat constitute the chief article of their diet, being found in 473 instances distributed through every month of the year. Poultry appears to be their second preference in this group. The grouse was most popular of game birds, having 207 records, though outnumbered by the 373 miscellaneous birds. Among the smaller animals, rabbits are most prominently represented with 1,462.

*Stomach Analysis—Laboratory*

Deep appreciation is expressed to Charles C. Sperry, long on the staff of the old Bureau of Biological Survey, and the present Fish and Wildlife Service, for portions taken from his manuscript on "The Food of the Bobcat."

Sperry examined in the Wildlife Research Laboratory at Denver, Colorado, a total of 3,538 bobcat stomachs, collected mainly by the field personnel of the Branch of Predator and Rodent Control of the Fish and Wildlife Service, from 30 states. The results are given in Table 10.

Approximately 70 percent of the 3,538 bobcat stomachs examined by Sperry were collected in 15 western states by Federal and cooperative trappers engaged in predatory mammal control, largely in the interest of livestock protection. Most of the stomachs from eastern and southern states, as well as a large number from California, were obtained through direct cooperation by the state game and fish departments, and the fine series of stomachs from Michigan and Vermont were delivered unsolicited and without cost to the Federal Government. A few stomachs from eastern and southern states were saved and donated by private trappers. Analysis of these stomachs showed these items:

*Rodents* (46 percent) distributed as follows: *Cricetidae,* 28 percent. Native rats and mice eaten by bobcats were chiefly wood rats, meadow mice, and cotton rats, but include also a number of deer mice and red-backed mice as well as a few harvest mice, muskrats, pine mice, and rice rats. *Sciuridae,* 10 percent. Both ground squirrels and tree squirrels are important sources of food for bobcats. Other squirrels eaten in appreciable numbers locally are chipmunks, flying squirrels, prairie dogs, and marmots. Many prairie dogs were eaten in New Mexico and a few in Colorado, Utah, and Wyoming. *Heteromyidae,* 5 percent. Kangaroo rats and pocket mice formed an appreciable part of the food of bobcats throughout the West and Southwest—high percentages being 17 for 19 stomachs from Nevada, and 9 for 1,202 stomachs from California. *Geomyidae,*

TABLE 10.

Bobcat Stomach Analysis

| State | Jan. | Feb. | Mar. | Apr. | May | June | July | Aug. | Sept. | Oct. | Nov. | Dec. | Total |
|---|---|---|---|---|---|---|---|---|---|---|---|---|---|
| Ala. | 23 | 19 | 9 | 1 | | | | 2 | 1 | 1 | 4 | 19 | 79 |
| Ariz. | 21 | 19 | 30 | 19 | 26 | 34 | 23 | 15 | 15 | 28 | 14 | 8 | 252 |
| Ark. | 3 | 7 | | 1 | | 1 | | | | | | 1 | 13 |
| Calif. | 137 | 116 | 116 | 113 | 119 | 99 | 57 | 43 | 44 | 98 | 146 | 114 | 1,202 |
| Colo. | 2 | 4 | 4 | 3 | 1 | 3 | 4 | 5 | 12 | 18 | 7 | 6 | 69 |
| Fla. | 2 | | 4 | 4 | 1 | | | | 2 | | 2 | 1 | 16 |
| Ga. | | 1 | 9 | 2 | 1 | 2 | | | | | | 1 | 16 |
| Idaho | 2 | 4 | | | | | | 1 | 3 | 5 | 2 | | 17 |
| Maine | 2 | 2 | 2 | | | | | | | | | | 6 |
| Mass. | | | | | | | | | | | 5 | 1 | 6 |
| Mich. | 31 | 8 | 6 | 1 | 6 | 2 | 1 | 1 | 3 | 9 | 7 | 16 | 91 |
| Minn. | 3 | 1 | 1 | | | | | | | 1 | 3 | | 9 |
| Miss. | | 2 | 1 | 1 | | | | | 2 | | | | 6 |
| Mo. | | | | | | | | | | | | 1 | 1 |
| Mont. | 9 | 8 | | | 1 | 1 | 3 | 2 | | 1 | 2 | 2 | 29 |
| Nebr. | | | | 1 | | | | | | | | 1 | 2 |
| Nev. | | | 3 | 1 | 1 | 3 | 2 | | 1 | 3 | 3 | 2 | 19 |
| N. Mex. | 51 | 29 | 60 | 68 | 64 | 34 | 27 | 46 | 58 | 76 | 53 | 37 | 603 |
| Okla. | 9 | 6 | 12 | 4 | 9 | 1 | 2 | 3 | 4 | 5 | 2 | | 57 |
| Oreg. | 13 | 8 | 7 | 2 | 5 | 3 | 7 | 3 | 5 | 8 | 5 | 3 | 69 |
| S. C. | | | | | 2 | | | | | | 3 | | 5 |
| S. Dak. | | | | | | 2 | 1 | | | 1 | | 2 | 6 |
| Tex. | 70 | 82 | 81 | 98 | 50 | 49 | 34 | 24 | 33 | 41 | 53 | 71 | 686 |
| Utah | 2 | 6 | 1 | | 1 | 8 | 2 | 7 | 1 | 7 | 1 | | 36 |
| Vt. | 28 | 10 | 5 | 3 | | | | | 1 | 3 | 31 | 19 | 100 |
| Va. | 1 | 3 | 3 | 2 | 2 | 1 | | | | 3 | 1 | | 16 |
| Wash. | 11 | 6 | 4 | 8 | 3 | 1 | | 3 | 3 | 3 | | 9 | 51 |
| W. Va. | | 2 | 3 | | | | | | | | | | 5 |
| Wis. | 1 | | | | 1 | | | | | | | | 2 |
| Wyo. | 10 | 4 | 10 | 3 | 6 | 4 | 1 | 2 | 7 | 8 | 8 | 6 | 69 |
| Totals | 431 | 347 | 371 | 335 | 299 | 248 | 166 | 154 | 195 | 319 | 353 | 320 | 3,538 |

2 percent. Most of the pocket gophers eaten by bobcats were *Thomomys,* although the larger *Cratogeomys* and *Geomys* were eaten occasionally. *Porcupine,* 1 percent. Porcupine proved to be an important food item in bobcat stomachs from Vermont (13% in 100 stomachs), Minnesota (11% in 9 stomachs), Michigan (8% in 91 stomachs), South Dakota (17% in 6 stomachs) and Idaho (6% in 17 stomachs). Porcupines were frequently found also in bobcat stomachs collected in Idaho, Oregon, Colorado, New Mexico, Arizona, Wyoming, and California, importance being in the order named. *Other rodents* occasionally eaten by bobcats were house mice and mountain beaver, the latter being the dominant spring and summer food of Washington bobcats.

*Rabbits* occurred in 45 percent of all the bobcat stomachs examined and contributed from 29% to 47% of the food in each of the 12 months. They were a major source of bobcat food in every section of the United States, as follows: New England (28% in 112 stomachs), East (40% in 21 stomachs), Southeast (40% in 122 stomachs), Lake States (28% in 102 stomachs), Midwest (57% in 71 stomachs), Rocky Mountain (43% in 211 stomachs), Northwest (39% in 137 stomachs), and West (32% in 1,221 stomachs). All forms of rabbits (brush rabbits, cottontails, jackrabbits, marsh rabbits, and snowshoe hares) were well represented in the bobcats' food.

*Deer* contributed from 2 to 4 percent of the bobcats' food from April to October and from 5 to 10 percent from November to March—annual average 5 percent. Bobcat feeding on deer was most pronounced in New England (25% in 112 stomachs), the Lake States, Minnesota-Wisconsin-Michigan (25% in 102 stomachs) and the Northwest, Washington-Oregon-Idaho (10% in 137 stomachs).

*Livestock* (largely sheep and goats, but mostly sheep) comprised 2 percent of the bobcats' food and was significant in Idaho (12% in 17 stomachs), Wyoming (7% in 69 stomachs), Colorado (6% in 69 stomachs) and Nevada (5% in 19 stomachs). Most of the goats eaten were taken in Oregon and Oklahoma.

Calf and colt were rarely found in the bobcat stomachs examined, while swine, although found more frequently, still comprised only a trace of the total food and was confined almost entirely to Florida, Georgia and Louisiana. Peccary was not found in any of the bobcat stomachs examined.

*Other mammals* contributed 2 percent to the bobcats' food. The bulk of this food was composed of shrews from Vermont, Michigan and Idaho; moles from Oregon and California; opossums and raccoons from Virginia, Arkansas, Oklahoma, Alabama and Mississippi; and skunks from Vermont, Michigan, Wyoming, and California.

*Game birds* (mostly upland species) were found in bobcat stomachs collected throughout the year and contributed 1 percent to the total food. The bulk of these birds were quail from Arizona, California, Florida and Texas; ruffed grouse from Michigan, Minnesota and Vermont; and sage grouse from Wyoming. Other species recorded included blue grouse, sharp-tailed grouse, doves, and wild turkey. Aquatic game birds composed only a trace of the total food and consisted largely of coots and ducks from California and Texas.

*Non-game birds* were eaten by bobcats in 24 of the 30 states in which bobcat stomachs were taken and composed 1 percent of the total food. Sparrows, (including goldfinch, house finch, junco and towhee) were found in 13 stomachs from 7 states. Other birds with 2 or more records were thrushes (including bluebird, mockingbird, and robin), flickers, jays, blackbirds, owls, hawks, and wrens.

*Poultry* (chickens, ducks and turkeys) was found in bobcat stomachs from 13 states and comprised one or more percent of the food of the animals collected in Alabama, Arizona, Massachusetts, Michigan, Nevada, Vermont and Wyoming.

*Snakes and lizards* were eaten by bobcats in every month except November, December, and January and formed 1 percent of the food during April, May, June, July and October. Most of this reptile food was obtained in Arizona (1% in 252 stomachs), California (1% in 1,202 stomachs), and Oklahoma (2% in 57 stomachs). Most of the snakes were bull-snakes, racers and rattlesnakes, while the only lizard found in more than one stomach was the fence lizard *(Sceloperus)* taken a number of times in Arizona, California, and Oklahoma.

*Invertebrates,* chiefly grasshoppers and beetles, occasionally are eaten by bobcats but usually constitute merely a trace of the food. Exceptional cases include a Texas bobcat collected in May and a California bobcat taken in July that made 20 percent and 10 percent respectively of their last meals on beetles, and an Oregon bobcat, trapped in August that had eaten eight large grasshoppers.

*Vegetable food* is rarely consumed by bobcats. A trace of green grass was found in 1 Florida and 3 Texas bobcat stomachs, collected during January, February, April and May, and grass composed 5 percent and 40 percent of the contents of 2 California bobcats collected in March and April, respectively. Cultivated fruit (grapes and pears) was eaten by two California bobcats in October and composed 35 percent and 90 percent of the food. Wild fruits, chiefly cactus apples, made up 5 percent of the food of a Florida bobcat collected in April and was found in three Texas bobcat stomachs as follows: May, 3 percent; July, trace, November, 20 percent.

Pollack's (1951) study of bobcat foods from 208 bobcats taken in New England and New York in 1948 and 1949 showed that predominant items were varying hare, deer, cottontail, and porcupine.

In 250 scats examined in Massachusetts, predominant items were cottontail, deer, varying hare, and field mouse.

Davis (1955) in his analysis of 239 bobcat stomachs taken in Alabama during the period 1937-1954, of which 145 were captured by dogs or by shooting, and the remaining 94 were trapped, showed that animal matter comprised 100 percent of the foods in these stomachs. His findings are similar to other studies previously completed for different areas of the United States in that the rabbit was foremost in food preference.

"Listed in order of importance by occurrence comprising 1%
or more of the diet in 145 stomachs are as follows:

| | |
|---|---|
| *rabbit* (Sylvilagus) | 66.9% |
| *deer* (Odocoileus) | 13.8 |
| *cotton rat* (Sigmodon) | 11.7 |
| *white-footed mice* (Peromyscus) | 6.9 |
| *squirrel* (Sciurus) | 6.2 |
| *wood rat* (Neotoma) | 2.8 |
| *poultry* (Gallus) | 2.8 |
| *raccoon* (Procyon) | 2.1 |
| *opossum* (Didelphis) | 2.1 |
| *black rat* (Rattus) | 1.4 |
| *harvest mice* (Reithrodontomys) | 1.4 |
| *chipmunk* (Tamias) | 1.4 |
| *quail* (Colinus) | 1.4 |

"Food items comprising 5% or more of the total food
of 239 bobcats are listed in order of importance as follows:

| | |
|---|---|
| *rabbit* (Sylvilagus) | 63.2% |
| *cotton rat* (Sigmodon) | 11.3 |
| *deer* (Odocoileus) | 10.5 |
| *squirrel* (Sciurus) | 9.2 |
| *white-footed mice* (Peromyscus) | 5.4" |

Thirty-eight bobcat stomachs examined in Missouri contained: Rabbit, 70.7 percent; fox squirrel, 10.8 percent; turkey, 8.6 percent; deer, 2.6 percent; opossum, 2 percent; quail, 1.9 percent; and house cat, 1.9 percent.

From all of the analyses made, both in the field and laboratories, it can be said that the bobcat goes with the rabbit (Plates 22, 22a), as does the puma with the deer, and the fox with the field mouse.

Since the cottontail rabbit is hunted for sport and food in many parts of the United States, and in some areas is the only game animal available, it has become a common practice at times to expend large amounts of game funds to replenish such game by rabbit transplants. In view of the bobcat's fondness for this rabbit, it has been necessary to conduct a limited amount of bobcat control for the protection of such rabbit transplants in those areas where the habitats of these two mammals coincide.

Again, the opposite may be true, for where rabbits increase to the point of becoming a pest from the standpoint of the farmer and fruit grower, certain of our predatory birds and mammals may become more beneficial than harmful.

## FIELD OBSERVATION OF FEEDING HABITS

### Deer

Over a long period, arguments pro and con on the deer-killing tendencies of the bobcat have been voiced by naturalists and others. To summarize information relating to this subject, references to the killing of deer by bobcats are arranged according to geographic localities both in Canada and the United States.

In *Rod and Gun in Canada,* published March 1948, it was stated that: "Officials of the New Brunswick game division had been hearing complaints from all sections of the Province that wildcats were becoming more plentiful and that deer, especially young fawns, were being dragged down in the deep snow and killed by the ferocious cats. The department did something about it. Hon. R. J. Gill, the minister of lands and mines, announced that effective January 15, the bounty would be $10 instead of $5, the old rate. The new edict will probably result in renewed activity among trappers for the remainder of the season, and will witness a year-round campaign on the 'bobcat.' "

A rare observation made during the New Brunswick 1949 hunting season, similar to the account given by Young (1928), adds to the ever-increasing evidence of the bobcat as a deer predator. Here again, *Rod and Gun in Canada,* March 1950, records that:

"A nature-in-the-raw drama of the backwoods that happened in the closing days of the 1949 hunting season is told by Earl Paget, of Hartland, N. B., a Carlton county guide and outfitter, who was a witness, along with a Rhode Island sportsman, Jonathan A. Chaffer. Hunter and guide were moving along an old logging road in territory that bore evidence of deer, when their attention was attracted by a loud noise in the woods just ahead. Paget had the idea at the time that it might be a

moose, or maybe an 'injun devil' (Eastern panther). While
the men waited, the brush parted about thirty feet ahead and
a deer bounded into the open. On its back was a bobcat,
hunched low over the deer's shoulder and struggling to bring
its quarry to the ground. This gruesome and one-sided contest
had apparently been going on for some time, for the deer was
badly winded and lurched unsteadily on its feet. Still trying
to 'shake' the ferocious cat, the deer ran about twenty-five yards
farther along the road. Then it collapsed in a heap. Chaffer
fired at the bobcat but raised only a bit of fur, and it disappeared into the bush. The deer was stone dead when the
men reached it. A jagged hole about three inches deep had
been chewed through the hide near the shoulders and there
were no other marks on it."

Rand (1944) records that bobcats were very plentiful in
all the Nova Scotian sanctuaries, "and were viewed with dis-
favor because they killed deer . . . it was pointed out that while
the chief food of the cats was rabbit, when rabbits failed, the
bobcats would turn to other game."

Foote (1945: 27) in his treatise on the Vermont Deer Herd
indicates the range of weights of deer killed by bobcats," . . .
in Vermont from 1939 to 1944 are as follows:

| Weight in pounds | Bucks | Does | Totals |
|---|---|---|---|
| 0- 49 ..................... | 2 | 4 | 6 |
| 50- 99 ..................... | 12 | 10 | 22 |
| 100-149 ..................... | 1 | 7 | 8 |
| 150-199 ..................... | 1 | .. | 1 |
|  | 16 | 21 | 37 |

"The largest deer killed by a bobcat was a 150 pound buck,
with several does from 100-140 pounds reported killed.

"In a series of 240 fall and winter bobcat stomachs which
were examined deer were a leading item . . . but in many instances the deer taken were thought to have died from other
causes, chiefly malnutrition or accidental. No doubt some were
deer that had been fatally wounded, perhaps with lingering
death, from gunshot wounds. With local exceptions, the bobcat
is definitely beneficial rather than detrimental. Local excep-

tion probably include parts of Essex County, where bobcats are more plentiful. Here they may exercise a definitely detrimental influence on the herd by heavy pressure upon yearlings and fawns. It appears significant that bobcat and deer apparently prefer similar cover types. . . ."

Leo K. Couch, formerly of the Fish and Wildlife Service (now retired), records:

"As per your memorandum of April 21, I looked through some of my old reports and diaries covering my assignment as inspector of wildlife CCC projects back in 1936-37.

"From January 30 to February 3, 1937, I inspected the game management areas on the Chattahoochie National Forest in Georgia, with A. E. Schilling and T. S. Seely, Forest Service Technicians. Efforts had been made to reintroduce whitetailed deer and wild turkey in the forest, and in one district particularly, the Blue Ridge Ranger District, the planting of 9 deer almost failed due to depredations by bobcats. Forest Ranger W. A. Woody called on the Biological Survey for help. Four of the deer had been killed within a few days after release.

"Quoting from my report:

" 'There is ample sign of bobcats on all the Units visited, indicating a need for some control work. The assigning of Mr. Andy Ray, Biological Survey hunter, to the forest to train forest officers in the best trapping procedure should be effective in handling the problem. Four of the deer fawns transplanted from the Pisgah National Forest were killed by bobcats on upper Waters Creek, Chestatee watershed.'

"Ranger Woody is one of the most practical native woodsmen I have ever met. He located each of the fawn kills, and determined from the sign they were made by bobcats. I personally accompanied Mr. Ray over his trap-line on January 31, and one large bobcat was taken in one of six sets hurriedly put out the night before on the ridge bordering the watershed where the four deer were killed. I understand several bobcats were trapped by Mr. Ray in the area, and further depredations on the deer ceased."

Similarly, Phil Goodrum of the Fish and Wildlife Service wrote me: "Below is an account of deer predation that I gave you verbally today.

"Quinton Breland (Refuge keeper, Leaf River Refuge for State of Miss. on the Desoto National Forest 60 miles north of Gulfport, Miss.) told me that on September 19, 1945 at 9:45 p.m. he heard a deer bleating as if caught by a dog, but felt sure that some other animal than a dog was the culprit. (Breland lives on refuge). The next morning and for two days following he searched for evidence of the kill or probable kill. On Sept. 21 he found the carcass covered with debris. Track around the carcass plainly showed that a bobcat had killed a yearling female deer. He set two traps around the carcass and that night caught a 31 pound bobcat. The cat had eaten about one half the deer. The dorsal part of the neck, throat, and hams of the deer were torn. The deer was in good physical condition."

Pennsylvania adds to the record as Matson (1948) wrote:

"It apparently is not common knowledge that bobcats (*Lynx rufus*) kill deer. Years ago, when small game was plentiful in Pennsylvania, and deer were scarce, bobcats did live largely on small game. During the several years just past, I have followed the nightly hunting trails of cats many miles, studying their motives, and have seen little indication of their interest in small game. During that time I have come upon many dead deer, killed by cats, where the evidence on fresh snow was unmistakable. This was in Pennsylvania State Lands, in areas not accessible by roads after the early snows and not visited by others than my party, including local foresters and wardens, during the winter months. These conditions preclude the possibility of the deer having been wounded or killed by men. In cases where there was the possibility of their having been killed or wounded during the deer season, such cases were discounted.

"In recent years, small game (rabbits and grouse) has become very scarce while deer have increased to the maximum. Although the cats are by no means numerous we have found as many as five deer in two weeks in a certain locality that were unquestionably killed by cats. Careful examination showed that these deer were unwounded and in good condition when killed. Most of these were fawns although occasionally a doe is killed. We have found several instances where a cat attacked a large deer which it could not overcome. A few cases have been reported, although such have not come under my personal observation, where cats have killed full grown bucks. In these cases evidence of considerable struggle was reported.

"Ordinarily the cat circles the bedded deer, creeps to within about ten feet, and pounces. It seizes the deer by the head with its forepaws and holds the head down. Fawns and small deer seized thus are seldom able to get to their feet and are killed in their beds, leaving little evdidence of struggle. The cat's killing hold is at the throat close behind the deer's jawbones. The skin is not broken except for the piercing by the four canine teeth. I have laid the throat skin back on deer and found the windpipe severed in some cases. Apparently this is done by grating the canine teeth thus cutting or pulling the windpipe apart. Frequently the cat then drags the deer a few feet, or a few yards. He usually begins feeding from the rear middle of the uppermost hind quarter, eating a portion about the size of the cat's head.

"In the case of a kill found (in January 1947) before the carcass had cooled, the cat had eaten the entire hind quarter, had detached the bone from the hip joint, had eaten the loin, up to the ribs, and the side and belly meat, including hide and hair, and exposed the intestines. This was a fawn and the cat was an unusually large one.

"On February 5, 1947, we studied the trail of a large cat which had followed three deer about a mile to where they had bedded down. The cat approached from several different angles (creeping). Finally, when about sixteen feet distant, the bedded deer bounded. It was in its second bound when struck by the cat. The deer was evidently too large (judging by its tracks and the size of its bed) and the cat could not make good his throat hold. The deer carried the cat forty to fifty feet into heavy brush where it was shaken off or more likely knocked off by saplings. There were slabs of deer hair the size of a man's hand, such as might be slashed off by the stroke of a razor. The cat did not chase the deer after being shaken off. Within another mile, this same cat's trail met the tracks of several deer traveling (walking) at right angles to his course. He made four or five bounds after the deer, but failed to catch it.

"In this locality (Slate Run, in Tioga and Potter Counties, Pennsylvania) the cats live almost exclusively on deer. Evidently the big cats do most of the killing, but they seldom return to the kill. In the case of two freshly killed deer (we were convinced both kills were made by the same large cat) the killer did not return, in one case during a two weeks period, in the other a four weeks period. On two or three occasions he passed within a few rods of them; no other cats found either of these two kills. Traps were set at the kills and visited daily. This, and the fact that all cats killed in this locality are very fat, indicates their ability to kill a deer when and where required.

"Indications are that they feed irregularly, gorging on occasion and at times not feeding for several days. They commonly remain in their resting places during a storm and appear to be reluctant to travel in deep, soft snow. On a recent hunt, following an eight inch snowfall, no tracks were found during the storm nor during the following week.

"A female, weight sixteen pounds, had one-eighth to one-half inch of fat under the hide on the belly; the abdominal cavity was completely filled with firm white fat. The stomach and intestine were empty except for a small amount of thick, dark, semi-fluid material in the intestine and a small wad of fine fur, probably rabbit or rat (rabbits are rare in that locality). This is the only specimen examined in that locality, during several years past, that showed stomach content other than deer meat.

"In a male, weight sixteen and one-half pounds, the stomach

was distended with deer meat and hair; no other material was present. The intestine contained wads of deer hair. A layer of fat one-half inch thick covered the belly. The stomach, intestines, and kidneys were completely encased in firm white fat. Porcupine quills were embedded in the fore legs and back of this specimen."

Stalnaker (1952), District Conservation Officer in West Virginia, records the killing of a deer on its bedding ground by a bobcat slipping up on it, jumping on its back, and in the following struggle succeeding in cutting the deer's throat and thrice puncturing its windpipe. Later examination of the deer showed that a tendon on one of the front legs had also been cut. The scene of this killing was on Cheat Mountain, where, on Christmas Day of 1951, Stalnaker succeeded in trapping a female bobcat weighing twenty-five pounds.

James S. Lindzey, Assistant Game Technician, Conservation Commission of West Virginia, reported in a letter to the author under date of March 16, 1948, that a male bobcat weighing 20 pounds was trapped near the carcass of a deer which it had killed near the Pocahontas County line in Greenbrier County, West Virginia.

Failing (1953), with respect to Michigan, states: "Once in a while a heavy 'cat will kill a full grown deer and it is done quickly and efficiently by biting the throat. Rarely does a deer travel over 30 ft. after the initial attack but sometimes we find where the deer has been successful in brushing off his assailant by making use of a convenient overhanging limb. This is similar to that antic sometimes apparent in a pack-horse or mule when trying to get rid of its load."

Failing, continues: "Each winter [in Michigan] we have reports of deer being killed by 'cats and upon investigation find that it actually happens."

Vernon E. Gunvalson (Pittman-Robertson Quarterly, January 1952, p. 43) records five authenticated kills of deer by bobcats in Minnesota during the winter of 1950-51. He further states that "verified reports show that even small bobcats have the ability to attack and kill large deer."

Near the mouth of Beaver Creek which flows into the Little Missouri River from the west near the northwest corner of Billings County, North Dakota, the Goldsberry children, Jerry age 11, Ronald age 10, and Loren age 5, while walking to school on the morning of October 12, 1953, observed three bobcats killing an adult doe deer on the ice approximately in the center of Beaver Creek. After the killing, these children saw the bobcats drag the deer into the brush on the south side of the creek, where later government hunter Howard J. Martin, stationed at Beach, North Dakota, observed it. In a subsequent investigation Martin found nine other deer carcasses in this same vicinity killed by bobcats.

In the language of hunter George Barnes, the killing of a yearling whitetail buck in the Buckthorn Mountains between 5 and 6 miles north of Custer, South Dakota on April 5, 1954 is of more than passing interest. Barnes' account follows:

"Near Wabash Spring this carcass of a yearling white tail buck was found. It had been dead a few hours. The remains were half covered with twigs and pine needles. The kill was almost instant there was some hair on the up slope about thirty feet. The ground was smooth no big trees or rocks, a few thin jack pines, on a slight slope. The attack was made from the ground. There was claw marks on the back from the shoulders forward. The first bite no doubt was close behind the ears thru the neck. The neck below and behind the jaws was a net work of teeth holes. The feeding started at the base of the neck going up and back. About eight ribs were chewed off. The meat gone on right shoulder and down to heart region. I would estimate five pounds. It was the work of one cat. I was fortunate enough to have a trail set less than 200 yards away, and there he was, full of venison and chipped deer ribs. I put the cat and deer on the jeep hood and went to Custer. It made an interesting exhibit. The cat was a good specimen long and sleek a nice tom weighing 27 lbs." (Plate 23.)

The late George M. Trickel, who was an assistant in the predatory animal work of the Bureau of Biological Survey,

U. S. Department of Agriculture, reported to me an interesting observation relative to an attack on a deer by a bobcat (Young, 1928). The deer, a yearling that would weigh possibly one hundred pounds, was found killed on Little Alkali Creek, west of Housetop Mountain, Colorado, in February, 1926. The snow in this area was about eight inches deep, and Trickel could see where the bobcat had caught the deer and floundered with it in the snow about fifty feet before the deer went down. From all appearances, the bobcat had attacked the deer at the throat, for this part of the animal was badly chewed up. After killing the deer the bobcat had proceeded to eat some of one of the hind quarters and had then completely covered up the carcass with snow, except for the head. In the immediate vicinity not a single track was noted besides those of the bobcat. At the time Mr. Trickel found the dead deer, coyotes had evidently not located it. From all indications, the killing had been done but a very short time before, possibly not over forty-eight hours.

From C. R. Landon, long familiar with predatory animal conditions in Texas, the following is cited:

"You requested that I furnish you the bobcat story related to me by the late Mr. Robert Real of Kerr County some 25 years ago. As I recall, the incident occurred several years prior to that time. When Kerr County was first being fenced with woven wire fences in order that sheep and goats might run loose without protection from herders, Mr. Real, then General Manager of the extensive Schreiner ranching properties, took much interest in running wolves and bobcats primarily for the control of these animals but incidentally for the pleasure it afforded him. He kept a good pack of the best purebred fox hounds and had his personal saddle horse of thorobred stock upon which he followed them.

"One morning when trailing conditions were good he jumped a bobcat from a recently killed yearling deer. The dogs soon treed this animal and after disposing of it Mr. Real returned to the deer to try to determine the cause of its death. At the carcass the dogs immediately picked up a second trail and after another short chase a second bobcat was captured. By skinning out the neck and shoulders Mr. Real found the numerous claw marks which proved to his satisfaction that the deer which was evidently in perfect health had indeed been pulled down by these two cats. The male bobcat was an unusually large specimen which later weighed on the ranch scales 32 pounds. Mr. Real was a very close observer and any statement of fact made by him could be accepted without question."

Barker (1946) records in the Vermejo Park area of New Mexico, near Castle Rock, the killing by a large bobcat, blind in one eye, of a long yearling doe deer that would hog-dress between 65 and 75 pounds. This kill was covered over with debris much as the puma does its uneaten prey.

W. O. Grimes, of the Fish and Wildlife Service, in writing from Clarkdale, Arizona, vouched for the following incident:

"During a part of the summer of 1951, my assignment as Assistant Mammal-Control Agent was to work Mingus Mountain and adjacent areas. In so doing, I frequently met Ranger Jones of the Forest Service who took a keen interest in the work. Late in August, I moved back to Camp Verde. A few days later I received a telephone call from Ranger Jones from the Look-Out Station on 'Mingus' saying: 'Come up, and bring some big traps. I've found a fresh lion kill.' Although it was then after 4:00 p.m., I told him I'd be on my way within ten minutes. I made the 45 mile run to the top of 'Mingus' and met him at the Look-Out Station. He got into my pickup and we drove to Dry Lake on the south end of 'Mingus' from which point we had to walk, following the old Cherry Creek trail for about one-half mile. There he showed me the 'kill' beside a fallen pine—a small buck deer, horns about two inches long. It had been partly eaten and then partially covered with pine needles. Looking the situation over, I said to Jones: 'That is the work of a bobcat, not a lion.' 'Oh, no,' he answered, 'a bobcat couldn't kill a deer that size.' Then I showed him the reason for my observation. I figured it was a small animal because in covering the carcass with pine needles, it had reached not more than fourteen inches from the carcass. A lion's reach would have been three feet or more. Jones was evidently still unconvinced, but I set a 4½ Newhouse trap. He agreed to watch it for me, but stated he had no gun of suitable caliber to kill a lion, so I left my 30-30 with him. Two days later came another telephone call from him: 'You were right about that kill,' he said. 'I went down the next morning and there was the biggest bobcat I ever saw.'

"My observation is that bobcats are really destructive to young animals, whether deer, calves, sheep or goats."

While observing deer in the Salmon River area during the interval March 20-26, 1950, Stewart M. Brandborg and Dwight R. Smith, of the Idaho Cooperative Wildlife Research Unit, reported that two bobcats were seen chasing a deer in the vicinity of Lake Creek by Frank Rood, Idaho state trapper, and Mal Rodgers, resident of the area. The deer escaped and swam to an island in the river.

In regard to bobcat predation upon deer, Robinette observed but four cases of where he was reasonably sure that a bobcat was responsible, as follows:

"One was an old mule deer doe found the morning of April 25, 1952 in the Duck Creek area of Nevada. The doe was still warm when found. Tooth marks and clotted blood were found on the back of her neck and in the throat region. About 2-3 pounds of flesh had been taken from the hind quarters and a small amount of debris had been raked up over the head and the hind quarters. The deer was in open sagebrush and had not been dragged, apparently being too large for the bobcat. Marrow in the doe's leg bones was of the yellow gelatinous type indicating a very poor condition. The ground was too rocky for clear impressions of tracks but the width of the claw marks and distance at which the cat had reached out when scraping twigs and dirt onto the deer indicated a bobcat rather than a cougar.

"Another instance involved a 6-7 month-old mule deer fawn which I found in the Oak Creek area of central Utah, January

4, 1952. The fawn had been killed the preceding night and an account of the struggle was easily read from signs in the 12 inches of loose snow that covered the ground. The fawn had been feeding on cliffrose when the bobcat sneaked up to within a few feet of the deer and jumped onto the fawn. The fawn went down as soon as it was hit but struggled to its feet and upon going down the third time was killed by the bobcat. Considerable blood marked the spot of the actual kill. Apparently the bobcat ate his fill from the neck and shoulder region before pulling the fawn down hill for about 25 feet and in under the low hanging branches of a juniper tree. This fawn appeared to be of normal size, and the bone marrow showed it to be in fair condition.

"On May 3, 1955 a group consisting of several members of the Colorado Game and Fish Commission as well as myself observed a fawn—probably 10-months of age—which had been killed by a bobcat, perhaps the previous day in one of the experimental deer pastures at the Little Hills Station in Colorado. The bobcat was observed fleeing from the carcass upon which it had been feeding. The fawn had definitely been killed by the bobcat as numerous tooth punctures in the neck region and blood clotting under the hide would testify. The bobcat had fed only on the hind quarters. The fawn appeared to have been a healthy individual although smaller than average for this time of year.

"On June 26, 1953, I found the remains of a young spotted fawn hidden under the low hanging branches of a fir tree within the Oak Creek area of central Utah. The manner of hiding and the fact that the chest organs, ribs and neck had been fed on suggested a bobcat. The fawn's stomach was full of curdled milk and had not been touched, further suggesting the work of a bobcat. Coyotes on the other hand, according to the professional trappers, show a predilection for lamb stomachs containing milk. I, also once surprised a coyote that was feeding on a young fawn that he had just killed and although the coyote had eaten but a part of the fawn the stomach and intestines were among the portions taken."

On March 9, 1946, in checking the mule deer range near the west side of the Ruby Lake National Wildlife Refuge, Nevada, Dill (1947) says:

"I found a rather unusual record of a doe *(Odocoileus hemionus)* being killed by a bobcat *(Lynx rufus)*. We were working through a bed ground at about 6,000 feet elevation in scattered clumps of juniper, service berry, bitter brush and heavy sage brush on a southern and eastern exposure where the sun had melted most of the snow leaving soft mud underfoot. From the tracks in the mud it was apparent that the bobcat had sneaked up on the deer, jumped her, grabbed her by the throat and brought her down just 14 feet from the bed. The bobcat ate one meal from a ham and neatly covered the place he had eaten from and the wound on the neck with grass and twigs. The doe had been dead about 12 hours when found and from all appearances was normal and in good condition when killed. She was estimated to weigh about 100 pounds.

"There were no other tracks near the kill, and since the ground was muddy at the time, it was not difficult to check the tracks and piece together the details of the attack. The bobcat (a male estimated to be about 3 years old and weighing 25 pounds) was caught the next day in a trap which had been set by the deer's carcass."

In his admirable paper on the mule deer of California, Dixon (1934: 229) gives a vivid account of a bobcat attacking a full-grown mule deer. This was evidently taken from Harwell's (1932) recording as follows:

"On February 2, electricians Sam Cookson and Joe Gann, while driving up the highway, one mile east of Arch Rock Ranger Station, at 3 o'clock in the afternoon, saw a full grown doe jump from a 20-foot bank to the soft snow at the side of the highway with a wildcat at her throat. They brought their car to a stop within 20 feet of the two animals . . . grabbed shovels from their car and hurried to the rescue. . . . The doe was striking the cat sharply with her fore feet. The men observed that the cat had his teeth deeply imbedded in the throat of the deer. Blood was streaming from the wound. When

Cookson and Gann got within a few feet, the cat loosened his hold and made an attempt to escape by scaling the bank. The deer trotted on down the road out of sight. The soft snow coupled with the steepness of the bank proved too much for the cat. When he saw he was cornered he turned on the men. A blow on the side of the head from a shovel quickly dispatched him. The wildcat was a male weighing 12 pounds, and is now a scientific specimen at the Yosemite Museum."

Harwell (1932) adds further to the record obtained in Yosemite National Park, stating:

"I have often heard old-timers in the mountains talk about wildcats riding on the backs of deer, seemingly with the purpose of tiring out their victim or getting them in such an excited condition that this smaller animal could make a kill. Assistant Chief Ranger John Wegner, one evening about 1925, while sitting on a bench at the Government saddle room, observed a four-point buck come dashing down the road by the Government barns. As he came closer Mr. Wegner noticed a bobcat was riding on the deer's back firmly gripping the back of the buck's neck, with his teeth. He also had a strong hold with his claws. The deer was making a frantic effort to shake off the cat. He disappeared on down the road still being firmly ridden.

"Ranger Henry Skelton tells me that during the winter of 1920, while he was stationed at Arch Rock, he found two carcasses of eight-month old fawns where all indications pointed toward a kill by a bobcat. In each case from the tracks in the snow and evidences of struggle he was sure of the fact. He followed the tracks of one of these deer back up the hillside and found one place where the deer had run under a low hanging tree in an attempt to scrape off the cat. Ranger Skelton found hair of both deer and wildcat on the limbs of this tree. He followed the tracks far enough to locate the exact spot where the cat had evidently jumped from a large boulder to the back of the fawn. As a finish to these observations he set traps near both carcasses and very soon caught a wildcat in each. These cats weighed 18 pounds each."

And finally, Marston (1942) says with respect to his study of bobcat-deer relationships in Maine: ". . . The toll is not limited to young or weak individuals; some cats perhaps kill wantonly more deer than they can utilize. . . . Smaller bobcats are fully as harmful to deer as the larger ones. Bobcats are not selective in hunting; ordinarily they kill any deer they are able to approach." This statement is in keeping with the author's findings concerning bobcat-deer relationships.

The foregoing represents a cross-nation series of observations and recordings of the bobcat's taste for deer, but it is by no means a complete one. To attempt to cite all the available records would only be a monotonous repetition of what has already been said. In any game management plan concerned with deer, particularly in the transplant of the young, as brought out by Couch aforementioned, consideration should be given to any necessary bobcat control before attempting the transplant.

Very often bobcat scat analysis and field observations give clues to what extent deer depredations may be taking place. (Fig. 6.)

*Mearns Quail*

While watching a waterhole in Middle Canyon near Canelo Pass, approximately 14 miles south of Elgin, Arizona, the author observed a bobcat drinking within a short distance of a flock of Mearns quail. It made no attempt to molest this covey as it was apparently full of food, nor did these quail appear at all alarmed by the cat's presence. Evidence of a bobcat killing of this bird, however, was noted at the head of Turkey Creek, approximately the same distance from Elgin.

*Bats*

Wherever the bobcat has access to caves containing bats, this animal makes full use of them as food, particularly young bats that have dropped to cave floors from ceilings. Numerous bat caves explored in the mountainous sections of various western states have invariably shown bobcat tracks and dung containing bat remains.

### Snakes

On July 17, 1949, former Secretary of the Smithsonian Institution, Alexander Wetmore, found a bobcat scat on the Skyline Drive, near Elk Wallow Picnic Area, Shenandoah National Park, Virginia, that contained portions of a snake and a mouse as its greatest bulk.

Charles W. Quaintance, during October of 1933, recorded the removal of a large bull-snake skin and its vertebrae from a bobcat stomach examined at Eagle, in Greenlee County, Arizona.

In 124 bobcat scats from Virginia examined by Progulske (1952: 56) frequency occurrence of the rattlesnake *(Crotalus horridus)* was 1.9 percent.

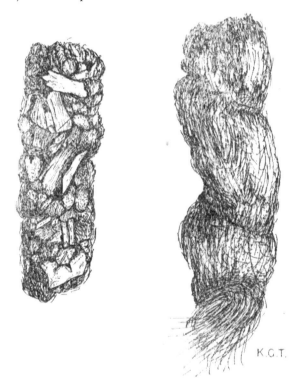

K.C.T.

FIG. 6. *Left.* Bobcat scat showing varying hare bones and some vegetation which was probably consumed with the hare. *Right.* Bobcat scat containing deer hair.

*Skunk*

Barton (1878: 628) records: "Observing in a late number of the *Naturalist,* the note 'Food of the Skunk,' reminds me that I have lately seen that the skunk is itself food for at least one animal. Discussing a wild cat *(Lynx rufus)* two days since, I found bunches of woolly hair in the intestine. These had no perceptible odor. Upon opening the gullet, however, near the stomach I found a roll of skin and hair which at once announced its proper belongings by a stifling wave of the peculiar mephitic stench of the skunk. I did not look further, but contented myself with the reflection *de gustibus,* etc.

"The lynx is said to feed upon rabbits, rats, squirrels and upon such birds as roost or breed on the ground, varying its diet from time to time with fish and frogs. The unusually mild winter through which we have passed and the absence of snow forbids the idea that hunger drove it to partake of skunk—besides which the lynx was very fat. The bunches of hair in the intestine may have been the remnants of some previous meal, or they may have been of the skunk but deodorized by bile. Perhaps strong alkalies may be found to destroy the odor of this stinking beast's secretion."

*House Cat*

Instances are on record in the Mississippi and Missouri Valley States where bobcats have been found to subsist in part on the domestic house cat. In some of these instances these cats were feral and used the same habitat as the bobcats.

*Opossum*

In the South a favorite bobcat food is the opossum.

*Porcupine*

Like the puma, the bobcat relishes the porcupine as food, and in areas where abundant, it is high on the preference list. Evidence of porcupine encounters in such areas is evinced from the pelts of trapped bobcats that contain the quills in the mouth, neck, and forelegs. Often the scats of the animal will contain quills, having apparently passed through the entire intestinal tract without noticeable injury as in the case of the puma. However, a superabundance of porcupine quills in the animal's mouth does lead to slow death from starvation.

L. T. S. Norris-Elye (1951) records a female bobcat trapped near a creek leading out of Mud Lake (Section 35-2-15 E.P.M.) in Manitoba that contained porcupine quills in the left fore and hind feet, and one had penetrated the soft palate and had reached the rear of the left eye-socket; all punctures had caused severe suppurations.

Some field observers incline to the opinion that while the bobcat will feed on the porcupine, this is done only when in dire circumstances of food shortage. When such is the case, the bobcat usually comes out of a porcupine attack second best. The resulting aftermath is usually a head and throat full of quills. When this happens the bobcat may be hindered in obtaining further prey and becomes very poor and emaciated.

A. de Vos (1953) mentions a small bobcat killed in the outskirts of Port Arthur, Canada that upon examination showed in its head six quills; from 15 to 20 on the right flank; 2 quills had pierced one eye, one quill the other, and two quills had penetrated the palate, and ". . . when skinned showed no fat."

## Otter (Land)

While photgraphing wolves in Madison Parish, Louisiana, southwest of Tallulah, I saw apparent evidence that the land otter may at times fall prey to the bobcat in our southern swamps. In a section along the Tensas River fresh otter feces were voided at a spot where bobcat tracks were much in evidence, indicating a surprise attack and the eventual kill of an otter.

## Weasel

Belden Lynn, a Federal trapper, and Leslie Robinette of the Fish and Wildlife Service were walking along a dusty trail in Weber Canyon, Morgan County, Utah, August 29, 1954, when they came onto a recently killed adult female weasel (long-tailed weasel—*Mustela frenata nevadensis*) lying in the trail. The fresh tracks of a bobcat and the tooth marks about the weasel's middle left no doubt as to how the weasel met its fate. The bobcat had made no attempt to feed on the weasel.

## Songbirds

While observing a robin roost near Winslow, Arkansas, which between November 7 and December 16, was estimated to contain 250,000 birds, Black (1932) witnessed a rare sight. Bobcats, barred and great-horned owls, and feral house cats were all preying on the robins. He stated: "The toll these raptores and cats collected from the flock was enormous," and further, "The deep gutteral 'meows' of the bobcats as they stalked their prey nearby and the most terrifying snarl as they made the kill furnished a regular thrill that served to make the nightwork [of banding and observing the flight of these birds] interesting."

Youngblood (1950) observed the bobcat making early morning and late evening forays into an area where robins were nesting during July in the vicinity of Mirror Lake in the lower Tenaya Canyon, Yosemite National Park, California. Numerous tracks and scattered robin feathers indicated a condition similar to the foregoing Arkansas observation.

## Great Blue Heron

Monson (1951) while in the vicinity of Devil's Elbow, in the Havasu Lake National Wildlife Refuge on the Colorado River, on January 8, 1951, observed a bobcat capture a great blue heron. The bird had alighted after flying from the Arizona to the California side of the river at approximately 5 o'clock in the afternoon. Apparently, the bobcat, secluded in a rocky bank at the point where this heron alighted, had only to spring at its unsuspecting prey and grasp it by the neck. In spite of the bird's struggles with outstretched wings, the cat was able to drag it up a rocky ledge and over the bank of the river, away from Monson's view.

## Wild Turkey

Wherever wild turkey range is subjected to periodic flooding causing turkeys to seek higher elevations, these birds are apt to be heavily preyed upon by bobcats if these predators happen to be common. Some southern states are faced with such a problem. In Louisiana, during the fall of 1934, examples of this were noted along the Tensas River drainage.

With regard to the Merriam turkey of our Southwest, E. M. Mercer adds to the record in Arizona by reporting that—

"I was hunting elk on the Ft. Apache Indian Reservation late in the afternoon on November 17, 1950, at a point on Tonto Creek, about two miles southwest of Tonto Lake. A flock of fifteen wild turkeys passed by while I stood watch at a bend in the canyon. They fed down the canyon at a brisk walk and finally disappeared from my sight where they went around a second bend in the canyon some three hundred yards away. They were just out of my sight when I heard quite a commotion among them and looking that way again, I saw four of the turkeys in the air, fifteen or twenty feet from the ground, but they seemed to be unable to take a course in flight. At about this instant I saw a turkey running up the canyon toward me. It took flight but the grade was rather steep and it was able to maintain itself in the air for only about 150 yards. When it lit on the ground it continued toward me as fast as its legs could carry it and it also continued to sound an alarm.

"After the turkey lit on the ground my attention was suddenly attracted to an animal some 35 or 40 yards behind it and running very fast. I first thought it was a fox, but as it came closer I determined that it was a bobcat. The turkey was running as fast as it could, but the bobcat was rapidly overtaking it. When within about 50 yards of where I was, the turkey tried to make it to a spruce tree a few yards to its right. The bobcat overhauled and killed it by severing the neck vertebrae just above the crop and then biting it through the head. When the turkey gave up the struggle, the bobcat stepped back about two feet from it and appeared not only to be looking the kill over, but also surveying its surroundings. I shot at the bobcat and apparently creased it across the withers as I saw some fur fly from its back. The bobcat let out a snarl and a 'spit' that I am sure could have been heard for several hundred yards. It started to run, but when 25 or 30 feet away, changed its mind and returned for the turkey. Seizing the turkey, it started to run again but apparently found that the eight or ten pound turkey was too much to take along on a hurried retreat. At this time the bobcat discovered me walking toward it. It dropped the turkey and attempted to hide behind it. All I could see of the bobcat was the top of its scalp. When I had approached to within 30 feet of it, the bobcat jumped up and beat a hasty retreat through jack pines on the hillside. I had passed this way the day before and noted that some animal, probably a bobcat, had eaten a turkey under the same spruce tree only a few hours before."

### Crustaceans

The late Luther J. Goldman reported that between the dates of March 15 to 19, 1937, he found evidence of bobcats subsisting on a diet of crustaceans, such as crayfish, in the Cape Sable region of Florida, which is further evidence of the animal's non-aversion to water.

In Oklahoma there is some evidence that, like the raccoon, the bobcat feeds on crayfish.

In northern Arizona it is known to work along creek beds containing shallow ponds, subsisting on any crayfish it finds.

### Prairie Dog

Gaut reported a bobcat seen carrying a prairie dog in its mouth near Tres Piedras, New Mexico, in early August of 1904.

The late Merritt Cary, author of 'A Biological Survey of Colorado' (N. Amer. Fauna No. 33, 1911) observed on August 8, 1907, a bobcat in the act of catching a prairie dog in the Hotchkiss region, on the western slope of Colorado.

On August 28, 1914, J. Stokley Ligon observed a bobcat chase a prairie dog into its hole, northeast of Springerville, Arizona.

Edward C. Cates similarly observed a bobcat attempting to catch a prairie dog during the late spring and summer of 1924, while he was employed in control work of this rodent on the Custer National Forest in Montana. He was of the opinion that prairie dogs are a favorite food of the bobcat whenever available, as they are also with the coyote.

## Sage Grouse

Early records, especially those concerned with the period during the late 1880's, mention the bobcat as very destructive to sage hens. I also found evidence of this while on a field trip through southern Wyoming and northwestern Nevada in the summer of 1930.

## California Quail

There is difference of opinion regarding effectiveness of bobcat control for the protection of California quail, particularly on lands surrounding watering areas managed for this game bird. Leach and Frazier (1953) did not find California quail of any importance to the diet of the bobcat. This conclusion was based on 55 bobcat stomachs taken from trap sites containing heavy quail populations, supplemented by 166 bobcat stomachs collected state-wide in California. In the 55 stomachs, but one adult quail was found, and in the 166 stomachs the quail occurred on only two occasions. Rodents and lagomorphs (rabbits) were found to be the main items of diet.

## Blue Grouse

J. A. Loring, in December, 1893, removed the remains of a blue grouse from a bobcat taken in a trap for marten in heavy timber near Chama, New Mexico.

## Owls

A bobcat taken at an elevation of 8,000 feet by Gaut on October 24, 1903, on the east slope of the Manzano Mountains in New Mexico, had as a stomach content the remains of a saw-whet owl, *Aegolius acadicus acadicus* (a small species of owl). One foot had been swallowed whole and was still in perfect shape.

## Mourning Dove

Bobcats have been observed preying on mourning doves that have been seeking water in certain of the desert areas of the Southwest. In such country, where water holes are few and far between, this bird is vulnerable to bobcat attack. (Plate 24.)

## Antelope

During the winter of 1948 a prong-horned antelope kid was found killed by a bobcat near Spanish Lake on Hart Mountain, Oregon. While on a trip through that area, Ellis Mason and Morse Murphy, the latter a Warner Valley resident, spotted this bobcat sitting behind a sagebrush clump not far from the antelope carcass.

The foregoing may or may not be the same incident as reported by Einarsen (1948: 76) where the bobcat was surprised while feeding on a freshly killed 2-point buck. The kill, made in a mahogany thicket some feet away, was dragged to the den area over boulders that averaged 6 feet high. This and other observations, Einarsen avers, proves that Oregon bobcats do feed on pronghorns and other game of equal size.

Nelson (1925) recounts an incident of a bobcat depredation at the then Wind Cave Game Preserve in South Dakota, where a full-grown buck antelope had been easily killed by the bobcat leaping upon its back and riding it to its death by the familiar pattern of biting and clawing explained elsewhere in the text.

The late Vernon Bailey recorded the loss of two antelope to bobcats just above Indian Garden on the Kaibab Plateau.

## Mountain Sheep

Vernon Bailey, on July 23, 1928, recorded the capture of a bobcat that had previously killed a full-grown mountain sheep at the north end of the Kaibab Plateau near a spring east of Kanab.

## Food as a Factor for Bobcat Concentration

During the period November 1 to 30, 1947, hunter Darrell W. Martin, trapping with 48 traps, took a total of 25 bobcats in an area of approximately 6 by 15 miles around the north edge and foothills of the Santa Rita Mountains in southern Pima County, Arizona. This concentration was probably caused by the abundance of such miscellaneous rodents as wood rats, kangaroo rats, pocket mice, round-tail ground squirrels, Harris ground squirrels, young jack rabbits, and Gambel quail.

Similarly, the bobcat take of hunter Walt E. Martin, working an area of approximately 10 by 12 miles on the Patterson Ranch, located northwest of Oracle, Pima County, Arizona for the period January 4 to June 30, 1944, totaled 129 bobcats. This is the greatest concentration for its size ever recorded in Arizona. A food factor consisting of heavy rodent and Gambel quail populations apparently was the reason for this concentration.

Bobcat scats examined in the field show that ground squirrels, field mice, and wild rabbits are devoured by bobcats wherever their habitats coincide. In the rows of newly raked alfalfa hay, in small valleys with precipitous rocky walls, in northwestern Colorado, scat remains of the bobcat showed a preponderance of field mice. It was evident at this period of midsummer that these rodents made up the bulk of the food consumed by bobcats.

Wood rats are often a favorite food. Live trapping of wood rats for study specimens often attracts bobcats to the scene of capture. When attempts are made by bobcats to get at the live rats, traps may be dragged some distance.

### Instances of Domestic Animals as Prey

Records of field observation on the feeding habits of the bobcat cover a long period of time and are from practically every section of the United States, as well as much material from Mexico and Canada. To avoid tiresome repetition of narrative, a few typical instances have been selected from the thousands of cases that have been reported and are included among carded and readily accessible information. These have been received from sources believed to be reliable, including field naturalists, hunters, and stockmen. Effort has been made to condense these into concise, direct statements as follows:

Roosevelt (1885), while ranching in North Dakota, relates that a bobcat "destroyed half of my poultry, coming night after night with most praiseworthy regularity."

A rancher in California reported having lost 175 chickens and 40 pigs to bobcats during two months.

On gaining entry into a flock of sheep at lambing time, commonly under cover of darkness, the bobcat carries on its depredations in such manner as to cause little commotion. The lamb is usually attacked by a characteristic bite on the back of the neck or head, and then it is pulled down to be eaten. If its lust for killing is not satisfied, the bobcat may kill other lambs by the same method, continuing its work quietly until a large number have been destroyed. A single bobcat has been known to kill 38 lambs in this manner in one night.

A rancher in Montana reported 23 lambs killed by a bobcat or lynx in two nights.

A hunter in Nevada reported catching a female bobcat which had killed 7 lambs on one ranch in the two nights previous to its capture.

A hunter in Washington reported trapping a bobcat which was known to have killed lambs owned by one sheep company which were valued at $750.

Progulske (1952) states that "in certain localities in Virginia the bobcat at least individually has become a serious nuisance, especially in the sheep raising areas . . . and in the control of this type of depredation it is essential to capture the individual predator rather than to undertake a control program affecting the entire population."

Those sheep and goat producers who lamb and kid in open canyons and draws have repeatedly reported heavy bobcat depredations. The following accounts are from Texas:

A hunter reported finding 8 lambs and 4 goats killed by a bobcat on a ranch near Sonora. A rancher reported 30 kids killed on his ranch by bobcats between October and December. Another rancher reported 17 pigs and 75 lambs killed by bobcats. During May of 1944 hunter William W. Dobson trapped a bobcat that had killed 50 lambs for Moody Bennett and N. B. Chaffin who ranch in the central part of Presidio County. These killings were done in approximately 6 weeks. On the ranch of Hugh Rideout, located in the southwestern part of Presidio County, hunter Dobson, during June of 1944, trapped a bobcat that had killed 30 lambs over a 45-day period. In 1947, a bobcat killed 50 lambs on one ranch in Presidio

County during the latter part of April. A 32-lb. female bobcat on a Culberson County Ranch in two weeks prior to its capture, killed 30 lambs. This animal was suckling 5 kittens which were later discovered and removed from a den near this ranch.

Joseph C. Moore (1946) states that bobcat depredations on turkeys were so severe on the Mount Royal estate, which borders the University of Florida Conservation Reserve near Welaka, Putnam County, Florida, that intensive trapping had to be inaugurated, resulting in the removal of 10 bobcats.

In the spring of 1907 on the Ward Ranch, 10 miles northwest of Saguache, Colorado, a bobcat worked a small rock out of the foundation of the chicken house and crawled through the small opening. In the house were 52 half-grown chickens, which had been moved there the night before from the brooder house. The bobcat killed 51 of these chicks by biting their heads. Then he ate part of their heads and lapped their blood.

The next morning Mr. Ward went to feed the chickens as his wife, who usually fed and took care of them, had fallen and sprained her ankle. When he opened the henhouse door he saw feathers and chickens strewn all over. Then he noticed the bobcat sitting back in one corner too full of chickens to get back out of the small opening.

Mr. Ward then went to the house, placed his wife in a wheelbarrow, and wheeled her to the chicken house where she disposed of the bobcat in short order with her shotgun. This was the only reward she received for her two months' work of raising chickens.

The Prince of Wied (1861-62) nearly a century ago reported that young pigs running the forests in Indiana were killed by bobcats. Even earlier, by approximately a century and a quarter, John Lawson (1718), the Carolina historian, wrote concerning the bobcat: "I knew an Island, which was possess'd by these vermine, unknown to the Planter who put thereon a considerable Stock of Swine, but never took one back; for the wild Cats destroy'd them all."

In Oklahoma, it has long been the practice on the part of hog producers to buy all breeds of pigs when two months old.

These are then turned loose to "root, hog, or die" by feeding on "mast" produced by the oak-pine and oak-hickory forests in such counties as Pushmataha, Le Flore, Latimer, McCurtain, Seguoyah and Adair. In normal years hickory nuts and acorns form the predominant "mast," and after two years of such foraging, the hogs are rounded up with pig dogs. They are then brought into ranch headquarters, topped off on corn feed for a period, and marketed.

The bobcat is one of the problems of this type of stock raising, for at times it works havoc on these porkers, particularly sows having young pigs. When her piglets are threatened, the old sow, as a protective measure, will attempt to cover her young as does a barnyard hen. A bobcat, constantly worrying the sow, will often expose a piglet to attack, permitting it to be captured. Remains of such bobcat prey have been found at times in the tops of old tree stumps where it has been carried and all devoured with the exception of ears and feet. One bobcat can thus take a whole litter of pigs.

Sam Boozer (1948) recounts that "On the cold frosty morning of an early December day I first saw the true characteristics of a killer cat. It was in Pearl River swamp in Rankin County, Mississippi while on patrol.

"There was no wind and sound traveled fast in the clear cold. While walking along the old log road and trail in the dense swampland I heard a pig squeal. The very nature of the squeal revealed that a horrible fright possessed the pig. At the sound I stopped instantly and stood motionless, trying to locate the exact position from which the frightened squeal came. Overhead a group of cardinals, fussily declaimed their alarm at something going on in the underbrush beyond my sight. Their cries of alarm and the squeal of the pig indicated that some marauder was on the prowl. It was off to my left about two hundred yards.

"As I stood still anxiously watching to see what was happening, I saw a big bobcat come into the trail about a hundred yards ahead. It had a small pig in its mouth. The cat put it down in the trail and returned to the underbrush. In a second

I heard another pig squeal and the old sow snapping her jaws.

"I moved down to the pig lying in the trail. Then I saw there were three pigs there, all dead. The cat had killed them and returned for another. When she returned with the fourth pig in her bloody jaws, I was ready for her. I eased my gun out of its holster and as she came in the opening, her only natural enemy, man, put an end to her killing spree."

An intriguing account comes from Parkersburg, West Virginia ("Blennerhasset," 1907), depicting the antics of a mother bobcat, her young, and a half wild razor-back boar while the observer was regarding a chestnut tree near a spot where he had been whipping a trout stream:

"While I was looking at the tree and admiring its beautiful proportions, a full grown Wild-cat with 2 kittens so small that they were barely able to keep up with the mother Cat emerged from a clump of underbrush a few yards below.

"The old Cat was doubtless giving her young a lesson in woodcraft, but she had committed a serious error in bringing her little ones to that particular spot, as she seemed to realize in a moment; for, after a few sniffs at the ground and in the air, the hair on her back went up in a line from the top of her head to the end of her short stubby tail. Then catching one of her kittens by the loose skin on the back of its neck, she sprang up the chestnut tree as quick as thought, and deposited the kitten upon a limb close to the bole of the tree.

"Leaving the startled kitten there, she quickly scrambled back to the ground, and caught up the other young one just as an enormous old half-wild Razorback Boar, with tusks at least 5 inches long, dashed out of the brush not a dozen feet away, closely followed by a wild Sow with a litter of Pigs about the size of Rabbits. The Cat barely made her escape, for before she had ascended the tree 10 feet, the old Boar was stamping and grunting in baffled rage at its foot.

"After depositing her kitten in the crotch of a limb, the Cat descended to one of the lower branches, overhanging the ground, but out of reach of the wild Boar, who was tearing around the tree, foaming at the jaws, and snapping his great teeth with rage. Neither of the animals saw me as I peered through the brush of laurel above them, and as I was on the leeward side, they could not scent me at that distance, and I sat there forgetful even of the big trout I had climbed the mountain to catch, and looked on, wondering what the old Cat was up to, for that she had some particular object in view when she took up her position so close to the ground, I was satisfied. That she intended springing upon the wild Boar and fighting it out then and there, I could not for a moment believe, for I knew—and she must have known even better than I—that she was no match for an animal that a full-grown Bear would have hesitated to tackle.

"But the old Wild-cat had no intention of testing the fighting qualities of the Boar, though she kept a close watch upon his movements. Meanwhile the Sow and her Pigs seemed to become satisfied that as long as they had the protection of the Boar they were entirely safe, and in a little while they began to feed upon the chestnuts, which literally covered the ground beneath the tree. Closer and closer some of the young Pigs approached to the ground beneath the limb upon which the Cat crouched, until at last one of the Pigs, while rooting around among the leaves, worked its way to a spot a little to the right and almost beneath the crouching Cat. I caught a slight movement of the latter as she crouched lower and lower, and a second later she sprang out and landed upon the unfortunate Pig. Then an agonized little squeal from the Pig, and the Cat was bounding away with the wild Boar in pursuit, the Cat carrying the victim in her mouth, much as a pointer Dog carries a fallen game bird, bounding along the mountain shelf in plain view, seeming barely able to keep out of reach of the formidable tusks of the Boar. Over fallen logs they ran, the Boar sometimes so close that it seemed to me that he would overtake her in another second; then around a clump of brush, a big log, or rock, they would disappear for a moment, to reappear with the Cat still ahead.

"How long the chase had lasted I do not know, so interested was I, but I saw her at last at the foot of a ledge of rocks a couple of hundred yards away. One glance must have convinced the cat that she should not ascend the cliff weighted down by the body of the pig, for she gave it a vicious crunch and threw it aside just as the old Boar crashed through the brush a few feet away. Then with a screech of rage and victory, she sprang up the rocks and disappeared, leaving her enemy champing and frothing over the body of the dead pig.

"Turning my attention now toward the chestnut tree, I found that the sow and her family had also disappeared in the undergrowth, and while I was looking, the old cat crept out of the brush and sprang up the tree to reappear a minute later with one of the kittens in her mouth. Dropping the little bobtailed fellow at the foot of the tree, she reascended and again returned with her remaining kitten, then after fondling and purring over them a few minutes, for all the world like an old house tabby, she trotted off, followed by her family, and disappeared in the forest."

Sometimes the bobcat will bury part of its prey as does the puma. Instances have been found where a pile of the intestines of a squirrel were covered with a mound of dust and pine needles scraped from a trail. Nearby were observed spots of blood showing where the animal had eaten its meal and in the dust along the used trail were plain cat tracks leading to the scratched-up mound of dust and pine needles.

From the foregoing field observations of the bobcats' feeding habits, it is certain this carnivore consumes a great variety of wild prey. This, coupled very often with the new and satisfying provender in the young of the flocks and herds of the stockman and the poultry of the farmer over much of its natural range, causes it to become a close second to the coyote in its adaptability to any modified habitat.

———CHAPTER SIX———

# HUNTING AND CONTROL

### Trapping

TRAPPING has been found to be one of the most effective methods of bobcat control. Bobcats are easily caught in traps of the common double-spring steel type, in sizes 2 and 3. Such traps have been used by many generations of trappers, and although deemed inhumane by some persons, no better or more practical device is yet available to take their place. The brief description here presented of trapping methods to be used in bobcat control is based on field experiences of Federal and cooperative trappers who have applied methods developed by the Fish and Wildlife Service.

107

*Where to Trap*

In selecting a site for trap sets, one should be guided to a large extent by the tracks of the animal and by other traces of its presence, which are commonly found in the rugged recesses of the open range. Such places as leached limestone ridges, limestone cap rock, or eroded granitic canyons containing an abundance of small caverns and holes surrounded by rather extensive underbrush form the ideal habitat of the bobcat. This may be in low-lying country or in adjacent higher mountainous areas. Though it is advisable to use the greatest caution in setting bobcat traps, the care with which the art is practiced need not be so great as in the case of the wolf or the coyote.

*"Blind" Trap Sets*

When the trail of a bobcat has been found, by track or sign, along or leading from its rocky lair, traps may be placed in either double or single sets (Fig. 7). If the trail is not also fre-

FIGURE 7. "Blind" or trail set being placed for bobcats. Trails used by both bobcats and cattle make ideal situations for placing the blind set for predators during periods when stock is removed from such parts of the range.

FIGURE 8. Details of setting trap for bobcat in trail; trap bedded just beyond a natural obstruction in the path; the working parts of trap are lightly packed with cotton to insure springing when the ground is frozen.

quently used by livestock, or such big game animals as deer, the so-called "blind" trap set may be employed. This set is called a blind because no lure or scent need be used around it when completed.

Whether single or double blind trap sets are employed, they should be placed in holes dug directly in the trail of the bobcat close to such obstructions as exposed roots, rocks, or clumps of weeds, for the bobcat seldom fails to step over rather than on such obstructions in its path (Fig. 8). If the double set is to be used, the trap holes should be only about one inch apart, separated just far enough to prevent interference of the jaws when the trap is sprung. Each hole should be dug only slightly larger than the size of the trap and just deep enough to hold the set trap and allow this to be slightly lower than the level of the surrounding ground. When two traps are used, they may be joined together with a lap link at the ends of their chains, which in turn may be attached to a stake pin driven slightly below the ground level; or a drag may be used either made of wrought iron or consisting of a fairly heavy stone. The drag should be bedded under the traps, in which case more excavating will be required. It is well to have a free-acting swivel at the top of the stake pin to prevent a captive animal from twisting and breaking the trap chains attached to it.

In some sections the traps are set far apart (Fig. 8a) so that the animal, if caught in both, is eagle-spread. If the traps are set close together as indicated in Figure 8 they can become entangled to the extent that the animal will be able to twist the foot off and escape.

FIGURE 8a. Blind trap sets in horizontal position often insure higher percentage of catch.

After the trap has been firmly bedded it is advisable to cover it with fine pulverized earth similar to that found in the mound of a pocket gopher. This will do for the spring of the trap. Dry dirt from under a nearby bush or finely pulverized horse or cow manure may be more advantageously used to cover the inside of the trap jaws. Care should be taken to keep all loose dirt from getting under the pan and to see that there is an open space beneath it of at least a quarter of an inch.

A trap pad made of canvas or of old unscented slicker cloth for finally covering the pan should now be placed on the inside of the jaws; then over all should be sprinkled dry dirt of the same color as the ground surrounding the trap to the depth of a quarter- to a half-inch. The spot where the trap is buried should be left in as natural a condition as possible.

### Scented Trap Sets

A scent attractive to bobcats may be used to advantage to lure the animals to trap sets. When scenting is resorted to, however, the traps should not be placed in the runway proper, but on either side of it, or on one side only, and parallel to the trail. They should be set in the same manner as described for the blind sets, between the trail and the spot selected for scattering the scent (Fig. 9). This spot should be no more than 6 to 8 inches from the trap. In placing the scent, advantage should be taken of any stubble, bunch of weeds, exposed root, or object known as a scent post. These are so termed because they are the places selected by the animal for voiding urine or feces. (See page 112a.)

Bobcats usually have their scent posts slightly off the trail, on stubble of range grasses, on bushes, or even on old bleached-out carcasses. Where the ground conditions are right for good tracking, natural scent posts may be detected by the claw scratches and the small mound of dirt where the bobcat has covered its excrement. Such habits are similar to those of house cats. In passing along its trails, the bobcat will usually revisit these scent posts.

When natural scent posts cannot be readily found, one may

be easily established along the determined trail of a bobcat by dropping scent (of a kind to be described) on a few clusters of weeds, spears of grass, stubble or low brush. The trap should be set between the trail and the place scented, about 6 or 8 inches from each (Fig. 10). Any number of such scent stations may be placed along a determined trail. The farther from the trail a trap is set, however, the more scent will be needed. For dropping the scent, a 2- to 4-ounce bottle fitted with a shaker cork may be used.

The "flag-set" also is widely used. In this procedure the trapper suspends an object, such as a rabbit, chicken or piece of hide, from a stake about 4 feet high and places a buried trap at the foot of the stake. The bobcat is attracted by the object waving in the wind. This set is more widely used in parts of Montana and Colorado than the "blind" and "natural scent" sets previously described. The efficacy of the flag-set is caused by the bobcat's keen vision and coyote-like curiosity.

### Preparation of Scent

The basis of the scent may be any kind of fish, but oily varieties such as sturgeon, eels, suckers, and carp, are preferred. The flesh should be ground in a sausage mill, placed in strong tin or galvanized-iron cans, and left in a warm place to decompose thoroughly. Each can must be provided with a small vent to allow the escape of gas, otherwise there is danger of explosion. The aperture, however, should be screened with a fold of cloth to prevent flies from depositing eggs, as the mixture seems to lose much of its scent quality when maggots develop in it. This preparation may be used within three days after mixing, but it is more lasting and penetrating when it is about a month old.

Fish scent alone gives excellent results, but several modifications have been found highly effective. For instance, mice, beaver castors, musk glands from minks, weasels, and muskrats, and the bladders of coyotes and bobcats may be added to the decayed fish. Oil gives body to the scent and to a certain extent prevents freezing. If the mixture appears too thin, glycerin,

FIGURE 9. Placing a scent set for bobcats: A, double trap set, placed as in blind sets, but a few inches off the trail instead of directly in it; B, traps bedded, and springs and jaws properly covered and pan unobstructed, ready for covering with a trap pad, on which the topsoil is to be spread. Scent sets are placed between the trail and a clump of weeds or other natural or artificial scent posts.

PLATE 26. Bobcat burying its nose into a catnip ball, Carmen Mts., Coahuila, Mexico. (Photo courtesy of Tappan Gregory, Chicago.)

PLATE 27. Bobcat takes a whiff of catnip. The catnip ball is directly under cat's nose. (Photo courtesy of Tappan Gregory, Chicago.)

brains, fish oil, butterfat, or other animal fat, such as that from woodchucks and ground squirrels, may be added.

The hunter may commence with a quantity of ground fish placed in a large galvanized-iron container, similar to a milk can, and as the original lot is used on the trap line, he may replenish it by adding more fresh fish and others of the ingredients mentioned. The addition of new material from time to time seems to improve the desirable qualities of the scent mixture.

FIGURE 10. Details of placing scent set on cleared space between the trail and a clump of higher weeds or grass used as a scent post. Between the trap set and the scent post may be buried a jar having perforated top and containing cotton saturated with oil of catnip; or other scent material may be sprinkled on the clump of weeds to lure the bobcat to the trap.

*Catnip Oil as a Lure*

Oil of catnip, diluted in the proportion of 35 drops of the pure oil to 2 ounces of petrolatum, has proved an effective lure in bobcat trapping. Catnip in this form has been used as a lure by some trappers with a fair degree of success. A few drops of the mixture or of the tincture, should be placed on the scent spot every third day.

Some Fish and Wildlife Service hunters employ this lure by burying at one side of a bobcat runway a small glass jar or bottle (Fig. 10) into which has been dropped gauze or cotton batting, saturated with catnip oil. The mouth of the container is left open, but level with the ground, and is protected by a perforated top. If the top is bright, it should be made inconspicuous by moistening it, and brushing it over with dust or sand while wet. Trap sets placed as described around such scent posts have accounted for the trapping of many bobcats.

At this point, for the record, it will be of interest to narrate further of the successful use of catnip oil in not only bobcat trapping, but also as an aid in photographing both the bobcat and puma.

The late Courtney Ryley Cooper, recalling his early experiences with the circus, in his interesting book "The High Country," said: "For years, in the circus, trainers found that the surest way in the world to make friends with their cat charges was to do the same thing that the proverbial old maid does with her pet tabby . . . feed him catnip." Whether the circus folk were the first to be aware of this fact I do not know, but so far my research points that way, and probably they should be so credited. Anyway, it became a matter of common knowledge that pumas, or mountain lions, and bobcats are attracted by the odor of the catnip plant.

Experiments, sponsored by the then United States Biological Survey, of the Department of Agriculture, were undertaken at various times during the period 1915 to 1920, to synthesize a chemical the odor of which would simulate that of catnip and serve as a lure. This proved unavailing. Knowledge of the anatomy and physiology of the catnip plant *(Nepeta cataria)* gave the clue to the secret. It was believed that an essential oil produced in the plant was the source of the characteristic odor. A member of the technical staff in the Biological Survey found a small group of plants of this species on the U. S. Fur Animal Experiment Station, located at the time near Keeseville, New York, and arranged for the harvesting of them at the proper time. Arrangements were also made with the Drug Division of the Bureau of Plant Industry, United States Department of Agriculture, to extract the oil from these plants. In 1923 the catnip was harvested and a small supply of the catnip oil was obtained. So far as is known this was the first catnip oil extracted in the United States. About a teaspoonful had been extracted by European chemists previous to that year, but it was pronounced of no commercial value.

It was evident that a large quantity of the plants was required to obtain a very small quantity of the oil. Catnip oil is highly volatile, and the odor of the pure oil is very heavy compared with that of the plant. Further experiments were undertaken to dilute the catnip oil with some neutral agent that would combine with it to produce a larger supply of oil which would have the desired fragrance and be more lasting when exposed to the open air. It was found that the desired result could be obtained by mixing the catnip oil with oil of petrolatum in the proportion of 35 drops of catnip oil to 2 ounces of oil of petrolatum. It was also discovered that when the pure catnip oil cannot be obtained, a mild tincture of catnip can be produced by boiling the leaves of the plant to a pulpy consistency in water. This concoction, however, as a lure, is not as efficient as the pure oil or the oil diluted with oil of petrolatum.

The question then arose as to where catnip oil could be obtained in sufficient quantities for use as a lure in trapping members of the cat family in predator control work on the western stock and big game ranges. To enable the Biological Survey to procure sufficient quantities of the oil, the Bureau of Plant Industry of the Department of Agriculture planted a small area on the Arlington Experimental Farm to catnip.

From the small crop that resulted, enough catnip oil was produced for a more thorough test in field operations conducted in the desert mountain ranges of Arizona and the Rocky Mountain of Colorado. In the spring of 1927 an acre of ground on the Biological Survey's Fur Animal Experiment Station, which had been relocated, at Saratoga Springs, New York, was planted. The harvesting of this crop yielded nearly a ton of the catnip plants in the late summer of that year. An expert on the distillation of fine oils from the Bureau of Plant Industry supervised the harvesting, and from the ton of the harvested catnip plants a pint of the pure catnip oil was extracted (Plate 25.)

This catnip lure retains its efficacy a long time after exposure. The writer found that pumas in Colorado, Arizona, and New Mexico were attracted to a place 6 months after one exposure of catnip had been made there. Members of the Provincial Game Conservation Board of British Columbia, in experimenting with a supply of the oil furnished by the Biological Survey also reported that it proved effective 6, and even 10, months after exposure.

Why catnip is so attractive to members of the feline family is not yet fully known. Experiments indicate that it produces sexual excitement and also that it has a soothing effect on the nervous system similar to that of mild opiates on man. Its use as a lure in the trapping of both bobcats and pumas committing depredations on livestock of the far western mountainous ranges has resulted in some remarkable catches.

Catnip oil has proved equally effective as a lure when photographing these animals in their own habitats. Enticing these mammals into a situation in which they will take their own pictures requires a trapping technique similar to that practiced by puma and bobcat trappers. In an attempt, among other objectives, to obtain self-photographs of puma and bobcats (Gregory 1938), an expedition was made by the writer during the fall of 1937 to the Carmen Mountains in northern Coahuila, Mexico. This effort was sponsored by the U. S. Bureau of Biological Survey, the Chicago Academy of Sciences represented by Tappan Gregory of Chicago, one of the outstanding wildlife photographers in the country, the Smithsonian Institution, and the National Zoo. To Gregory, a self-taken picture of the prince of predators, the puma, was the sole objective. Coupled with this, however, I also wished particularly to find out just what the big cat, as well as the bobcat, looks like when sniffing catnip oil. My dozens of experiments in the field with the wild cats and catnip oil had conjured up different pictures in my mind as to the attitude the puma and bobcat might assume. We were successful in attaining both objectives, and as far as we are aware, this was the first time a puma and bobcat ever were led to take their own picture in their own undisturbed habitat.

The Carmen Mountains are situated in northern Coahuila, Mexico, south and a little west of Del Rio, Texas, on the Rio Grande, and are reached by a desert road of about 130 miles over rough, rocky country, crossed by many arroyos. The Carmens present a formidable array of eroded granitic peaks, cut with many deep, steep-walled canyons. On the mountain slopes are live oaks bedecked with the parasitic mistletoe alternating with fine stands of ponderosa pine. Here and there are interspersed small, flat, open parks carpeted with succulent grama grass, often knee high. It is a botanist-zoologist paradise. At the time we were there, in September and October, the forest floor with its profusion of wild flowers was a riot of color. They were a forester's dream of what real forest litter should be like. Clear, cool, forest streams pitch off the mountains and flow through the canyons, to work their way eventually north and sink into the desert sands. This entire area of the Carmens at that time was fully protected from livestock grazing, and was disturbed only by man, and that to a limited extent during the Mexican seasons for deer hunting. Deer are found there in large numbers, and pumas and bobcats in abundance. In a 12-mile ride from the northern part of the range to our base camp at the head of the Carbonera Canyon to the south, we counted nearly one hundred puma and bobcat "scratches," places where the animal defecates or voids its urine and covers the whole by heaping forest litter over it with its front paws.

The puma and to a certain extent the bobcat are great night wanderers, and they generally have well-defined crossing points where they pass from one watershed to another in search of food. Many of these are commonly found in the low saddle of local drainage divides, and at such crossings it is not uncommon to find puma and bobcat scratches. For instance, as many as eight such scratches of the puma were found in the Carmens within an area of 4 to 6 square feet. These were sometimes 6 to 8 inches high, and at least 6 inches in diameter. Frequently old or fresh feces were noticed near them. Bobcat scratches are, of course, much smaller because of the proportionate size of its paws.

These scratches make ideal places for setting the so-called camera tread. This is buried at a distance of 14 to 22 feet from a set camera which is placed 5 to 6 feet up in a tree. The camera tread consists of two metal plates about a foot square. The bottom plate carries a dozen or so copper nails that point upward. The top plate of the tread rests on four springs strong enough to resist a certain degree of pressure so that when the tread is buried the weight of the earth will not produce an electrical contact. This resistance to pressure also prevents a camera from being "shot" by the smaller mammals and birds that may step or alight upon the tread. The metal plates are held together by a waxed string, and the whole device is then encased in an oiled-silk envelope. From these plates run insulated positive and negative electric cables connected to a dry cell, which was also connected with the flash powder, hermetically sealed in a small box approximately 2 inches in diameter and the same in height. We used a thin sheet of aluminum to seal the powder box. The metal tread was buried an inch below the surface of the ground and all wires were camouflaged or hidden from view. As the animal stepped on the tread the electric circuit was closed, an electric spark thus produced exploded the flash powder, and enough energy was released to trip the shutter of the camera and take the picture. In most of the shots thus made the shutter on the camera was set at 1/100 of a second speed. If care is exercised this kind of photography may be employed at any time of the year.

In burying the metal treads every precaution was taken to avoid leaving any human odor in the vicinity of the place selected to set the camera, or on any of the equipment. A canvas cloth was used to kneel on while burying the tread, and descented gloves were worn when handling the apparatus and in removing the surplus earth in covering the metal plates.

Wherever a scratch was found within 14 to 22 feet (our focusing distance) of a tree that would serve to hold the camera securely, which was fastened with set screws to a small platform, a camera tread was sunk close to the scratch. The scratch was in no way disturbed, but was left just as the puma or bobcat had left it. A few drops of catnip oil were then sprinkled on a small ball of cotton, the size of a filbert, and this was placed near the center of the scratch. A small dried leaf was placed carefully over the top of the catnip ball to serve as a miniature shingle in protecting it from mountain fogs, dews, or rains.

The reason for thus "framing" the cats is that as they pass over their travelways they may instinctively stop at the scratch, either to void urine or to defecate, or perhaps only to sniff these spots. Attracted by the odor of catnip they invariably step on the tread, and their picture is taken. The reader may say that they would stop at such points anyway, even if no catnip were present! That may or may not be true, for pumas and bobcats often pass up scratches or may perhaps sniff at only one out of several in a group. But photographic evidence seems to bear out the contention that catnip will hold the puma and the bobcat where you want them and cause them to put their feet just where you hoped they would. Moreover, with the catnip lure we obtained pictures when no puma or bobcat scratches were in evidence by placing the tread at one side of a game trail, the catnip ball being so placed as to cause the animal to step upon the tread while extending its neck and nose for a good whiff.

It all sounds so easy but the chances of success are very small.

Why? Because the first and most important requisite is that the photographer must know the habits of the animal and must be able to recognize the scratches. Then, after completing all the refinements necessary in placing the tread and the camera in proper position, a leaf may drop down unnoticed over the lens. Or again, fog may dim the lens or a fallen limb may smash the camera in the course of a windstorm. Chipmunks may dance on the aluminum-covered flash-powder box resulting in their sharp toenails penetrating to the powder, thus admitting moisture and ruining it, as they did for us in the Carmens. And rodents may dig out the treads, or rabbits may land on them with all four feet, as did some of the big Mexican rabbits, coming down on the treads with sufficient force to make them contact, explode the flash, and trip the camera shutter, making a camera useless that might have taken a striking picture sometime later. These are just a few of the trials and tribulations. Hence the thrill is all the greater when one day you find evidence at the tread that indicates a visit from old *Felis concolor,* or *Lynx rufus,* and you hurry back to base camp with the negative, develop it, and at last find success. The camera that took our first bobcat picture was out but a few nights, but our first puma was taken by a camera that had been set in a tree above eight puma scratches 20 feet away for nearly three weeks before the picture we were working so strenuously to obtain was finally taken. Bobcats were more easily photographed as they were not so long in coming by certain points along their travelways which were chosen for camera sets.

A well-known western stockman to whom photographs were shown of the puma and bobcat self-photography in Coahuila asked, "How did you lure him into the field of the camera?"

"We used oil of catnip," I replied.

"Let me smell some," he said.

I produced a small vial of it. He took one whiff and exclaimed, "Great gods, that's what must make the wild cat wild!"

Who but a westerner could say it as well? (Plates 26 and 27.)

### Care in Details

Success in trapping, whether for bobcats or for other predators, is in many respects dependent upon the trapper's attention to what might seem to be minor details. While digging holes for the sets it is well for the trapper to stand or kneel on a "setting cloth," which is made of canvas or a piece of sheepskin or calf hide about 3 feet square. Human scent on the canvas may be avoided by previously burying the cloth in an old manure pile. The dirt removed from the place where the trap is bedded may be piled on the setting cloth. Surplus dirt not needed for covering the trap should be scattered evenly on the ground at some distance from the set. It is well, also, to wear gloves while setting traps, and to use them for no other purpose. However, the precautions against arousing the suspicion of bobcats are less necessary than those in trapping wolves and coyotes.

*Rust on traps.*—Rust is often the cause of the failure of traps to spring properly, particularly when the trap pan rusts on its post. Most steel traps are so constructed that when the trap pan is moved back and forth it will spread the joint and thus permit the pan to work freely. Putting a few drops of fine oil on the post, as well as in the slots that hold the jaws at the base of the trap, will overcome such difficulties.

*Frozen ground.*—When the ground is frozen it is difficult to keep the traps in working order. Some hunters overcome this difficulty by lining the bottom of the hole in which the trap is to be bedded with clean, coarse cotton or wool, and by packing more of this material around the pan, springs, and jaws after the trap is placed. When the ground is frozen, the dirt cover for the set can be made of such debris as is found on ant hills, or by using dead leaves or the fine earth obtained under spruce, fir, hemlock, or aspen trees.

*Deodorizing traps.*—When received from dealers or manufacturers, traps frequently smell of grease, perspiration from human hands, or other odors caused by contact with various kinds of merchandise in the course of shipment. As some of these odors are likely to arouse the suspicion of predators, it is advisable to clean all traps before using them. This may be done by boiling them in a tincture of sage leaves, or of leaves from other native trees. Common soil is a good deodorizer, but it acts slowly. Simply burying the traps for a few days in a manure pile (the odor from which does not arouse the predator's suspicion) will often remove all other odors. It is better, however, before using traps to clean them by boiling, as mentioned. Never attempt to burn off an odor over a fire, as this may destroy the temper of the springs and make the trap worthless.

*Paper trap pads.*—Paper pads are not dependable, as they are usually too smooth to hold the covering of soil. This is soon swept off the paper when the trap is set in a windy place, and when this is gone the trap is exposed. Furthermore, rain will readily soak a paper pad, causing it to break or collapse and expose much of the set. Another objection to paper pads is that when an animal steps lightly into a trap jaw, resting its toes barely inside of it but not on the trap pan, it is likely to hear the rustle of the paper under its foot as well as to feel its smoothness. The result is that it will be shy of that particular spot, and thus a catch is lost. Trap pads made of fairly thick canvas or woven wire of fly-screen consistency are preferable to paper pads. Such trap pads should be free from all odor, and when not in use should be kept in a clean container, such as the 1-pound cans used for coffee.

### Use of Live Poultry as Bait

A unique scheme, long practiced, particularly in parts of the South and in the Great Lakes area, involves the use of live hens or roosters, preferably the latter. These are placed in a box frame enclosed with poultry wire. Where roosters are used, one or more boxes are employed and placed some distance apart so that the birds may hear each other crow. Steel traps are then set on opposite sides of the boxes. When the bobcat seeks entrance to the boxes to capture the penned bird, it seldom fails to step into the trap.

Cory (1912) says: "Wild Cats are very fond of poultry. I

have trapped many of them by placing a live hen in a box frame covered with wire netting and setting steel traps on opposite sides. In running around the cage trying to find an entrance, the animal is almost certain to be caught in one of the traps; but they are very suspicious of a bait over a steel trap and are not nearly so likely to be taken as by the method above described." (Plate 27a.)

### Resetting Traps

The trap may be reset after a bobcat has been caught, the same spot being used if the ground and the natural surroundings have not been too badly scratched up or otherwise defaced, and if evidences of disturbance can be cleared away. It may be highly desirable to reset the trap in the same place, particularly if other good spots are not available.

### Novel Trapping Procedure

Much could be written on the humorous side of bobcat trapping episodes. One rather hazardous procedure, however, must suffice here. C. A. Keeler reported to the Biological Survey in May of 1889 regarding bobcat conditions in the Carson River Valley of Nevada where the animals were numerous. It appears that some years previously a large herd of goats was pastured in the valley and the "wildcats" were very destructive to the young kids. A one-armed goat herder had a novel method of taking them alive. When one was caught in a trap he would force a wooden arm (which had replaced his lost appendage) down the animal's throat so it could not bite and then hold it fast. Four or five thus caught were kept on exhibition at some of the hot springs in the valley. I am sure anyone who has ever attempted to hog-tie a trapped bobcat and remove it alive can appreciate this goat herder's intestinal fortitude. (Plate 28.)

## THE BOUNTY AS A CONTROL MEASURE

Most of the early colonies established a bounty on the bobcat (which sometimes included the lynx).

Massachusetts, by 1727, placed a bounty of 20 shillings for every full-grown wildcat. This bounty was off and on for many years. By 1903 the bounty was $3, and in 1951 it was as high as $10, per animal.

Pennsylvania's bobcat bounty is of long duration. It began in 1819 at $1 for an adult and 25 cents for young. From time to time changes were made as follows: 1841, $1.50 for adult, 75 cents for young; 1869, $2 for adult, $1 for young; 1885, $2 for adult, nothing for young; 1907, $4 for adult, nothing for young; 1915, $6 for adult, nothing for young; 1919, $8 for adult, nothing for young; and 1923, $15 for adult, nothing for young. The $15 bounty continued until 1937 when it was removed on October 1 of that year, and up to the present writing (1952) has not been reinstated. The passage of the act of July 25, 1913, that placed a bounty on certain animals and birds in Pennsylvania was bitterly opposed by the Pennsylvania Game Commission. This law empowered the various counties to pay the claims and then be reimbursed for such by the State from a fund collected from sportsmen of the State through the so-called Resident Hunters' License Act. Up until the winter of 1915-16 the various Pennsylvania counties were empowered to pay bounty, after which time the Pennsylvania Game Commission took over this function. From this time until the bobcat bounty removal in 1937, a total of 7,305 bobcats were bountied to the Commission. At the rate of $15 per bobcat, the take for the year 1923 totaled 617, and from then on the payments show a gradual diminution for each succeeding year until the bounty was discontinued. During the period 1937-38, only 3 of these predators were bountied.

In Virginia, bobcat bounty is paid from county funds and the amount is set by the various Boards of County Supervisors. At this writing, of the 40 counties authorized to levy a bounty in Virginia, only 5 have actually done so, the amount of which ranges from $1.50 to $5.00 for each animal.

In common with bounties on other predators, the bobcat bounty has not been paid without attendant frauds. Some examples of these are related in the following paragraphs.

Several counties in the State of Washington paid bounties of $5 on bobcats upon presentation of the pelts to the proper county official who removed the right front foot when he allowed the bounty. The claimant retained the skin. One day an auditor of Whitman County asked the government hunter how many bobcats he usually caught in the county in a season. The hunter replied that ordinarily he did not take more than four or five in three seasons. The auditor intimated that perhaps the Federal hunter was not fully acquainted with local conditions, because that day a man had presented for bounty 34 bobcats, declaring on affidavit that he had caught them in the immediate vicinity within a period of 30 days. The matter was reported to the sheriff, who apprehended the man. It was found that this man had collected $652 in bounties on 129 bobcats and 7 coyotes (at $1 per coyote), but that most of the skins presented as bobcats were small ocelots, animals of the far Southwest, and of small southern wildcats, also taken outside the State.

Not long after this incident, another bounty hunter entered the State and proceeded to present for bounty 35 bobcats in one county, 48 in another, 30 in another, and 40 in still another. Investigation by the county officials, whose suspicions were thus aroused, led to the mans' arrest. In his car were 75 bobcats and a sack containing 356 extra bobcat feet. Close examination showed that bobcat feet had been sewed onto some of the skins. And this man had strongly condemned to the Whitman County Game Commissioner the Biological Survey's (now Fish and Wildlife Service) paid hunter method of predatory animal control!

In Pennsylvania, a justice of the peace once certified that two raccoon skins were actually bobcat skins, and the owner thus received a bounty of $8.00. In other instances, evidence was found that certain justices, instead of destroying the skins presented to them as provided by law, saved some and afterwards probated same before another justice. These and other incidents of fraud in that State gave rise to the following statement made in the annual report of the Board of Pennsylvania Game Commissioners prepared by Dr. Joseph Kalbfus, Secretary and Chief Game Protector for the year

1915 (pp. 25-34): "No one could have made me believe that so many men in public life were as lax in the handling of public interest entrusted to them as has been demonstrated they undoubtedly have been in the handling of these claims for bounty . . ."

It was such fraudulent occurrences that led finally, in 1915, to the payments of Pennsylvania bounty claims by the Pennsylvania Game Commission from its headquarters in Harrisburg, and in the later passage of the act of May 24, 1923, that enabled the Game Commission to not only set the various bounties on certain animals when "in its opinion . . . it is desirable or necessary for the better protection of game . . . throughout this Commonwealth." The exactness of procedures which the Game Commission now follows in the payment of any bounty makes Pennsylvania's bounty payments as free from fraud as is humanly possible under such a plan of predator control, be it for bird or mammal.

Many states which had the bobcat bounty on their statutes, but failed to appropriate sufficient funds to keep it in effect, are facing a possible swindle if and when funds are again provided. This could come about because many defunct state bounty warrants have been purchased from the original holders at a fraction of their original value by speculators. The purchasers, of course, hope for a substantial profit though they had nothing whatever to do with the original capture of any bobcat.

It makes no difference which animal has a bounty on its head, fraud will in some way be perpetrated. An example concerns a bounty of $5 offered by the Forest Service of British Columbia for the removal of both ears of each wild horse presented. It appears:

"These animals had increased to such an extent that they were ruining the range. One operator took out his horse-shooting permit and went hunting. He was back in a very short time with a suspiciously large sack full of horse's ears. When the Forest Ranger examined them he became suspicious because some of the ears were not only a little bit the worse for wear, but were quite mouldy. He questioned the hunter, who had been out only a few days and must have done some mighty heavy hunting to bag such a large number of horses in such a short time. It turned out that the hunter had a brother working in a down-country abattoir and more than 1,200 pairs of horses' ears had been saved up so that they could be presented for bounty later.

"If the hunter had not been too greedy, it is quite possible that he would have collected."

A different situation was encountered in the case of a bounty on the so-called Modoc ground squirrel of northern California. For each squirrel tail brought in, a sum of 10 cents was paid. This went on for a considerable time, until the authorities were taken aback by reports of a preponderance of bob-tailed squirrels appearing on the ranges. What had happened was that as each squirrel was captured it was turned loose after its tail had been cut off. Thus another crop of squirrels would be assured; a sort of bounty deal not far removed from perpetual motion.

The bounty plan of control has been carried on by many commonwealths for several centuries in a more or less desultory manner, and with little success. Arnold (1952) stated that "Michigan bobcats are a splendid example [of the ineffectiveness of the bounty system]. The bounty was removed from Lower Peninsula bobcats in 1941, while the bounty remains in the Upper Peninsula. Lower Peninsula bobcats have not increased since the bounty was removed. In fact, some hunters are complaining that there are more 'cat hunters than 'cats, at the same time, the bobcats in the Upper Peninsula have not been exterminated or reduced by the bounty. The presence or absence of a bobcat bounty in Michigan has apparently had no effect on populations. Funds expended on any bounty, be it bobcat or otherwise, would improve a lot of game habitat, would acquire a lot of public shooting ground, or could materially aid in better compensation to the large army of game technicians living on starvation salaries."

In some states, particularly Pennsylvania, where evidence

of serious predation has been found lacking, removal of the bounty has occurred because the trophy value of the animal is high, and it has been felt that needed control of an excessive bobcat population can be attained by the sport of hunting with dogs.

From the foregoing, and from additional evidence on file concerning bounties on predatory animals, it may be concluded that the bounty as a measure of control not only creates opportunities for fraud, but is usually ineffective and a waste of funds that might be better used toward improvement of game management. When confronted with a bounty issue, stockmen, sportsmen and conservationists should demand the facts as to how successful this method of control has been.

## HUNTING BOBCATS WITH HOUNDS

Since Colonial times bobcat hunting with hounds has been an exhilerating form of sport. At times, considerable expense results from this recreation in the maintenance of packs of hounds. One of the favorite breeds is the Kentucky foxhound, though any breed of hound may become a good "bobcat hound," depending on the owner and his ability to train the dog from puppyhood, for the task is not particularly an easy one. Furthermore, there are hound pups and hound pups. Just any pup does not necessarily develop into a fine "cat" dog even after the best of training. When a hunter endeavors to combine a hound as a runner of both bobcats and puma, his work of training the animal is most difficult. The reason for this is that a bobcat leaves less scent in its travelways than does a puma. Hence seldom indeed does one ever encounter an owner with the so-called "bobcat-puma dog."

With some hunters the opinion is held that the bobcat is more difficult to tree with dogs than is the puma. Much like a fox, some bobcats are prone to pull all the tricks known against running dogs. This consists at times of circling to throw dogs off the scent by doubling back on its track. When half-grown young accompany a mother cat and all are run with dogs, the young will often soon take to separate trees (Plate 29)

PLATE 27a. Box trap enclosed with poultry wire. In partitioned center, live poultry are used as lure; steel traps are placed at opposite sides.

PLATE 28. Bobcat in defending mood. Twenty pounds of dynamite.

PLATE 29. Bobcats are good tree climbers beginning when very young.

to avoid the dog while the mother, instead of delaying to fight off the pursuers, will run on apparently to draw attention away from the treed youngsters. Unless the hunter is very much on the alert, he may easily miss seeing the treed young while following the dogs chasing on after the old one.

One example of bobcat back-tracking is interestingly described by State Senator G. W. "Dub" Evans (1951), long known for his expertness with bear, puma and bobcat hounds in southwestern New Mexico. He records:

"There was a certain bobcat that ranged in the upper Indian Creek country that was trailed many times by my hounds. Judging by the size of his tracks, I figured he was a large male. I wondered why the hounds always lost this particular cat, and one day while they were after him I learned the reason.

"The trail was fresh but the area was too rough for me to follow the hounds closely on horseback, so I worked around ahead of them and took a stand on a point where I had a good view of three or four rough hillsides. I could hear the hounds, hot on the cat's trail, coming in my direction. About that time I saw the cat running, straight across the canyon from me. While I was watching him, he went up a big tree. The hounds were not yet in sight, but were coming fast.

"To my surprise, the cat didn't stay up the tree; he came down and went right back over his own trail away from the tree and toward the hounds, in spite of the fact that the hounds were getting close and making a lot of noise. The cat backtracked about fifty yards, then turned off sharply at right angles and went over the top of the ridge into the next canyon.

"About the time the cat went out of sight, the hounds reached the tree which he had climbed and left. The tree was tall and had a brushy top in which it would have been very difficult for the hounds to have seen the cat even if he had stayed there, and certainly they couldn't tell whether he was there or not. The scent must have been very strong on the base of the tree where the cat had gone up and down, and the hounds barked "treed" with complete confidence. I gave them time, waiting to see if they would straighten out the trail, but they were so sure that this was the trail's end that they made no attempt to do it. I figured that cat had taught me something and had earned a reprieve, so I called the hounds off and made no effort to put them on the trail where the cat had climbed over the ridge."

Hunting the bobcat with one or more trained dogs often requires much endurance on the part of both man and dog. Much patience, persistence, and a full understanding of the animal's habits are likewise essential requirements. Finally, an old tom bobcat that sometimes will bay instead of treeing can give a dog a terriffic clawing. So, a hunter needs to be close to the scene of action to prevent what might prove a fatal injury to a well-trained and favorite as well as high-priced dog.

## POISONING

It is the feeling of many trappers and woodsmen that it is an extremely rare occasion when the bobcat may be induced to take poisoned baits. Of interest in this connection are the findings of three Arizona hunters working in widely separated ranges of that State. Says Marion Maxwell, of Amado; Tennis C. Creighton, of Bowie; and Cy Mangum, of St. Johns, respectively:

"In regards to bobcat picking up drop baits around decoy stations placed for coyotes, it seems that bobcats are pretty much on killing fresh meat for themselves, although at Springerville cats were visiting a station and eating a little of it but refused to take the drop baits until first being covered with rotted fish. The baits were gone but couldn't find the cats and they never returned to the station."

"I have been unable to ever find one yet, and I have tried pretty hard to find where one has picked up a bait. I don't believe they will do it only on very rare occasions."

"I don't think we are killing very many bobcats with drop baits. I don't think they have the keen scent to find the baits as a coyote. I have had bobcats come to my stations and walk straight to the decoy and go straight on. I have never seen where one of them ever picked up a bait or ever found one.

They seem to see decoy and go to it. I have never had a bobcat eat on a decoy station."

The foregoing bears out the experiences of the author with regard to experiments dealing with various poisoned baits as a control measure. This predator's eyesight is its foremost aid in obtaining prey, closely coupled with its rather keen hearing. This may account for its avoidance of poisoned bait placed around decoy stations. It is also felt that any attempt to utilize poison, where deemed necessary in preference to trapping or hunting with dogs, had best be entrusted to a Federal or State agency fully versed in predator control poisoning techniques.

———CHAPTER SEVEN———

# RACES OF THE BOBCAT

THE following races of the bobcat together with their describer, type locality, synonymy, and geographic range are taken from Miller and Kellogg (1955).

Races occurring in California *(californicus* and *pallescens)* were revised by Grinnell and Dixon, Univ. California Publ. Zool., vol. 21, No. 13, pp. 346-353, Jan. 24, 1924.

*Lynx rufus rufus* (Schreber). *Eastern Bobcat*

> 1777. *Felis rufa* Schreber, Die Säugthiere . . ., Theil 3, Heft 95, pl. 109b. (For use of the name *rufus* Schreber 1777 in place of *ruffus* Güldenstaedt 1776 (not a scientific name) see J. A. Allen, Journ. Mamm., vol. 1, No. 2, p. 91, Mar. 2, 1920.)
>
> 1817. *Lynx rufus* Rafinesque, Amer. Monthly Mag., vol. 2, No. 1, p. 46, November 1817.
>
> 1884. *Lynx rufus* True, Proc. U. S. Nat. Mus., vol. 7 (App., Circ. 29), p. 611, Nov. 29, 1884. (Part).

*Type Locality.*—New York. *Range.*—Formerly southern Ontario and Quebec, but now rare, Anderson, Nat. Mus. Canada Bull. 102, 1946, p. 76, Jan. 24, 1947; Maine south to Georgia, the Great Smoky Mountains (Komarek and Komarek, Bull. Chicago Acad. Sci., vol. 5, p. 151, Aug. 15, 1938), and south-central Tennessee; west through Michigan, Wisconsin, and Minnesota to eastern North Dakota (V. Bailey, North Amer. Fauna No. 49, p. 149, December 1926); south to Arkansas (Dellinger and Black, Journ. Mamm., vol. 21, No. 2, p. 189, May 16, 1940) and eastern Kansas (Hibbard, Trans. Kansas Acad. Sci., vol. 47, p. 71, 1944).

*Lynx rufus gigas* Bangs. *Nova Scotia Bobcat*

    1897. *Lynx gigas* Bangs, Proc. Biol. Soc. Washington, vol. 11, p. 50, Mar. 16, 1897.

    1952. *Lynx rufus gigas* Peterson and Downing, Contr. Roy. Ontario Mus. Zool., No. 33, p. 11, Apr. 8, 1952.

*Type Locality.*—Fifteen miles back of Bear River, Nova Scotia, Canada. *Range.*—From Nova Scotia and New Brunswick westward through southern Quebec to southeastern Ontario.

*Lynx rufus superiorensis* Peterson and Downing. *Lake Superior Bobcat*

    1952. *Lynx rufus superiorensis* Peterson and Downing, Contr. Roy. Ontario Mus. Zool., No. 33, p. 1, Apr. 8, 1952.

*Type Locality.*—McIntyre Township, near Port Arthur, Ontario, Canada. *Range.*—In Ontario north and east at least to Kenogami River and from southwestern Algoma and western Manitoulin Island Districts westward to southeastern Manitoba; Upper Peninsula of Michigan westward across Wisconsin and Minnesota; western and southern limits as yet unknown.

*Lynx rufus floridanus* Rafinesque. *Florida Bobcat*

    1817. *Lynx floridanus* Rafinesque, Amer. Monthly Mag., vol. 2, No. 1, p. 46, November 1817.

    1858. *Lynx rufus* var. *floridanus* Baird, Mammals, in Rep. Expl. Surv. Railr. to Pacific, vol. 8, pt. 1, (Washington, 1857), p. 91, July 14, 1858.

1897. *Lynx ruffus floridanus* Bangs, Proc. Biol. Soc. Washington, vol. 11, p. 49, Mar. 16, 1897.

1911. *Lynx floridanus* Gifford, Florida Rev., vol. 6, No. 6, p. 461, December 1911. (Shore of Biscayne Bay, 6 miles south of Miami, Dade County, Fla.)

*Type Locality.*—Florida. *Range.*—Florida north at least to Randolph County, southwestern Georgia (Harper, Journ. Mamm., vol. 10, No. 1, p. 84, Feb. 11, 1929) and southeastern Virginia (Peterson and Downing, Contr. Roy. Ontario Mus. Zool., No. 33, p. 3, April 8, 1952), west across Alabama and Mississippi to alluvial swamps of eastern, southern and southeastern Louisiana (Lowery, Occ. Pap. Mus. Zool. Louisiana State Univ. No. 13, p. 235, Nov. 22, 1943), and thence northward to western Kentucky and southeastern Missouri (Peterson and Downing, loc. cit.).

*Lynx rufus uinta* Merriam. *Mountain Bobcat*

1902. *Lynx uinta* Merriam, Proc. Biol. Soc. Washington, vol. 15, p. 71, Mar. 22, 1902. (Regarded by Grinnell and Dixon, Univ. California Publ. Zool., vol. 21, No. 13, p. 350, Jan. 24, 1924, as identical with *Lynx rufus pallescens.*)

1932. *Lynx rufus uinta* V. Bailey, North Amer. Fuana No. 53 (December 1931), p. 294, Mar. 1, 1932.

*Type Locality.*—Bridger Pass, Carbon County, Wyo. *Range.* —From southern Alberta, Glacier National Park in Montana (V. Bailey, The mammals, *in* Wild animals of Glacier National Park, U. S. Nat. Park Service, p. 82, 1918), and western North Dakota along Missouri River and in Badlands (V. Bailey, North Amer. Fauna No. 49, December 1926, p. 148, Jan. 8, 1927), south in Rocky Mountains to higher mountains of northern New Mexico and along Manzano and Sacramento chain of ranges between Pecos and Rio Grande Valleys to southcentral New Mexico (V. Bailey, 1932, loc. cit.).

*Lynx rufus pallescens* Merriam. *Pallid Bobcat*

1899. *Lynx fasciatus pallescens* Merriam, North Amer. Fauna No. 16, p. 104, Oct. 28, 1899.

1901. [*Lynx rufa*] *pallescens* Elliot, Field Columb. Mus. Publ. 45, Zool. Ser., vol. 2, p. 297, Mar. 6, 1901.

1905. *Felis rufa pallescens* Elliot, Field Columb. Mus. Publ. 105, Zool. Ser., vol. 6, p. 371, Dec. 6, 1905.

1924. *Lynx ruffus pallescens* Grinnell and Dixon, Univ. California Publ. Zool., vol. 21, No. 13, p. 350, Jan. 24, 1924.

1933. *Lynx rufus pallescens* Grinnell, Univ. California Publ. Zool., vol. 40, No. 2, p. 116, Sept. 26, 1933.

*Type Locality.*—South side of Mount Adams, near Trout Lake, Skamania County, Wash. *Range.*—From southern British Columbia south on both slopes of the Cascades through Washington and Oregon (V. Bailey, North Amer. Fauna No. 55, June, p. 268, Aug. 29, 1936) to Siskiyou (Mount Shasta) and Lassen (Plumas Junction) Counties in northern California (Grinnell, Dixon, and Linsdale, The fur-bearing mammals of California, vol. 2, p. 605, Aug. 10, 1937), east through central and northern Nevada (Hall, Mammals of Nevada, p. 277, July 1, 1946) into Idaho (Davis, The Recent mammals of Idaho, p. 150, Apr. 5, 1939) and Utah, except southern and southeastern parts (Durrant, Univ. Kansas Publ. Mus. Nat. Hist., vol. 6, p. 441, Aug. 10, 1952).

*Lynx rufus fasciatus* Rafinesque. *Northwestern Bobcat*

1817. *Lynx fasciatus* Rafinesque, Amer. Monthly Mag., vol. 2, No. 1, p. 46, November 1817.

1897. *Lynx fasciatus* Merriam, Mazama, Portland, vol. 1, p. 224, October 1897.

1901. [*Lynx rufa*] *fasciata* Elliot, Field Columb. Mus. Publ. 45, Zool. Ser., vol. 2, p. 297, Mar. 6, 1901.

1905. *Felis rufa fasciata* Elliot, Field Columb. Mus. Publ. 105, Zool. Ser., vol. 6, p. 371, Dec. 6, 1905.

1924. *Lynx ruffus fasciatus* Grinnell and Dixon, Univ. California Publ. Zool., vol. 21, No. 13, p. 348, Jan. 24, 1924.

1933. *Lynx rufus fasciatus* Grinnell, Univ. California Publ. Zool., vol. 40, No. 2, p. 115, Sept. 26, 1933.

*Type Locality.*—Northwest Coast; based on Lewis and Clark's description of specimens obtained near the mouth of the Columbia, on Netul River (now Lewis and Clark River) near Astoria, Oreg. (V. Bailey, North Amer. Fauna No. 55, June, p. 269, Aug. 29, 1936). *Range.*—Humid and heavily forested area west of Cascade Mountains from southwestern British Columbia south through Washington, Oregon (V. Bailey, North Amer. Fauna No. 55, June, p. 269, Aug. 29, 1936), and the humid redwood coast belt of northwestern California to Mendocino County (Grinnell, Dixon, and Linsdale, The fur-bearing mammals of California, vol. 2, p. 599, Aug. 10, 1937).

*Lynx rufus californicus* Mearns. *California Bobcat*

1897. *Lynx rufus californicus* Mearns, Preliminary diagnoses of new mammals of the genera *Lynx, Urocyon, Spilogale,* and *Mephitis,* from the Mexican boundary line, p. 2, Jan. 12, 1897. (Preprint of Proc. U. S. Nat. Mus., vol. 20, p. 458, Dec. 24, 1897.)

1899. *Lynx (Cervaria) fasciatus oculeus* Bangs, Proc. New England Zool. Club, vol. 1, p. 23, Mar. 31, 1899. (Nicasio, Marin County, Calif. Regarded as indistinguishable from *californicus* by Grinnell and Dixon, Univ. California Publ. Zool., vol. 21, No. 13, p. 347, Jan. 24, 1924.)

*Type Locality.*—San Diego, San Diego County, Calif. *Range.*—Southcentral Oregon, south through main part of California west of the Great Basin and southeastern desert and southeast of extreme humid coast belt, except on open plains, to and across the Mexican boundary in the San Diegan subfaunal district (Grinnell, Dixon, and Linsdale, The fur-bearing mammals of California, vol. 2, p. 590, Aug. 10, 1937) into northwestern Baja California; and the Sierra Nevada and eastern foothills in the vicinity of Lake Tahoe in extreme central western Nevada (Hall, Mammals of Nevada, p. 278, July 1, 1946).

*Lynx rufus peninsularis* Thomas. *Peninsular Bobcat*
　　1898. *Lynx rufus peninsularis* Thomas, Ann. Mag. Nat.
　　　　Hist., ser. 7, vol. 1, p. 42, January 1898.
　　*Type Locality.*—Santa Anita, Baja California, Mexico. *Range.*
—Cape region of Baja California.

*Lynx rufus baileyi* Merriam. *Desert Bobcat, Plateau or Bailey's Bobcat*
　　1890. *Lynx baileyi* Merriam, North Amer. Fauna No. 3,
　　　　p. 79, Sept. 11, 1890.
　　1897. *Lynx rufus eremicus* Mearns, Preliminary diagnoses
　　　　of new mammals of the genera *Lynx, Urocyon, Spilo-
　　　　gale,* and *Mephitis,* from the Mexican boundary line,
　　　　p. 1, Jan. 12, 1897. (Preprint of Proc. U. S. Nat. Mus.,
　　　　vol. 20, p. 457, Dec. 24, 1897. New River, near Laguna
　　　　Station, Colorado Desert, Imperial County, Calif.
　　　　Regarded by Grinnell and Dixon, Univ. California
　　　　Publ. Zool., vol. 21, No. 13, p. 349, Jan. 24, 1924,
　　　　as a synonym of *baileyi.*)
　　1901. [*Lynx rufa*] *baileyi* Elliot, Field Columb. Mus.
　　　　Publ. 45, Zool. Ser., vol. 2, p. 297, Mar. 6, 1901.
　　1905. *Felis rufa baileyi* Elliot, Field Columb. Mus. Publ.
　　　　105, Zool. Ser., vol. 6, p. 372, Dec. 6, 1905.
　　1932. *Lynx rufus baileyi* V. Bailey, North Amer. Fauna
　　　　No. 53 (December 1931), p. 291, Mar. 1, 1932.
　　*Type Locality.*—Moccasin Spring, north of Colorado River,
Coconino County, Ariz. *Range.*—Western Baja California;
southeastern arid region of California, including both Colorado and Mohave Deserts, from east slopes of Coast Ranges
in extreme eastern San Diego County and Antelope Valley in
northern Los Angeles County north along east flank of Sierra
Nevada in Inyo and Mono Counties and desert mountains east
of Owens Valley (Grinnell, Dixon, and Linsdale, The fur-
bearing mammals of California, vol. 2, p. 603, Aug. 10, 1937)
into southern and low western area of Nevada as far as
Carson Sink, Churchill County (Hall, Mammals of Nevada
p. 282, July 1, 1946), and across Arizona and New Mexico to
Kansas west of Flint Hills (Hibbard, Trans. Kansas Acad.

Sci., vol. 47, p. 71, 1944), Oklahoma west of Osage savanna biotic district (Blair, Amer. Midl. Nat., vol. 22, p. 109, July 1939) and western Texas; south at least to Mojarachic in west-central Chihuahua (Knobloch, Journ. Mamm., vol. 23, No. 3, p. 297, Aug. 14, 1942) and Sonora north of Rio Yaqui (Burt, Univ. Michigan Mus. Zool. Misc. Publ. 39, p. 35, Feb. 15, 1939); and north to southern and southeastern Utah (Durrant, Univ. Kansas Publ. Mus. Nat. Hist., vol. 6, p. 443, Aug. 10, 1952).

*Lynx rufus texensis* J. A. Allen. *Texas Bobcat*

> 1884. *Lynx maculatus* True, Proc. U. S. Nat. Mus., vol. 7 (App., Circ. 29), p. 611, Nov. 29, 1884.

> 1895. *Lynx texensis* J. A. Allen, Bull. Amer. Mus. Nat. Hist., vol. 7, p. 188, June 20, 1895. (Based on *Lynx rufus* var. *maculatus* Audubon and Bachman. The viviparous quadrupeds of North America, vol. 2, p. 293, 1851.)

> 1897. *Lynx rufus texensis* Mearns, Preliminary diagnoses of new mammals of the genera *Lynx, Urocyon, Spilogale,* and *Mephitis,* from the Mexican boundary line, p. 2, Jan. 12, 1897. (Preprint of Proc. U. S. Nat. Mus., vol. 20, p. 458, Dec. 24, 1897.)

*Type Locality.*—Vicinity of Castroville, on headwaters of Medina River, Medina County, Tex. *Range.*—From Natchitoches Parish, northwestern Louisiana (Lowery, Occ. Pap. Mus. Zool. Louisiana State Univ. No. 13, p. 235, Nov. 22, 1943), west to big bend of Rio Grande in Kinney County, and north at least to Montague and Cooke Counties, Tex. (V. Bailey, North Amer. Fauna No. 25, p. 169, October 1905); south presumably in Tamaulipas biotic province of Mexico.

*Lynx rufus escuinapae* J. A. Allen. *Sinaloa Bobcat*

> 1903. *Lynx rufus escuinapae* J. A. Allen, Bull. Amer. Mus. Nat. Hist., vol. 19, p. 614, Nov. 14, 1903.

*Type Locality.*—Escuinapa, Sinaloa, Mexico. *Range.*—Southern Sinaloa north at least to Rio Mayo in southern Sonora, Mexico (Burt, Univ. Michigan Mus. Zool. Misc. Publ. 39, p. 34, Feb. 15, 1939).

## CONCLUSION

As mentioned in the "Foreword" this monograph on the bobcat completes the author's attempt to bring together the pertinent natural history of, and economic role played by, our four main North American predators. It has been a task that embodies most of my field experiences dealing with the predators for the past thirty-eight years of official life with the former Biological Survey and the present Fish and Wildlife Service.

These four monographs are far from being the last word on the wolf, puma, coyote, and the bobcat, but they all, I hope, will be of some aid to our future workers who may be interested enough to take it from here and come forth with additional findings that will further enlighten us all on the often too-little understood part played by the larger predators in the great out-of-doors. May these animals never cease to have a place in our North American fauna, a condition that I am sure can be made possible in view of the vast domain yet remaining on this continent where they all roam at will and where their presence is not in conflict with human welfare. In other regions may they be tolerated in reasonably controlled numbers. To that end I have through these many past years given every support.

# REFERENCES AND SELECTED BIBLIOGRAPHY

A———, F.
   1908. Ruffed grouse and lynx. Forest and Stream 70: 331.
Abbot, Charles C.
   1868. Catalogue of vertebrate animals of New Jersey. *In* Cook, George H.,
      Geology of New Jersey, Newark, pp. 751-830; 753.   (Bobcat rare
      in this state.)
   1884. A naturalist's rambles about home. D. Appleton & Co., New York
      485 pp.; 447.
Adams, Charles C.
   1906. An ecological survey in northern Michigan. Rept. Univ. Mich. Mus.
      Zool. Pub. by State Bd. Geol. Survey for 1905, pp. 1-133; 130.
Aikman, Duncan
   1927. Calamity Jane on The Lady Wildcats, 347 pp., New York. 1st edition.
Aldous, C. M., and H. L. Mendall
   1941. The status of big game and fur animals in Maine. Maine Coop.
      Wildlife Research Unit, Univ. Maine, Orono. September 1.
Allen, Glover M.
   1904. Fauna of New England. III. List of the Mammalia. Boston Soc.
      Nat. Hist. Occas. Pap. 7: 1-35; 22. June.
Allen, J. A.
   1869. Catalogue of the mammals of Massachusetts, with a critical revision
      of the species. Mus. Comp. Zool. Bull. 1 (8): 143-252; 153.
   1870. Notes on the mammals of Iowa. Boston Soc. Nat. Hist. Proc. 13:
      178-194; 181.
   1871a. The fauna of the prairies. Amer. Nat. 5: 4-9; 5. March.

1871b. On the mammals and winter birds of East Florida. Mus. Comp. Zool. Bull. 2 (3): 168.

1874a. Notes on the natural history of portions of Dakota and Montana Territories, being the substance of a report to the Secretary of War on the collections made by the North Pacific Railroad Expedition of 1873, Gen. D. S. Stanley, Commander. Boston Soc. Nat. Hist. Proc. 17: 33-91; 37.

1874b. Notes on the mammals of Kansas, Colorado, Wyoming, and Utah. Essex Inst. Bull. 6: 43-66; 45, 58.

1876. Geographical variation among North American mammals especially in respect to size. U. S. Geol. & Geog. Survey Terr. Bull. 2 (4): 309-344; 325. July 1.

1891. On a collection of mammals from southern Texas and northeastern Mexico. Amer. Mus. Nat. Hist. Bull. 3: 219-228; 219.

1893. List of mammals and birds collected in northeastern Sonora and northwestern Chihuahua, Mexico on the Lumholtz Archeological Expedition, 1890-1892. Amer. Mus. Nat. Hist. Bull. 5: 27-242; 32, 84.

1894. On the mammals of Aransas County, Texas, with descriptions of new forms of Lepus and Oryzomys. Amer. Mus. Nat. Hist. Bull. 6: 165-198; 197. May 31.

1895a. On a collection of mammals from Arizona and Mexico made by Mr. W. W. Price, with field notes by the collector. Amer. Mus. Nat. Hist. Bull. 7: 193-258; 253. June 29.

1895b. List of mammals collected in the Black Hills region of South Dakota, and in western Kansas by Mr. Walter W. Granger, with field notes by the collector. Amer. Mus. Nat. Hist. Bull. 7: 259-274; 274. August.

1896a. On mammals collected in Bexar County and vicinity, Texas, by Mr. H. P. Attwater, with field notes by the collector. Amer. Mus. Nat. Hist. Bull. 8: 47-80; 78. April 22.

1896b. List of mammals collected by Mr. Walter W. Granger in New Mexico, Utah, Wyoming, and Nebraska, 1895-1896, with field notes by the collector. Amer. Mus. Nat. Hist. Bull. 8 (15); 241-258; 258.

1903a. A new deer and a new lynx from the State of Sinaloa, Mexico. Amer. Mus. Nat. Hist. Bull. 19: 613-615.

1903b. List of mammals collected by Mr. J. H. Batty in New Mexico and Durango, with descriptions of new species and subspecies. Amer. Mus. Nat. Hist. Bull. 19: 587-612; 590. November 12.

1906 Mammals from the States of Sinaloa and Jalisco, Mexico, collected by J. H. Batty during 1904 and 1905. Amer. Mus. Nat. Hist. Bull. 22: 191-262; 222, 223.

1920. Notes on Gueldenstaedt's names of certain species of Felidae. Jour. Mammal. 1 (2): 90-91. (Correct name for bobcat is *Lynx rufa* (Schreber) and not *Lynx ruffus* (Gueldenstaedt).)

Allen, Ross, and Wilfred T. Neill
1955. The Florida bobcat. Florida Wildlife 8 (9): 20. February. Illus. Florida Game and Fresh Water Fish Commission. (An account of the bobcat as found in Florida.)

Allin, A. E.
  1940. The vertebrate fauna of Arlington township, Durham County,
    Ontario. Roy. Canad. Inst., Toronto, Trans. 23 (49): pt. 1, pp.
    83-118; 88. October.
  1942. Cat-bite wound infection. Jour. Canadian Medical Assoc. 46: 48-50.
    Prov. Lab., Ft. William, Ontario.
Amundson, Geno A.
  1943. Bobcat swims. Jour. Mammal. 24 (3): 399-400. August 8.
Amundson, Rod
  1950. The bobcat. Wildlife in North Carolina 14 (12): 4-7, illus. Decem-
    ber. Raleigh, N. C. (A good general account on the natural history
    of the bobcat.)
Anburey, Thomas
  1789. Travels through the interior parts of America in a series of letters.
    London, 2 vols. Vol. 2, p. 433.
Anderson, James R.
  1893. Second report of the Department of Agriculture of British Colum-
    bia for the year 1892. British Columbia Sess. Papers, Victoria, pp.
    717-978; 930.
  1894. Third report of the Department of Agriculture of the Province of
    British Columbia, 1893. Victoria, B. C., pp. 1882-1892; 1884.
Anderson, R. M.
  1934. The distribution, abundance, and economic importance of the
    game and fur-bearing mammals of western North America, rep-
    resented from the Proc. of the 5th Pacific Science Congress, Vic-
    toria and Vancouver, B. C., Canada. 1933. Univ. of Toronto Press,
    pp. 4055-4075. (Bobcats presumed not to occur on Cape Breton
    Island, Nova Scotia.)
  1935. Annual report of National Museum of Canada for 1934. Division
    of Biology, Ottawa, pp. 10-18; 14.
  1947. Catalogue of Canadian Recent Mammals. Natl. Mus. Canada Bull.
    102 (Biol. Ser. No. 31), pp. 76-77. (Bobcat distribution in Canada.)
Anonymous
  1891. Notes from Northampton, Mass. Orn. & Ool. 16 (1): 15. January.
  1892. The bay lynx. Forest and Stream 39: 465. December 1.
  1896. Some Texas mammals.—II. Forest and Stream 46 (23): 454. June 6.
  1898. An Adirondack wildcat. Forest and Stream 50: 365. May 7.
  1903. Notes. [Wildcats in County]. Amer. Field 60 (11): 244. September 12.
  1904a. Notes. [Wildcats killing in private deer park]. Amer. Field 61 (9):
    201. February 27.
  1904b. Notes. [Lynx killed in Gibson County, Indiana]. Amer. Field 61
    (9): 203. February 27.
  1906a. A wildcat that turned. Forest and Stream 66: 670. April 28.
  1906b. Wild animals of Indiana. Indiana Mag. Hist. 2: 13-16. March.
    (Records in 1859 by A. B. Cole of Noblesville, an agent who bought
    from local trappers 48 wildcat skins.)
  1907a. Notes. [Wildcats unusually plentiful in Vermont.] Amer. Field 67
    (4): 76. January 26.

1907b. In field and forest. Saint Louis Sportsman 10 (21): 4. February 23.

1908. Notes. Wildcats still found in Illinois. Amer. Field 69 (26): 597.

1909. Exceptionally large wildcat taken. Amer. Field 72 (22): 502. November 27.

1910. Hunting bobcats. Forest and Stream 75: 883. December 3.

1913a. Notes from counties. Oregon Sportsman 1 (4): 14. November.

1913b. Wildcat follows hunters. Forest and Stream 81: 639. November 15.

1914a. Notes from counties. Oregon Sportsman 2 (4): 18-20. April.

1914b. Bounties on predatory animals. Oregon Sportsman 2 (6): 19. June.

1914c. Notes. [Wildcat killed near Clinton, Kentucky]. Amer. Field 82 (22): 500. November 28.

1914d. Game conditions on the Upper Clackamas. Oregon Sportsman 2 (12): 16. December.

1914e. Pussy was a wildcat. Forest and Stream 83: 592. November 7.

1914f. Big lynx killed on Seven Mountains. Forest and Stream 83: 625. November 14.

1914g. Notes from counties. Oregon Sportsman 2 (3): 15-17; 2 (4): 18-20.

1916a. Many coyotes and bobcats killed in Wasco County. Oregon Sportsman 4 (1): 58. January.

1916b. Notes. [Number of Utah predators reported killed]. Amer. Field 86 (14): 395. January 30.

1918. Notes. [Bobcat taken in Fayette County, Pa.] Amer. Field 90 (1): 4. July 6.

1919a. Notes. [Forty-pound wildcat taken in New Hampshire.] Amer. Field 91 (24): 581. June 14.

1919b. Hints on the care of peltries. U. S. Dept. Agr., Bureau of Biological Survey Bi-148; mimeographed, p. 1. (Instructions for proper skinning and drying pelt of the bobcat.)

1920. Monster wildcat killed in swamp. Washington, D. C., Herald, November 5.

1921a. Notes. [Woman and child attacked by wildcat.] Amer. Field 95 (14): 374. April 2.

1921b. Notes. [Wildcat taken near Painterville, Pa.] Amer. Field 95 (3): 65. January 15.

1922. Ludlow, Vt. bobcat disputes right of way on mountain trail. The Washington Post, p. 1. January 31.

1926. Wildcat is killed on South Mountain, Md. The Evening Times, Washington, D. C., June 30.

1931. Bobcats kill deer. Field and Stream 36 (3): 43. July.

1932. Wildcats invade town. Vermont community terrorized. The Washington Evening Star, April 29.

1939. Fur production. Wis. Conserv. Bull. 4 (4): 49-50. April.

1940. Documentary material on native protection and wildlife preservation in Latin America. Prepared for use of Comm. of Experts in Nature Protection, May 13-16; vol. 1 (pt. 1): 103-125 (Mexico). Pan-American Union, Washington, D. C. (Status of the bobcat, among other animals.)

1941. Cats differ in Michigan. Detroit News, June 30.

1942. Mountain bobcats. North Carolina Wildlife Conserv. 6 (9): 7. September.

1943. [Wildcat shot near Driftwood, Elk Co., Pa.] Pa. Game News 15 (1): 31. illus. April.

1944a. Wildcats sent to museum. North Carolina Wildlife Conserv. 8 (3): 7. March.

1944b. Fur animals of Texas. Texas Game and Fish 2 (4): 10, illus. March.

1945. Bobcats aid farmers by helping control rabbits. Science News Letter 47 (16): 248. April 21.

1947. Wildcat hunting in Southeast Missouri. Missouri Conservationist 8 (9): 8-9, illus. September. (Tom Phelps of Butler County, ardent bobcat hunter, largest cat killed was 5 ft. long, wt. 40 lbs.; picture shows 1 litter of 4.)

1948a. Bounty on wildcats [bobcat] raised from $5.00 to $10.00. Rod and Gun in Canada 49 (10): 36. March.

1948b. Bobcat. The Hunter's Encyclopedia, Raymond R. Camp, Ed. The Stackpole Company, Harrisburg, Pa., pp. 127-129, illus.

1948c. Predator bounties paid July 1, 1947 to June 30, 1948. Oregon State Game Commission Bull. 3 (11): 5. November. (Gives bobcats bountied in Oregon for this period.)

1949a. Bounty claim payments now stand at $15,500. West Virginia Conservation 12 (10): 20. January. Charleston, W. Va. (Total bounty paid on fox and bobcats March 1-December 1, 1948, W. Va. of which $4.00 is paid per bobcat year around.)

1949b. Bobcat hunters team up on a deer killer. Outdoor Life 103 (7): 51-53, illus. February.

1949c. Wild fur catch decreasing. Texas Game and Fish 7 (3): 11. February. (Six year summary of take bobcats, Texas, 1941-48.)

1949d. Bobcat record. The Explorer. Cleveland Mus. Nat. Hist. Bull. 99: 7. Spring. (Bobcat occurrence in Cleveland area of Ohio.)

1949e. Play it smart for that perfect trophy. Wyo. Wild Life 13 (8): 23. September. (40-lb. bobcat killed sneaking up on some new born calves 6 miles south of Worland, Wyo.)

1950a. A killer is caught in act. Texas Game and Fish 8 (2): 12-13. January. (Illustration of bobcat trapped at scene of a dead doe.)

1950b. Nature in the raw. Rod & Gun in Canada 51 (10): 35. March. (Deer killing by bobcat, New Brunswick.)

1950c. The bobcat. Maryland Conservationist 27 (1): 9, 28, illus. Baltimore, Md. (Records a Maryland bobcat weighing 43 lbs. and overall length of 53 inches.)

1950d. Beleaguered bobcat arouses Sterlingites, (Illinois). Outdoors in Illinois 16 (2): 14, illus. Department of Conservation, Springfield, Ill. Spring. (Killing of 40-lb. bobcat.)

1951a. The curious cat. New Mexico Magazine 29 (7): 30, illus. July. (Bobcat as a pet.)

1951b. B. M. (Bobcat) Dietz, 103 won title in Civil War, Washington, D. C. Evening Star. November 19.

1952. Feline felicity. Oklahoma Game and Fish News 8 (12): 22, illus. December.

1954. Old Bob; Iowa's Wild Ghost. Iowa Conservationist 11 (9): 65, 70. (A short but good natural history account of the bobcat.)

Anthony, H. E.
1913. Mammals of northern Malheur County, Oregon, Amer. Mus. Nat. Hist. Bull. 32: 1-27; 24. March 7.

1928. Field book of North American mammals. 625 pp.; 166-167. G. P. Putnam's Sons, New York and London.

Arant, Frank Selman
1939. Status of game birds and mammals in Alabama. Ala. State Conserv. Dept., Montgomery, 38 pp.; 13, maps. September.

Arnold, Bridgewater M.
1927. Dictionary of fur names. Nat. Assoc. of the Fur Industry, N. Y., pp. 1-22; 5, 13. (Terminology used for the bobcat in the fur trade.)

Arnold, David A.
1952. The fox bounty. Michigan Conservation 21 (4): 28-31. (Comments on the asininity of bounty plan for control of harmful species.)

Arnold, Walter L.
1947. The bobcat. Fur-Fish-Game Harding's Magazine 35 (10): 38, 40-42, illus. October.

Arthur, Stanley C.
1926. Louisiana's fur-bearing mammals. 7th Bien. Rept., La. Dept. Conserv. 1924-26: 63-113.

1928. The fur animals of Louisiana. La. State Conserv. Bull. No. 18, pp. 1-433, illus.; 139. November.

1931. The fur animals of Louisiana. Louisiana State Dept. of Conserv. Bull. 18: 139-144.

Asdell, S[ydney] A[rthur]
1946. Patterns of mammalian reproduction. xii+437 pp.; 174. Comstock Publishing Co., Ithaca, N. Y.

Ashbrook F. G., and H. J. McMullen
1928. Fur-bearing animals of the United States. Fur Jour. 10: 12, 35, 41, illus.

Ashe, Thomas
1808. Travels in America made in 1806. London pp. 1-366; 17.

Aspey, L. S.
1918. [Wild-cat in Fayette County.] In the Open 8 (5): 20. May.

Audubon, J. J., and John Bachman
1851-54. The quadrupeds of North America. 3 vols. Vol. 1, pp. 13, 14. New York.

Austin, Mary
1906. The flock. Houghton-Mifflin Co., Cambridge, Mass., p. 176. (Bobcat attack on young lambs.)

Avery, Carlos
  1916. Minnesota State Game & Fish Commission, Biennial Rept.

B——, W. N.
  1889. Death from wildcat's bite. Forest and Stream 33: 433. December 26.

Bachman, Rev. Dr.
  1849. Catalogue of the mammals of the State of Georgia. *In* White, Statistics of Georgia, App. 3-5; App. 3.

Badger, G. B.
  1894. Lynxes and their names. Forest and Stream 42: 488. June 9.

Bagster, C. Birch
  1861. The progress and prospects of Prince Edward Island. Charlotte-town, Prince Edward Island, 139 pp.; 21, 24.

Bailey, Bernard
  1929. Mammals of Sherburne County, Minnesota. Jour. Mammal. 10 (2): 153-164; 158.

Bailey, B. H.
  1917. The mammals of our state. Iowa Conserv. 1 (1): 14-15. January-March.

Bailey, H. H.
  1930. Correcting inaccurate ranges of certain Florida mammals and others of Virginia and the Carolinas. The Bailey Mus. & Library Nat. Hist., Miami, Bull. 5: 1-4; 3. December 1. (Distribution of Florida bobcat.)

Bailey, John Wendell
  1946. The mammals of Virginia. 413 pp.; 171-173. (Description of the bobcat; its occurrence in Virginia.)

Bailey, Vernon
  1888. Report on some of the results of a trip through parts of Minnesota and Dakota. Annual Rept. U. S. Dept. Agr. for year 1887; report of the ornithologist, pp. 413-454; 431.

  1895. The pocket gophers of the United States, Division of Ornithology and Mammalogy, U. S. Dept. Agr. Bull. 5: 1-40; 20. (Pocket gopher eaten by bobcat.)

  1896. List of mammals of the District of Columbia. Biol. Soc. Washington Proc. 10: 93-101; 98.

  1905. A biological survey of Texas. U. S. Dept. Agr., Bur. Biol. Survey, North Amer. Fauna 25: 1-222, illus., p. 169. October 24.

  1908. Harmful and beneficial mammals of the arid interior. U. S. Dept. Agr. Farmers' Bull. 335: 1-31, illus; 26.

  1918a. General information on Yellowstone National Park, U. S. Dept. Interior Leaflet, 84 pp.; 58.

  1918b. General information on Glacier National Park. U. S. Dept. Interior Leaflet, 76 pp.; 49.

  1919. Wild animals of Glacier National Park. U. S. Dept. Interior, Natl. Park Service, pp. 25-102; 82. (Weight of type specimen of *Lynx rufus uinta* 31½ lbs.)

1923. Mammals of the District of Columbia. Biol. Soc. Washington Proc. 36: 103-138; 121. May 1.

1927. A biological survey of North Dakota. I. Physiography and life zones. II. The mammals. U. S. Dept. Agr., Bur. Biol. Survey, North Amer. Fauna No. 49, pp. vi + 226, 21 pls, illus.; 148-149. January 8.

1929. Government report of game survey in Bath and Highland Counties. Va. Game and Fish Conservationist 9 (1): 3-6; 5. June.

1930. Animal life of Yellowstone National Park. Chas. C. Thomas, Springfield, Ill., and Baltimore, Md. 241 pp., illus.; 132.

1931a. Mammals of New Mexico. U. S. Dept. Agr., Bur. Biol. Survey, North Amer. Fauna No. 53: 1-412, illus.; 291.

1931b. A trip down Tanner Trail. Grand Canyon Nat. Notes 5 (12): 119. October.

1933. Cave life of Kentucky. Amer. Midland Nat. 14 (5): 385-635; 429. September.

1935. Mammals of the Grand Canyon region. Grand Canyon Nat. Hist. Assoc., Nat. Hist. Bull. 1: 1-42; 31. June.

1936. Mammals and life zones of Oregon. U. S. Dept. Agr., Bur. Biol. Survey, North Amer. Fauna No. 55: 1-416; 269. June.

1940. Our fur bearing animals. Amer. Humane Assoc., Albany, N. Y. pp. 1-8, illus.; 6. (Trapping of bobcat with chain-loop known as the Verbail trap.)

Bailey, Vernon, William B. Bell, and Melvin A. Branson

1914. Preliminary report on the mammals of North Dakota. N. Dak. Agr. Expt. Sta. Circ. 3: 1-20; 16. December.

Bain, Francis

1890. The natural history of Prince Edward Island. 123 pp.; 122. Charlottetown, Prince Edward Island.

Baird, S. F.

1857. Mammals of North America. Expl. and Surveys R. R. Route to Pacific 8 (pt. 1): 1-757, illus.; 92.

Bancroft, C. C.

1907. Game along the Mexicala River. Forest and Stream 69: 415. September 14.

Bangs, Outram

1897. Notes on the lynxes of eastern North America, with descriptions of two new species. Biol. Soc. Washington Proc. 11: 47-51; 49.

1898. The land mammals of peninsular Florida and the coast region of Georgia. Boston Soc. Nat. Hist. Proc. 28 (7): 157-235, illus.; 233.

1899. A new lynx from the coast of California. New England Zool. Club Proc. 1: 23-25.

Barber, Edwin A.

1882. Mound pipes. Amer. Nat. 16: 265-281; 269.

Barger, N. R.

1948. Bobcat-wildcat (*Lynx rufus rufus*). Wisconsin Conserv. Bull. 13 (5): 29-30, illus. May. (Bobcats not plentiful in Wisconsin, but fair number are trapped annually for their pelts.)

Barker, Elliott S.
    1946. When the dogs bark "treed." Univ. of New Mexico Press, Albuquerque, pp. xviii + 209. (One of best puma books ever written; also contains excellent bobcat lore.)

Barnes, Claude T.
    1922. Mammals of Utah. Univ. Utah Bull. 12 (15): 1-166; 111. April.

Barton, B. W.
    1878. The skunk eaten by a lynx [bobcat]. Amer. Nat. 12: 628. September.

Bartram. Wm.
    1928. The travels of William Bartram. Macy-Masius Publishers, N. Y. 414 pp.; 34, 109.

Beck, Herbert H.
    1924. Ornithology of Lancaster County, Pennsylvania, with supplementary notes on the mammals. The Lewis Historical Publishing Co., Inc., New York, N. Y., pp. 1-39, map; 37.

Beesley, Thomas
    1857. Lyncus rufus New Jersey. Rare. Geology of the County of Cape May, State of New Jersey, Trenton, p. 137.

Bennitt, Rudolf, and Werner O. Nagel
    1937. A survey of the resident game and fur-bearers of Missouri. Univ. Missouri Studies 12 (2): 1-215; 26, 176. April 1.

Benson, Seth B.
    1933. Concealing coloration among some desert rodents of the southwestern States. Univ. Calif. Pub. Zool. 40 (1): 1-70; 22. June 13.

Best, R. E.
    1890. Brief notes. [Wildcat taken in mountains near Kingston, N. Y.] Orn. & Ool. 15 (2): 29. February.

Beverly, Robert
    1722. The history of Virginia. London, 4 pts., 284 pp.; 135.

Black, J. D.
    1936. Mammals of northwestern Arkansas. Jour. Mammal. 17 (1): 29-34; 31. February. (Bobcat depredations on robin roosts.)

Black, J. W.
    1932. A winter robin roost in Arkansas. Wilson Bulletin 44 (1): 13-19; 18-19. March. (Severe depredations by bobcats and feral house cats on robin roosts near Winslow, Ark.)

Blair, W. Frank
    1935. The mammals of a Florida hammock. Jour. Mammal. 16 (4): 271-277; 274. November.

    1938. Ecological relationships of the mammals of the Bird Creek region, northeastern Oklahoma. Amer. Midland Nat. 20 (3): 473-526; 498. November.

    1939. Faunal relationships and geographic distribution of mammals in Oklahoma. Amer. Midland Nat. 22 (1): 85-133; 109. July.

    1940. A contribution to the ecology and faunal relationships of the mammals of the Davis Mountain region, southwestern Texas. Univ. Mich. Mus. Zool., Misc. Pub. No. 46; 1-39; 26, June 28.

Blennerhassett
1907. Wildcat and boar. Forest and Stream 68 (24): 935. June 15.

Boardman, Geo. A.
1886. A black lynx. Forest and Stream 27: 163. September 3.

Boozer, Sam
1948. Bobcat a killer. Mississippi Game & Fish 12 (1): 11. July.

Borell, Adrey E.
1933. Rare fur-bearing mammals in Yosemite. Yosemite Nat. Notes 12 (6): 62-63. June.

Borell, A. E., and Monroe D. Bryant
1942. Mammals of the Big Bend area of Texas. Univ. Calif. Pub. Zool. 48 (1): 1-62; 19. August 7.

Borell, Adrey E., and Ralph Ellis
1934. Mammals of the Ruby Mountains region of northeastern Nevada. Jour. Mammal. 15 (1): 12-44, illus.; 23. (Bobcat habitat and use of woodrat in trapping a bobcat.)

Brackett, A. G.
1881. The lynxes. Amer. Field 16 (24): 413.

Bramble, Chas. A.
1887. Sport in New Brunswick. Forest and Stream 28: 150.

Bransom, Paul, and T. Donald Carter
1952. The cats of North America. Field and Stream 57 (4): 36-41, illus. August. (Differences in bobcat, lynx, puma, jaguar range, foods and habits.)

Brayton, A. M.
1882. Report on the Mammalia of Ohio. Rept. Geol. Survey of Ohio 4 (pt. 1): 1-185; 12, 180.

Brimley, C. S.
1905. A descriptive catalogue of the mammals of North Carolina, exclusive of the Cetacea. Jour. Elisha Mitchell Sci. Soc. 21 (1): 1-32; 28. March.

Brimley, H. H.
1942. A few random notes on wild cats. North Carolina Wildlife Conserv. 6 (9): 5-6, 14, illus. September.

Brooks, Allan
1902a. Plateau wildcat. Recreation 17 (3): 174, illus. September.
1902b. Mammals of the Chillawack District, B. C. Ottawa Nat. 15: 239-244; 242. February.
1905. The Mammalia of northern Wellington County, Ontario. Ontario Nat. Sci. Bull. 1: 25-26.
1909. The lynxes of British Columbia. Forest and Stream 72 (11): 412. March 13.
1930. Early big-game conditions in the Mount Baker District, Washington. The Murrelet 11 (3): 65-67; 66. September.

Brooks, A. B.
1932. The mammals of West Virginia. W. Va. Wild Life 10 (5): 1, May; 10 (6): 2-4, June.

Brooks, Fred E.
1911. The mammals of West Virginia. Notes on the distribution and habits of all our known native species. Rept. W. Va. Bd. Agr. for quarter ending Dec.. 30, 1910, p. 23.

Brown, C. Emerson
1913. A pocket list of mammals of eastern Massachusetts, with especial reference to Essex County. Peabody Acad. Sci., Salem, pp. 1-48; 22.

Brown, J. S.
1923. The Salton Sea region, California. U. S. Geol. Survey Water-supply Paper No. 497: 19-21; 20.

Brown, Perry E.
1932. Game survey of Walhalla Plateau. Grand Canyon Nat. Notes 7 (4): 33-35; 33. July.

Brown, Louis G., and Lee E. Yeager
1943. Survey of the Illinois fur resource. Ill. Nat. Hist. Survey Bull. 22 (6): 434-504; 490. September.

Browning, Meshach
1928. Forty-four years of the life of a hunter. J. B. Lippincott Co., Philadelphia. 400 pp.

Brunner, Josef
1909. Tracks and tracking. xii + 219 pp., illus.; 101-106. Outing Publishing Co., New York, N. Y. (What the puma is as an enemy of useful big game, the bobcat is to small game, and the young of big game.)

Buck, Storey
1906. Notes. [Exciting contest with wildcat.] Amer. Field 65 (15): 336. April 14.

Buckley, S. B.
1859. Mountains of North Carolina and Tennessee. Amer. Jour. Sci. (ser. 2) 27: 286-294; 292.

Burks, Arthur J.
1950. Bloodthirsty bobcats of Sagebrush Flat. Western Sportsman 10 (2): 11, 22. January-February. Austin, Tex. (The killing of 30 lambs in one night by bobcats in Grand Coulee area of Washington State.)

Burr, J. G.
1948. Fanged fury. Even ferocious bobcats are easy prey for coyotes. Texas Game and Fish 6 (6): 4, 18, illus. May. (Coyotes treeing the bobcat.)

Burres, W. A.
1893. Wildcat and falcon. Nidiologist 1: 7.

Burroughs, Julian
1907. A wildcat in the Highlands. Forest and Stream 68: 174. February 2.

Burroughs, A. L., R. Holdenried, D. S. Longanecker, and K. F. Meyer
1945. A field study of latent tularemia in rodents with a list of all known naturally infected vertebrates. Jour. Infectious Diseases 76: 115-119.

Burt, Wm. H.
  1933. Additional notes on the mammals of southern Arizona. Jour. Mammal. 14 (2): 114-122; 116.
  1934. The mammals of southern Nevada. San Diego Soc. Nat. Hist. Trans. 7 (36): 375-427; 402. May 31.
  1938. Faunal relationships and geographic distribution of mammals in Sonora, Mexico. Univ. Mich. Mus. Zool., Misc. Pub. No. 39: 1-77; 35, map. February 14.

Butler, A. W.
  1895. The mammals of Indiana. Ind. Acad. Sci. Proc. 1894: 81-86; 85. October.

C———, F. D.
  1907. Game in Maine. Forest and Stream 69: 574. October 12.

Cahalane, Victor H.
  1928. A preliminary wild life and forest survey of southwestern Cattaraugus County, New York. Roosevelt Wild Life Bull. 5 (1): 9-144, illus.; 81.
  1939. Mammals of the Chiricahua Mountains, Cochise County, Arizona. Jour. Mammal. 20 (4): 419-440; 427. November.
  1947. Mammals of North America. x + 692 pp., illus.; 290-297. Macmillan Co., New York.
  1948. The status of mammals in the U. S. National Park system, 1947. Jour. Mammal. 29 (3): 247-259; 252. (On occurrence of bobcat in national park areas.)

Cahn, Alvin R.
  1921. The mammals of Itasca County, Minnesota. Jour. Mammal, 2 (2): 68-74; 70.
  1937. The mammals of the Quetico Provincial Park of Ontario. Jour. Mammal. 18 (1): 19-30; 25. February 14.

Carpenter, W. L.
  1876. Field notes on the natural history of the Big Horn Mountains. Forest and Stream 7 (2): 196. November 2.

Carson, Burch
  1941. Desert bighorn mountain sheep. Texas Game, Fish and Oyster Commission Bull. 21: 1-23. (Wild sheep wool found in bobcat feces.)

Carter, T. Donald
  1955. Remarkable age attained by a bobcat. Jour. Mammal. 36 (2): 290. May.

Cary, Merritt
  1911. A biological survey of Colorado. North Amer. Fauna No. 33: 1-256, illus.; 168.

Cecil, Salome
  1901. Hunting in northern Mexico. Field and Stream 6 (3): 163-165; 165.

Chamberlain, Montague
  1884. List of the mammals of New Brunswick. Nat. Hist. Soc. New Brunswick Bull. 3: 37-41; 38.

1892. Mammals of New Brunswick. Nat. Hist. Soc. New Brunswick Bull. 10: 30-33; 31.

Chandler, Asa C.
1942. *Mesocestoides manteri* n. sp. from a lynx, with notes on other American species of mesocestoides. Jour. Parasitol. 28 (3): 227-231.

Chapman, Frank M.
1894. Remarks on certain land mammals from Florida, with a list of the species known to occur in the State. Amer. Mus. Nat. Hist. Bull. 6: 336-346; 345, 346.

Chase, Harry
1909. A panther reported from Vermont. Forest and Stream 73: 251. August 14.

Chestnut, W. T.
1904. A New Brunswick caribou hunt. Field and Stream 8 (11): 918-923; 921. March.

Chitwood, B. G.
1932. Physaloptera praeputialis is reported as a parasite of *Urocyon* sp. from Virginia and *Lynx rufus* from Nevada. Jour. Parasitol. 18 (1): 531.

Church, J. E., Jr.
1909. Up from "The Land of Little Rain" to the land of snow. Sierra Club Bull. 7 (2): 105-118; 117.

Clapp, Henry
1868. Notes of a fur hunter. Amer. Nat. 1: 652-666; 653. February.

Clark, C. C.
1935. Report on the zoology of Navajo Mountain. Rainbow Bridge-Monument Valley Exped. NYA Proj. No. 3968-Y-1, Berkeley, Calif., pp. 1-15; 2. (Mimeog.)

Clark, Mary Lou
1952. The unknown origin and early history of the domestic cat. Cat's Magazine 8 (3): 7, illus. December. (Discusses prehistoric cats, their origin, and place in early Egyptian culture dating from 5383 B.C.)

Clarke, C. H. D.
1942. Investigation of Cape Breton Highlands National Park. Mimeographed by National Parks Bureau, released for limited use. (Based on field work in 1941.) (On the occurrence of the bobcat in this area.)

"Coahoma"
1887. Bruin in the canebrake. Forest and Stream 28: 179. March 24.

Coape, A. P. F.
1893. Experience with a bay lynx. Forest and Stream 40: 318. April 13.

Cockerell, T. D. A.
1927. Zoology in Colorado. Univ. Colo. Semi-Centennial Ser. 3: 1-262, illus.; 24. August.

Cockrum, E. Lendell
1952. Mammals of Kansas. Univ. Kans. Pub., Mus. Nat. Hist. 7 (1): 1-303; 263-268. August 25.

Collins, J. Parker
1954.  Bobcat bird dogs. Western Sportsman 14 (7): 9, 19-20. November-December. (Use of pet bobcats in hunting Arizona quail.)

Conneautville Courier
1920.  Wildcat killed in Pymatuning Swamp in western Crawford County, Pa. Jefferson Gazette, Jefferson, Ohio. December 9.

Cooley, C. H.
1918.  "Varmint" dogs clean out bobcats. Calif. Fish and Game 4 (2): 98-99. April.

Cooper, J. G.
1860.  Reports of explorations and surveys to ascertain the most practicable and economical route for a railroad from the Mississippi River to the Pacific Ocean, 1853-1855. Pacific R. R. Repts., 12 (2): 73-139, illus.; 74-75.

1869.  The naturalist in California. Amer. Nat. 3: 470-481; 477. November.

1873.  The fauna of California and its geographical distribution. Calif. Acad. Nat. Sci. Proc. 4: 61-81; 74.

Cope, E. D.
1870.  Observations on the fauna of the southern Alleghanies. Amer. Nat. 4: 392-402; 395. September.

1895.  The fossil vertebrata from the fissure at Port Kennedy, Pa. Acad. Nat. Sci. Philadelphia Proc., pp. 446-450; 447.

Copeland, Manton
1912.  Notes on the mammals of Mt. Greylock, Massachusetts. Biol. Soc. Washington Proc. 25: 157-162; 161. December 4.

Cory, Charles B.
1896.  Hunting and fishing in Florida, including a key to the water birds known to occur in the State. 304 pp.; 110. The Barta Press, Boston.

1912.  The mammals of Illinois and Wisconsin. Field Mus. Nat. Hist. Pub. 153, zool. ser. 11: 1-505, illus.; 293, 295. (Distribution of bobcat in Illinois and Wisconsin with description of its habits and ways of control.)

Coues, Elliott
1867.  Notes on a collection of mammals from Arizona. Acad. Nat. Sci. Philadelphia Proc. 19: 133-136; 134. November.

1871.  Notes on the natural history of Fort Macon, North Carolina and vicinity. No. 1. Acad. Nat. Sci. Philadelphia Proc. 23: 12-18; 12.

Coues, Elliott, and H. C. Yarrow
1875.  Report upon the collections of mammals made in portions of Nevada, Utah, California, Colorado, New Mexico, and Arizona, during the years 1871, 1872, 1873, and 1874. Geog. & Geol. Expl. West of 100th Mer. 5: 37-129; 43.

Cox, Ross
1832.  Adventures on the Columbia River, 1811-1817. Pp 25-330; 94.

Crabb, Ed. D.
1921.  Some unexpected findings in the stomach of predatory birds and mammals. Okla. Acad. Sci. Proc., Univ. Okla. Bull., pp. 65-66. July 15.

Craig, John L.
  1926. The fighting cat of "Old Hickory." Forest and Stream 96: 671, 694-696; 671.
Cram, Wm. Everett
  1925. Notes on New England carnivores. Jour. Mammal. 6 (3): 199.
Cramer, C. A., Jr.
  1951 Battling a wildcat. Outdoor Life 108 (6): 68. December. (A true tale, told in pictures, of a trapped bobcat attacking a human being.)
Crane, Jocelyn
  1931. Mammals of Hampshire County, Massachusetts. Jour. Mammal. 12 (3): 267-272; 269.
Creech, John D.
  1923. In a "nest" of bobcats. Outdoor Life 51: 215. March.
Criddle, Norman
  1929. Memoirs of eighties. Canad. Field-Nat. 43: 176-181; 181. November. (Comments on scarcity of bobcat in Province of Mantioba.)
Criddle, Stuart
  1929. An annotated list of the mammals of Aweme, Manitoba. Canad. Field-Nat. 43: 155-159; 157. October 1.
Cross, E. C., and J. R. Dymond
  1929. The mammals of Ontario. Royal Ont. Mus. Zool. Handbook, No. 1, pp. 1-56, illus.; 20. (Bobcat once ranged over southern Ontario, as far north as Georgian Bay. Still found in parts of its former range.)
Cross, R. H., Jr.
  1948. The bobcat. Virginia Wildlife 9 (3): 19-20, illus. March.
Culbertson, A. E.
  1938. Large wild mammals of California. Sci. Guide for Elem. Schools, Calif. State Dept. Education 5 (3): 1-26; 7. October.
Dalquest, W. W.
  1939. Abnormal mammal skulls from Washington. Murrelet 20 (1): 19. January-April. (Lynx rufus fasciatus, Odocoileus hemionus.)
  1948. Mammals of Washington. Univ. Kans. Pub., Mus. Nat. Hist. 2: 1-444, illus.; 241-243. April 9.
"Dan"
  1882. Ten days in the mountains of western North Carolina. Amer. Field 18 (3): 207.
Darling, J.
  1892. The Canada lynx. Forest and Stream 39: 421.
Davis, James Richard
  1955. Food habits of the bobcat in Alabama. M.S. Thesis, Mar. 17, Alabama Polytechnic Institute, pp. viii + 74; 2 illus. pp. v, vi.
Davis, John
  1803. Travels of four years and a half in the United States, 1798-1802. London, 454 pp.; 91.
Davis, Wm. B.
  1940. Mammals of the Guadalupe Mountains of western Texas. La. State Univ. Mus. Zool., Occas. Pap. No. 7, pp. 69-84; 76. July 10.

Davis, Wm. B., and J. L. Robertson, Jr.
1944. The mammals of Culberson County, Texas. Jour. Mammal. 25 (3): 266-272; 265.

Dearborn, Ned
1919. Trapping on the farm. U. S. Dept. Agr. Yearbook 1919: 451-484, illus.; 463-464. (Recommendations for trapping the bobcat with steel traps).
1932. Foods of some predatory fur-bearing animals in Michigan. Univ. Michigan School of Forestry and Conservation, Bull. No. 1, pp. 1-52; 29.

Dellinger, S.C., and J. D. Black
1940. Notes on Arkansas mammals. Jour. Mammal. 21 (2): 187-191; 189. May 14. (On bobcat occurrence in certain parts of this State.)

Denyse, T.
1919. The bobcat and coyote as game destroyers. Outdoor Life 44: 375.

de Vos, A.
1953. Bobcat preying on porcupine? Jour. Mammal. 34 (1): 129-130. February.

Dice, Lee R.
1919. The mammals of southeastern Washington. Jour. Mammal. 1 (1): 10-22; 13. November. (Bobcat along Walla Walla River.)
1920. The mammals of Warren Woods, Berrien County, Michigan. Univ. Mich. Mus. Zool., Occas. Pap. No. 86, pp. 1-20; 18.
1925. A survey of the mammals of Charlevoix County, Michigan, and vicinity. Univ. Mich. Mus. Zool., Occas. Pap. No. 159, pp. 1-33; 22. April 11.
1930. Mammal distribution in the Alamogordo region, New Mexico. Univ. Mich. Mus. Zool., Occas. Pap. No. 213, pp. 1-32; 22. April 24.

Dice, Lee R., and H. B. Sherman
1922. Notes on the mammals of Gogebic and Ontonagon Counties, Michigan, 1920. Univ. Mich. Mus. Zool., Occas. Pap. No. 109, pp. 1-46; 29. February 25.

Dill, Herbert H.
1947. Bobcat preys on deer. Jour Mammal. 28 (1): 63. (Bobcat attack on a doe deer in Nevada.)

Dixon, Joseph S.
1925. Food predilection of predatory and bur-bearing mammals. Jour. Mammal. 6 (1): 34-46; 36. February.
1934. A study of the life history and food habits of mule deer in California. Calif. Fish and Game 20 (3): 229, 272, July (Eye witness account of 12-lb. bobcat attacking full grown mule deer doe; bobcats kill deer in winter time.)

Dobie, J. Frank
1949. The voice of the coyote. Saturday Evening Post 221 (34): 30, 140-142, illus.; 142. February 19. (Description of 2 coyotes baying a bobcat.)

Dodge, Richard I., et al.
1886. Hunting at army posts. Forest and Stream 26: 44-45, 68, 85.

Donohue, Frank Laurence
1896. On Back Creek, New York. Forest and Stream 46: 72.

Douglas, D.
1836. A sektch of a journey to the northwestern parts of the continent of North America, during the years 1824-1827, *in* Hooker, W. J., Companion to Botanical Magazine. London 2: 83-140; 101.

Downing, S. C.
1948. Provisional check-list of the mammals of Ontario. Royal Ontario Museum Zoology, Misc. Pub. No. 2, p. 10. Toronto.

Duke, Kenneth L.
1949. Some notes on the histology of the ovary of the bobcat (lynx) with special reference to the corpora lutea. Anat. Rec. 103 (1): 111-132. January.

Dunn, Harry H.
1907. On foot across the California desert with a rifle. Field and Stream 11 (9): 793-799; 797.

Dutcher, Wm.
1887. Old-time natural history. Forest and Stream 28: 105-106. March 3.

Dwight, Henry E.
1820. Account of the Kaatskill Mountains. Amer. Jour. Sci. (ser. 1) 2: 11-29; 29.

Editor
1886. Range of the American bison. Amer. Nat. 20 (1): 177.

Edson, J. M.
1930. Wild animal population of the Mount Baker National Forest, Washington. Murrelet 11 (2): 14-15. May.

Edwords, Clarence E.
1893. Camp-fires of a naturalist. 304 pp., illus.; 103. New York.

Einarsen, Arthur S.
1948. The pronghorn antelope and its management. Wildlife Management Inst., Washington, D. C., 238 pp.; 75-79; 76. The bobcat feeds on antelope and other games of equal size if the opportunity occurs.)

El Comancho
1909. Some cats! Outdoor Life 23: 385. April.

Elliot, D. G.
1899. Catalogue of mammals from the Olympic Mountains, Washington with descriptions of new species. Field Columb. Mus. Pub. 32, zool. ser. 1: 239-276; 265. March.
1907. A catalogue of the collection of mammals in the Columbian Museum. Field Columb. Mus. Pub. 115, zool. ser. 8: 1-694; 394, 395.

Elye-Norris, L. T. S.
1951. The bay lynx in Manitoba. Canada Field-Nat. 65 (3): 119. May-June. (On occurrence of bobcat in Manitoba, and bobcat containing porcupine quills.)

Enders, Robert K.
1930. Some factors influencing the distribution of mammals in Ohio. Univ. Mich. Mus. Zool., Occas. Pap. No. 212, pp. 1-27; 11. April 23.

160    THE BOBCAT OF NORTH AMERICA

Evans, G. W. "Dub"
    1951. Slash ranch hounds. Univ. New Mexico Press, Albuquerque. Pp.
        1-244, illus.; 38-39.

Evermann, B. W.
    1917. A century of zoology in Indiana, 1816-1916. Ind. Acad. Sci. Proc. 1916:
        189-224; 190.

Evermann, B. W., and H. W. Clark
    1911. Notes on the mammals of the Lake Maxinkuckee region. Wash-
        ington Acad. Sci. Proc. 13 (1): 1-34; 27.
    1920. Lake Maxinkuckee—A physical and biological survey. Ind. Dept.
        Conserv., Indianapolis, 2 vols. Vol. 1, p. 460.

Failing, Otto
    1949. Bobcat hunt. Michigan Conservation, Lansing 18 (1): 21-22. Janu-
        ary-February. (Bobcat hunting with dogs in Michigan a strenuous
        sport requiring "perseverance, luck, and maybe not too many brains.")
    1953. The bobcat—hunter and hunted. Michigan Conservation, Lansing
        22 (1): 7-9, illus. January-February. (Regarding killing of deer in
        Michigan.)

Fannin, John
    1898. A preliminary catalogue of the collections of natural history and
        ethnology in the Provincial Museum, Victoria, British Columbia,
        p. 6.

Favour, Alpheus H.
    1936. Old Bill Williams, Mountain Man. 229 pp., illus.; 42. Univ. North
        Carolina Press. (Early fur inventory showing 355 "wildcat" skins
        held at Fort Osage 1808-1810.)

Felger, A. H.
    1910. Birds and mammals of northwestern Colorado. Univ. Colo. Studies
        7 (2): 132-146; 145.

Fisher, A. K.
    1896. The mammals of Sing Sing, New York. The Observer, Portland,
        Conn. 7 (5): 193-200; 198. May.

Fisher, G. Clyde
    1910. Some winter birds about Lake Wimlico, Florida. Wilson Bull.
        (old ser.) 22 (1): 41-47; 43.

Fitch, Henry S.
    1948. Ecology of the California ground squirrel on grazing lands. Amer.
        Midland Nat. 39 (3): 513-596; 592, 593. May. Bobcat probable
        predator at times on California ground squirrels.)

"Flanagan"
    1925. Capturing a wild cat. Forest and Stream 95: 486-487.

Fleming, James H.
    1913. The natural history of the Toronto region, Ontario, Canada.
        Canad. Inst., 419 pp., illus.; 211.

Foote, Leonard E.
    1945a. The Vermont deer herd. A study in productivity. Vt. Fish and Game
        Service, Fed. Aid. in Wildlife Restoration Proj. No. 1-R, State Bull.,

Pittman-Roberston Ser. No. 13, pp. 1-125, illus.; 27. (States with local exceptions, the bobcat is definitely more beneficial than detrimental.)

1945b. Sex ratio and weights of Vermont bobcats in autumn and winter. Jour. Wildlife Mgt. 9 (4): 326-327.

Frost, Jack
1944. [Bobcat trapped near Warrensburg, Mo.] Mo. Conservationist 5 (3): 7. March.

Frye, O. Earl, and Daniel W. Lay
1943. Fur resources and fur animals of Texas. Texas Game, Fish and Oyster Comn., Bull. No. 25: 1-42, illus.; 34.

Fuller, Arthur B., and B. P. Bole, Jr.
1930. Observations on some Wyoming birds. Cleveland Mus. Nat. Hist. Sci. Pub. 5 (2): 37-80; 42. September 27.

G———, J. A.
1894. Big tracks and a large yell. Forest and Stream 42: 91. February 3.

Garman, H.
1894. A preliminary list of the vertebrate animals of Kentucky. Essex Inst. Bull. 26 (1-3); 1-63; 3.

Garnier, J. H.
1882. Natural history of Lucknow (Bruce County), Ontario. Canadian Sportsman and Naturalist 3: 125-126. April. (Killed 4 bobcats that year, *Lynx canadensis* not known on peninsula or south of Ottawa River.)

Garrison, Lon
1938. A cycle of plenty. Yosemite Nat. Notes 17 (5): 71-72. May.

Gates, William H.
1937. Spotted skunks and bobcat. Jour. Mammal. 18 (2): 240. May.

Gehr, Agnes Robbins
1952. Jared Potter Kirtland. The Explorer 2 (7): 1-33, illus.; 12. Cleveland Mus. Nat. Hist. (Bobcat in captivity.)

Gerstell, Richard
1937. The Pennsylvania system. Pa. Game News 7 (8): 8-10, 15, 24.

Gill, S. L.
1948. Treed bobcat. Texas Game & Fish 6 (10): 18. September.

Gilman, C. E.
1896. The Olympic country. Natl. Geog. Mag. 7: 133-140; 138. April.

Gilmore, Raymond M.
1946. Mammals in archeological collections from southwestern Pennsylvania. Jour. Mammal. 27 (3): 227-234; 230. August 14. (Six bone fragments identified as bobcat.)
1947. Report on a collection of mammal bones from archeologic cavesites in Coahuila, Mexico. Jour. Mammal. 28 (2): 147-165; 156. May. (Fragmentary bone material of the bobcat.)

Gilpin, J. Bernard
1872. On the Mammalia of Nova Scotia. Nova Scotia Inst. Nat. Sci. Trans. 3 (pt. 2): 109-126; 122.

Glading, Ben
1938. Studies on the nesting cycle of the California valley quail in 1937.
Calif. Fish & Game 24 (4): 318-340; 338. October.

Goff, John B.
1901. The Roosevelt lion hunt. Outdoor Life 7 (4): April; 7 (5): May.
Illus. (Gives one bobcat weight and number killed.)

Goldman, E. A.
1951. Biological investigations in Mexico. Smithsn. Miscl. Coll. Pub. No.
4017, vol. 115, 476 pp.; 413, 416, 417, 418, 423, 425, 426, 427.
(Bobcat occurrence in Mexico).

Goodpaster, Woodrow
1941. A list of the birds and mammals of southwestern Ohio. Jour.
Cincinnati Soc. Nat. Hist. 22 (3): 1-47; 46. June.

Goodwin, George G.
1932. New records and some observations on Connecticut mammals. Jour.
Mammal. 13 (1): 36-40; 39. February.
1935. The mammals of Connecticut. Conn. Geol. & Nat. Hist. Survey
Bull No. 53, 221 pp., illus.; 88.

Gordon, C. E.
1908. The otter in Massachusetts. Science 28 (726): 772-775; 775. November 27.

Gowanloch, James Nelson
1950. Bobcat—Predator. Louisiana Conservationist 2 (7-8): 10-12, 25, illus.
March-April.

Grafton Sentinel
1929. Wild cat killed in Taylor County. W. Va., Wild Life 7 (2): 19.
February.

Grange, Wallace B.
1932. Observations on the snowshoe hare, Lepus americanus phaeonotus
Allen. Jour. Mammal. 13 (1): 1-19; 19. February. (Bobcat as an
enemy of the snowshoe hare.)

Grant, Madison
1906. Notes on Adirondack Mammals, with special reference to the furbearers. Rept. N. Y. Forest, Fish and Game Comm. for 1903, pp.
319-334; 326.
1907. Game animals in the Adirondacks. Outdoor Life 19: 365-374; 372.
April.

Grater, Russell K.
1935. Some wildlife observations on the canyon floor. Grand Canyon Nat.
Notes 9 (10): 365-367; 366. January.
1936. Bailey bobcat contributes new mammal records. Jour. Mammal. 17
(2): 170-171. (On the stomach contents as well as parasites.)

Green, Morris M.
1930. Contribution to the mammalogy of North Mountain region of
Pennsylvania. Ardmore, Pa., privately published. 19 pp.; 14, March
31.

Greenwood, Charles
1894. The wolverine at home. Forest and Stream 42: 333-334. April 21.

Gregory, Tappan
    1938. Lion in the Carmens. Chicago Acad. Nat. Sci. 1: (3) 70-81; (4) 110-120.
    1939. Eyes in the night. 243 pp., illus.; 157-185. Thomas Crowell Co., N. Y.

Griffith, John R.
    1918. Robert and the wild-cat. In the Open 8 (4): 18-20; 18. April.

Grinnell, George Bird
    1875a. Report on the zoology and palaeontology of the Black Hills of Dakota, 1874, In Ludlow, Reconnaissance Black Hills of Dakota 1874. Pp. 79-102; 79.
    1875b. Reconnaissance from Carroll, Montana to Yellowstone National Park. In Ludlow, Zoological report. Pp. 63-92; 90-92.
    1929. Pronghorn antelope. Jour. Mammal. 10 (2): 135-141; 140. (Antelope killed by bobcat.)

Grinnell, Joseph
    1908. The biota of the San Bernardino Mountains. Univ. Calif. Pub. Zool. 5 (1): 1-170; 135.
    1913. A distributional list of the mammals of California. Calif. Acad. Sci. Proc. 3: 265-390; 298. August 28.
    1914. An account of the mammals and birds of the lower Colorado Valley, with especial reference to the distributional problems presented. Univ. Calif. Pub. Zool. 12 (4): 51-294; 253.
    1937. Mammals of Death Valley. Calif. Acad. Sci. Proc. (ser. 4) 23 (9): 115-169; 133. August 7.

Grinnell, Joseph, and Joseph S. Dixon
    1924. Revision of the genus Lynx in California. Univ. Calif. Pub. Zool. 21 (13): 339-354; 349.

Grinnell, Joseph, Joseph Dixon, and Jean M. Linsdale
    1930. Vertebrate natural history of a section of northern California through the Lassen Peak region. Univ. Calif. Pub. Zool. 35: 1-594; illus.; 475. October.
    1937. Fur-bearing mammals of California, their natural history, systematic status, and relations to man. 2 vols. Vol. 2, pp. 617-618.

Grinnell, Joseph, and Jean M. Linsdale
    1936. Vertebrate animals of Point Lobos Reserve, 1934-35. Carnegie Inst. Washington, Pub. No. 481: 1-159, illus.; 135. December 10.

Grinnell, Joseph, and Tracy I. Storer
    1924. Animal life in the Yosemite. Univ. Calif., Berkeley, pp. xviii + 752, illus.; 99.

Grinnell, Joseph, and H. S. Swarth
    1913. An account of the birds and mammals of the San Jacinto area of southern California with remarks upon the behavior of geographic races on the margins of their habitats. Univ. Calif. Pub. Zool. 10 (10): 197-406; 370.

Grubb, E. H.
    1882. Shooting in the Elk Mountains. Amer. Field 17 (23): 280-381; 17 (24): 399.

Guthrie, John D.
  1925.  Wild life in the national forests of the Pacific Northwest. Forest
    and Stream 95: 472-473, 496; 496.
H———, H. B.
  1894.  Wildcat kittens. Forest and Stream 43: 4.
H———, W. F.
  1888.  A wild cat hunt in Connecticut. Amer. Field 29 (12): 268-269.
Hahn, Walter L.
  1907.  Notes on mammals of the Kankakee Valley. U. S. Natl. Mus. Proc.
    32: 455-464; 462. June 15.
  1909.  The mammals of Indiana. 33rd. Ann. Rept. Indiana Dept. Geol.
    and Natl. Resources, 1908, pp. 417-663; 545, 547.
Haley, Wm. D.
  1861.  Phelp's Washington described. Washington, 239 pp.; 22.
Hall, E. Raymond
  1946.  Mammals of Nevada. Contrib. Museum of Vertebrate Zool., Univ.
    Calif., Berkeley. Pp. xi + 710, illus.; 275-279. July 1. Univ. Calif.
    Press, Los Angeles and Berkeley. (Description and account of 3 races
    of bobcat occurring in Nevada: Lynx rufus baileyi, L. r. californicus.
    L. r. pallescens.)
Hall, F. S.
  1932.  A historical resume of exploration and survey—mammal types and
    their collectors in the state of Washington. The Murrelet 13 (3):
    63-91; 76. September.
Hall, Maurice C.
  1920.  The adult taenoid cestodes of dogs and cats, and of related
    carnivores in North America. U. S. Natl. Mus. Proc. 55 (2258): 1-94,
    illus.; 55.
Hallock, Charles
  1891.  Winter sports in North Carolina. Forest and Stream 37: 346.
Halloran, Arthur F.
  1946.  The carnivores of the San Andres Mountains, New Mexico. Jour.
    Mammal. 27 (2): 154-161; 160-161. (Length of unborn bobcats, and
    weights of adults.)
Hamilton, W. J., Jr.
  1930.  Notes on the mammals of Breathitt County, Kentucky. Jour. Mam-
    mal. 11 (3): 306-311; 309. (On occurrence of bobcat in this part of
    Kentucky.)
  1939.  American mammals: their lives, habits, and economic relations.
    434 pp., illus. McGraw-Hill Book Co., Inc., New York and London.
  1940.  Weights of eastern bobcats. Jour. Mammal. 21 (2); 218. (Results
    on weights of 74 bobcats taken during winters of 1936-38 in Vermont.)
  1941.  Notes on some mammals of Lee County, Florida. Amer. Midland
    Nat. 25 (3): 689-691; 689. May (Comments on 2 black bobcats taken
    in Palm Beach County, Fla.)
  1943.  The mammals of eastern United States. Comstock Publishing Co.,
    Inc., Ithaca, N. Y. 432 pp., 184 figs.

Hamilton, W. J., and Russell P. Hunter
  1939. Fall and winter food habits of Vermont bobcats. Jour. Wildlife Manag. 3 (2): 99-103. April.
Handlan, John W., and W. R. DeGarmo
  1946. Trapping in West Virginia. Conservation Commission of West Virginia, pp. 1-46, illus.; 26-29. (A good concise description of the bobcat and its control under conditions as found in West Virginia.)
Hardy, Campbell
  1855. Sporting adventures in the New World. Vol. 1, p. 54.
Hardy, Manly
  1900. Weights of game. Forest and Stream 55: 510. December 29.
  1907. Canada lynx and wildcat. Forest and Stream 68 (26): 1010-1011, June 29; 69 (4); 131-132. July 27. (Discusses experiences with bobcats and Canada lynx in Maine.)
Harlow, Jim
  1900. An adventure with a moose. Forest and Stream 55: 206.
Harper, Francis
  1920. Okefenokee Swamp as a reservation. Amer. Mus. Jour. 20: 29-30.
  1927. The mammals of the Okefenokee Swamp region of Georgia. Boston Soc. Nat. Hist. Proc. 38: 191-396, illus.; 320.
  1929a. Mammal notes from Randolph County, Georgia. Jour. Mammal. 10 (1): 84-85; 84. (Bobcat fighting dogs while prowling around slaughtering pen of a local butcher.)
  1929b. Notes on mammals of the Adirondacks. New York State Mus. Handbook No. 8, pp. 51-118; 79. May.
Harris, Wm. P., Jr.
  1929. The mammals. In The Book of Huron Mountain. Huron Mountain Club. Marquette Co., Mich., pp. 191-212, illus.; 201.
Harwell, C. A.
  1930. Yosemite animal report for December. Yosemite Nat. Notes 9 (2): 15-16. February.
  1932. Winter wildlife observations. Yosemite Nature Notes 11 (3): 1-2. March.
      (Records of bobcat killing deer Yosemite National Park, Calif.)
Hatt, Robert T.
  1924. The land vertebrate communities of western Leelanau County, Michigan. Papers Mich. Acad. Sci., Arts, and Letters 3: 369-402; 395.
  1930. The relation of mammals to the Harvard forest. Roosevelt Wild Life Bull. 5 (4): 625-671; 640. August.
Hayden, F. V.
  1862. On the geology and natural history of the Upper Missouri; with a map. Amer. Philos. Soc. Trans. 12 (pt. 1): 1-218; 140.
Henshaw, H. W.
  1908. The policemen of the air. Natl. Geogr. Mag. 19 (2): 77-118; 93. February.
Henshaw, Henry W., and Clarence Birdseye
  1911. The mammals of Bitterroot Valley, Montana, in their relation to spotted fever. U. S. Dept. Agr., Biol. Survey Circ. No. 82, pp. 3-24, illus.; 21. August 3.

Hersey, H. B.
1893. Lynxes in captivity. Forest and Stream 40: 4. January 5.
Hibbard, Claude
1933. A revised check list of Kansas mammals. Kans. Acad. Sci. Trans. 36: 230-249; 237.
1944. A checklist of Kansas mammals, 1943. Kans. Acad. Sci. Trans. 47: 61-88; 71.
Hildreth, S. P.
1826. Notes on certain parts of the State of Ohio. Amer. Jour. Sci. (ser. 1) 10: 319-331; 326.
Hill, E. H.
1913. A wildcat makes her home close to town. Outdoor Life 32: 145. August.
Hill, John Eric
1942. Notes on mammals of northeastern New Mexico. Jour. Mammal. 23 (1): 75-82; 78. February 14. (Bobcat common near Cimarron at elevation above 7,800 ft.)
Hills, E. C.
1917. Cougars and wildcats killed in Lane County. Oreg. Sportsman 5 (2): 134. April.
Hitchcock, Charles H.
1862. Catalogue of the mammals of Maine. Portland Soc. Nat. Hist. Proc. 1: 64-66; 65.
Hofer, Elwood
1887. Winter in wonderland. Forest and Stream 28: 246-247, 270, 294.
Hoffman, W. J.
1878. List of mammals found in the vicinity of Grand River, Dakota Territory. Boston Soc. Nat. Hist. Proc. 19: 95-102.
1880. On a supposed instance of hybridization between a cat and a lynx. London Zool. Soc. Proc., p. 380.
1885. Hugo Reid's account of the Indians of Los Angeles County, California. Essex Inst. Bull. 17 (1): 1-33; 9.
Hollister, Ned
1910. A check list of Wisconsin mammals. Wis. Nat. Hist. Soc. Bull. 8: 21-31; 26.
Hooper, E. T.
1941. Mammals of the lava fields and adjoining areas in Valencia County, New Mexico. Univ. Mich. Mus. Zool., Misc. Pub. No. 51, pp. 1-47, illus.; 23. June 14.
Hopkins, John M.
1947? Forty-five years with the Okefenokee Swamp 1900-1945. Georgia Soc. Naturalists Bull. No. 4, pp. 1-69, illus. Atlanta.
Hornaday, Wm. T.
1909. The wild animals of Hudson's day and the zoological park of our day. N. Y. Zool. Soc. Bull. No. 35, pp. 533-542; 539. September.
Howard, William Johnston
1937. Notes on winter foods of Michigan deer. Jour. Mammal. 18 (1): 77-80; 77. (The bobcat as an enemy of deer.)

Howell, Arthur H.
1909. Notes on the distribution of certain mammals in the southeastern United States. Biol. Soc. Washington Proc. 22: 55-68; 65.
1921. A biological survey of Alabama. U. S. Dept. Agr., Bur. Biol. Survey, N. Amer. Fauna No. 45, pp. 1-88; 42.

Hubbard, D. H.
1941. The vertebrate animals of Friant Reservoir Basin with special reference to the possible effects upon them of the Friant Dam. Calif. Fish and Game 27 (4): 198-215; 209. October.

Huey, Laurence M.
1942. A vertebrate faunal survey of the Organ Pipe Cactus National Monument, Arizona. San Diego Soc. Nat. Hist. Trans. 9 (32): 353-376; 360. February 17.

Hughes, E. B.
1898. Lynx maculatus. [Photograph.] Recreation 8: 355.

Hughes, Wallace
1950. Trapping bobcats in Kay County [Okla.]. Okla. Game and Fish News 6 (12): 12-13, illus. December. Oklahoma City. (Good bobcat habitat pictures.)

Hunt, H. H.
1920. Food of the bobcat. Calif. Fish and Game 6 (1): 37. January.

Hutton, Hubert
1917. Wildcat hunting in Kentucky. Outdoor Life 39 (2): 153-155. February.

Ingles, Lloyd Glenn
1947. Mammals of California. Pp. xix + 258; illus.; 84. Stanford University Press, Calif. (On bobcat occurrence in California; food; its role as a predator.)

Jackson, C. F.
1922. Notes on New Hampshire Mammals. Jour. Mammal. 3 (1): 13-15; 15.

Jackson, Hartley H. T.
1908. A preliminary list of Wisconsin mammals. Wis. Nat. Hist. Soc. Bull. 6 (1-2): 13-34; 25. (Distribution of bobcats in Wisconsin.)
1910. The distribution of certain Wisconsin mammals. Wis. Nat. Hist. Soc. Bull. 8: 86-90; 86.

Jacobs, Orange
1884. The Puget Sound region. Amer. Field 21 (19): 456. May 10.

Jaeger, Ellsworth
1948. Tracks and trailcraft. Pp. vii + 381, illus.; 62. Macmillan Co., N. Y. (A fine illustration of bobcat and lynx tracks showing differences.)

Jarrell, Myrtis, and J. N. B. Hewitt
1937. Journal of Rudolph Friederich Kurz. Smithsn. Inst., Bur. Amer. Ethnol. Bull. 115: 1-382; 331.

Jefferson, Isaac
1951. Memoirs of a Monticello slave as dictated to Charles Campbell in the 1840's. William and Mary Quarterly 8 (4): 580. October. Third Series. (Regarding wildcats and wolves near Jefferson's colonial home at Monticello, Va.)

Jennings, Art S.
1900. In the wilds of the Badger State. Field and Stream 5 (1): 38-40.

Johnson, Carl T.
1951. This bobcat needed a lesson. Outdoor Life 107 (2): 37, 122-123, illus. February.

Johnson, Charles E.
1916. A brief descriptive list of Minnesota mammals. Fins-Feathers-Fur, No. 8, pp. 2-12; 5. December.
1922. Notes on the mammals of northern Lake County, Minnesota. Jour. Mammal. 3 (1): 33-39; 38.
1925. The muskrat in New York: Its natural history and economics. Roosevelt Wild Life Bull. 3 (2): 205-320; 208. March.

Johnson, M. S.
1930. Common injurious mammals of Minnesota. Univ. Minn. Agr. Expt. Sta. Bull. 259: 1-67; 59. January.

Johnson, Odin S.
1944. Bobcats at Arch Rock. Yosemite Nat. Notes 23 (4): 44. April.

Jones, Joseph
1869. The aboriginal mound builders of Tennessee. Amer. Nat. 3: 57-73; 67.

Jones, George C.
1884. Wildcat captured at Brookfield Centre, Conn. Ornithologist and Oologist 9: 36.

Jones, John
1951. Sketch book story of a Michigan bobcat hunt. Mich. Out of Doors 1 (9): 11-13, illus. February. Lansing.

Jones, Sarah V.
1923. Color variations in wild animals. Jour. Mammal. 3 (3): 172-177; 174.

Kellogg, Louise
1916. Report upon mammals and birds found in portions of Trinity, Siskiyou, and Shasta Counties, California. Univ. Calif. Pub. Zool. 12 (13): 335-398, illus.; 360.

Kellogg, Remington
1937. Annotated list of West Virginia mammals. U. S. Natl. Mus. Proc. 84 (3022): 443-479; 457. October 7. (Good account of bobcat in West Virginia.)
1939. Annotated list of Tennessee mammals. U. S. Natl. Mus. Proc. 86 (3051): 268-269. (On the occurrence of bobcat in Tennessee.)

Kelson, Keith R.
1946. Notes on the comparative osteology of the bobcat and the house cat. Jour. Mammal. 27 (3): 255-264, illus.

Kennicott, Robert
1855. Catalogue of animals observed in Cook County, Illinois. Illinois State Agr. Soc. Trans. 1853-54 1: 577-580; 579.

Kermode, F.
1905. Game of British Columbia with a check-list of birds and mammals. Bur. Prov. Inform. British Columbia, Bull. No. 17, pp. 63-68; 66.

Kirk, George L.
1916. The mammals of Vermont. Vt. Bot. & Bird Clubs. Bull. No. 2, pp. 28-34; 31. April.

Klugh, A. B.
1911. Notes on the mammals of the Bruce Peninsula. Ontario Nat. Sci. Bull. No. 7, pp. 58-60; 60.

Knobloch, Irving W.
1942. Notes on a collection of mammals from the Sierra Madres of Chihuahua, Mexico. Jour. Mammal. 23 (3): 297-298; 297. August. (Destruction of domestic fowl at Mojarachic and Barranca de Cofre.)

Knox, M. V. B.
1875. Kansas mammalia. Kans. Acad. Sci. Trans. 4: 18-22; 19.
1897. Additions to Kansas mammalia. Kans. Acad. Sci. Trans. 5: 64.

Komarek, E. V.
1932. Mammals of Menominee Reservation. Jour. Mammal. 13 (3): 203-209; 205. August.

Kopman, H. H.
1921. Wildlife resources of Louisiana, their nature, value, and protection. La. State Conserv. Dept., Bull. No. 10, pp. 23-39; 29. December.

Krefting, Laurits, and Alton Bramer
1944. Wildlife conservation at Grand Portage. Indians at Work, U. S. Dept. Interior 12 (3): 19-21; 21. September-October.

Kudlacek, J. J.
1911. Woodsloafing in Wyoming. Outdoor Life 28: 307-315; 312. October.

L——, A. L.
1908. Game in Connecticut. Forest and Stream 71: 377. September 5.

L——, H.
1911. Hunting the bobcat. Forest and Stream 76 (2): 55. January 14.

LaDue, Harry J.
1921. The future of the northwest's fur supply. Fins-Feathers-Fur, No. 28, pp. 1-2. December.

Lamster, E. R.
1943. A deer hunt in the Black Hills. S. Dak. Conserv. Digest 10 (12): 14. December.

Lancaster, I.
1886. Animal traits. Amer. Nat. 20 (9): 757-766; 758.

Langdon, Frank W.
1881. The mammalia of the vicinity of Cincinnati—A list of species with notes. Jour. Cincinnati Soc. Nat. Hist. 3: 277-313; 299.

Lanman, Charles
1856. Adventures in the wilds of the United States and British America. Philadelphia, 2 vols. Vol. 2, pp. 139, 194, 486.

Lantz, D. E.
1905a. A list of Kansas mammals. Kans. Acad. Sci. Trans. 19: 171-178; 176.
1905b. Kansas mammals in their relation to agriculture. Kansas State Agr. College, Expt. Sta. Bull. 129: 331-404; 380.
1907. Additions and corrections to the list of Kansas mammals. Kans. Acad. Sci. Trans. 20 (pt. 2): 214-216.

Latham, Roger M.
1951. Ecology and economics of predator management. Pa. Game Commission. Pp. 1-96; 39.

Lawrence, Robert H.
1891. In the great wood of Washington. Forest and Stream 37 (13): 246. October 15.

Lawrence, W. B.
1922. Predatory animal control on Spring Valley Water Company property. Calif. Fish and Game 8 (4): 230-231. October.

Lawson, John
1718. The history of Carolina; containing the exact description and natural history of that country, etc. Pp. 4 + 258, map; 118.

Leach, Howard R., and Walter H. Frazier
1953. A study on the possible extent of predation on heavy concentration of valley quail with special reference to the bobcat. Calif. Fish and Game 39 (4): 527-538. October.

Lee, Kenneth Fuller
1929. In the Allagash country. Natl. Geogr. Mag. 55 (4): 505-520, illus.; 514.

Leopold, Aldo
1936. Game management. Pp. xxi + 481, illus.; 35, 36, 248, 251.

Le Raye, Charles
1812. A topographical description of the state of Ohio, Indiana Territory, and Louisiana by Jervis Cutler, including the journal of Mr. Chas. Le Raye. 219 pp.; 190. Boston.

Lewis, John B.
1940. Mammals of Amelia County, Virginia. Jour. Mammal. 21 (4): 422-428; 425. November 14.

Lewis, M., and Wm. Clark
1893. History of the expedition under command of Lewis and Clark. Harper's New York, Coues Ed., 4 vols. Vol. 3, p. 912.

Lewiston Journal
1911. Wildcats kill deer. Forest and Stream 76 (4): 135. January 28.

Libby, Allie I.
1944. An oversize bobcat. Outdoorsman 86 (2): 7. March-April.

Lien, Carl
1921. [Mammals of Clallam County, Washington.] Murrelet 2 (2): 7. May.

Linsdale, Jean M.
1938. Environmental responses of vertebrates in the Great Basin. Amer. Midland Nat. 19 (1): 1-206; 176. January.

Lippincott, Wm.
1926. Siskiyou County pays bounty on coyotes. Calif. Fish & Game 12 (2): 108. April.

Longhurst, Wm. M.
1940. The mammals of Napa County, California. Calif. Fish & Game 26 (3): 240-270; 256.

Longhurst, Wm. M., A. Starker Leopold, and Raymond F. Dasmann
1952. A survey of California deer herds, their ranges and management problems. Calif. State Dept. Fish & Game, Game Bull. No. 6, pp.

1-136, illus.; 73-74. (Bobcat considered as of minor importance in California as deer predator.)

Loomis, Clarke Helme
 1898. In the West with note book and kodak. Field and Stream 4 (2): 112 115; 114, 115.

Loomis, F. B., and D. B. Young
 1912. On the shell heaps of Maine. Amer. Jour. Sci. (ser. 4), 34: 17-42; 27.

Lowery, George H., Jr.
 1936. A preliminary report on the distribution of the mammals of Louisiana. La. Acad. Sci. Proc. 3 (1): 1-39, illus.; 24. March.
 1943. Check-list of the mammals of Louisiana and adjacent waters. La. State Univ. Mus. Zool., Occas. Pap. No. 13, pp. 213-257; 235. November 22.

Lum, S. K.
 1878. The sewellel or show'tl. Amer. Nat. 12: 10-13; 12. January.

Luttringer, L. L., Jr.
 1931. An introduction to the mammals of Pennsylvania. Pa. Bd. Game Commissioners, Bull. 15, pp. 1-66; 40.

Lyon, Marcus Ward
 1934. Origins of Indiana's mammals. Indiana Acad. Sci. Proc. 43: 27-43; 38. April. (Bobcat once common throughout Indiana, but believed to be now extinct in this state.)
 1936. Mammals of Indiana. Amer. Midland Nat. 17 (1): 1-384; 164. (An excellent account of the bobcat's occurrence in Indiana.)

Lyon, Marcus W., Jr., and W. H. Osgood
 1909. Catalogue of the type specimens of mammals in the United States National Museum including the Biological Survey collection. U. S. Natl. Mus. Bull. 62: 1-325; 206.

Mailliard, Joseph
 1927. The birds and mammals of Modoc County, California. Calif. Acad. Sci. Proc. 16 (10): 340-359; 345.

Major
 1907. Colorado game notes. Amer. Field 67 (15): 340. April 13.

Manville, Richard H.
 1942. Notes on the mammals of Mount Desert Island, Maine. Jour. Mammal. 23 (4): 391-397; 394. November 14.
 1958. Odd items in bobcat stomachs. Journ. Mammal. 39 (3): 439. August.

"Marin"
 1902. San Francisco as a big game center. Forest and Stream 59: 427. November 20.
 1903. California jottings. A record wildcat. Forest and Stream 60: 105.

Marshall, Wm. H.
 1940. A survey of the mammals of the islands in Great Salt Lake, Utah. Jour. Mammal. 21 (2): 144-159; 154. May 14.

Marston, M. A.
 1942. Winter relations of bobcats to white-tailed deer in Maine. Jour. Wildlife Mgt. 6 (4): 328-337. October.

Martin, E. T.
 1914. Cats, catamounts, and bears. Forest and Stream 83: 363-365.

Mast, J. F.
1931.   A few pointers on bobcat trapping. American Trapper 3: 14-15.
1932.   Coyote and wildcat trapping. 78 pp., illus. Ontario, Calif.

Matheson, Colin
1948.   History of the lynx. Jour. Soc. Preserv. Fauna Empire, Hertford, England, n.s. (pt. 58), pp. 18-27. December.

Matson, J. R.
1948.   [Bob] cats kill deer. Jour. Mammal, 29 (1): 69-70. (Bobcat deer killing in Pennsylvania: Tioga and Potter Counties.)

Matthews, L. H.
1941.   Reproduction in the Scottish wildcat, Felis silvestrisgrampia Miller. Zool. Soc. Proc. London, Series B, 11: 59-77. Maxey, D. W.
1920.   Wildcat eats chickens. Calif. Fish and Game 6 (1): 37. January.

Maxwell, Hu
1898.   The history of Randolph County, West Virginia. 531 pp., illus.; 216. Morgantown. (Bounty payments on bobcat before Civil War, showing the animal apparently very abundant.)

Maynard, C. J.
1872.   Catalogue of the mammals of Florida, with notes on their habits, distribution, etc. Essex Inst. Bull. 4 (9): 135-136; 4 (10): 137-150; 137.

McCandless, A. D.
1907.   Western lynx and wildcat. Forest and Stream 69 (11): 413. September 14.

McChesney, Charles E.
1879.   Report on the mammals and birds of the general region of the Big Horn River and Mountains of Montana Territory. Rept. Sec'y. War 2 (pt. 3): 2371-2383; 2372.

McCurdy, H. M.
1912.   On certain relations of the flora and vertebrate fauna of Gratiot County, Michigan, with an appended list of mammals and amphibians. 14th Rept. Mich. Acad. Sci., pp. 217-225; 223.

McGuire, J. A.
1905.   The President's bear hunt. Outdoor Life 16: 533-538. July.

McIntosh, Allen
1937.   New host records for Diphylobothrium mansonoides Mueller, Jour. Parasitol. 23 (3): 313-315.

McKee, Edwin D.
1930.   Preliminary check list of mammals of Grand Canyon. Grand Canyon National Park, Natl. Park Service, U. S. Dept. Interior, 13 pp. (mimeog.).

McLean, Donald D.
1919.   Wildcat eats birds. Calif. Fish and Game 5 (3): 160. July.
1934.   Predatory animal studies. Calif. Fish and Game 20 (1): 30-36. January.

McQueen, A. S., and Hamp Mizell
1926.   History of Okefenokee Swamp. Press of Jacobs and Co., Clinton, S. C. 191 pp.; 94.

Mearns, Edgar A.

1897. Preliminary diagnosis of new mammals of the genera Lynx, Urocyon, Spilogale, and Mephitis, from the Mexican boundary line. U. S. Natl. Mus. Proc. 20 (1126): 457-461; 458. December 24.

1898a. Notes on the mammals of the Catskill Mountains, New York, with general remarks on the fauna and flora of the region. U. S. Natl. Mus. Proc. 21 (1147): 341-360; 359. November 4.

1898b. A study of the vertebrate fauna of the Hudson Highlands, with observations on the Mollusca, Crustacea, Lepidoptera, and the flora of the region. Amer. Mus. Nat. Hist. Bull. 10: 303-352; 351.

1900. The native mammals of Rhode Island. Newport Nat. Hist. Soc., Circ. No. 1, 4 pp. July 1.

Merriam, C. Hart

1884. The mammals of the Adirondack region, northeastern New York. Linn. Soc. Trans, New York, pp. 9-312; 41. (Highly recommends palatability of bobcat meat, besides gives good account of the animal in this area.)

1888a. Report of the ornithologist and mammalogist. Ann. Rept. Dept. Agr. for year 1887, pp. 399-456.

1888b. Remarks on the fauna of the Great Smoky Mountains, with description of a new species of red-backed mouse. Amer. Jour. Sci. (ser. 3) 36: 458-460; 459.

1890. Results of a biological survey of the San Francisco Mountain region and Desert of the Little Colorado, Arizona. North Amer. Fauna No. 3: 1-136; 79-80; pls., maps.

1891. Results of a biological reconnaissance of Idaho, south of latitude 45° and east of the thirty-eighth meridian, made during the summer of 1890, with annotated lists of the mammals and birds, and descriptions of new species. North Amer. Fauna No. 5, pp. 1-113; 81-82.

1892. The zoology of the Snake Plains of Idaho. Amer. Nat. 26 (303): 218-222; 221.

1897. The mammals of Mount Mazama, Oregon. Mazama 1 (2) 204-230; 224.

1899. Results of a biological survey of Mount Shasta, California. North Amer. Fauna No. 16: 1-179, illus.; 104 (First description of pallid barred bobcats, Lynx rufus pallescens.)

1902. A new bobcat (Lynx uinta) from the Rocky Mountains. Biol. Soc. Washington Proc. 15: 71-72.

Mershon, W. B.

1894. Bears and wildcats 12 miles from Saginaw. Forest and Stream 42: 73. January 27.

Michaux, F. A.

1904. Travels west of Alleghany Mountains, 1802. Thwaites Ed., Cleveland, pp. 117-306; 234.

Miller, Gerrit S., Jr.

1897. Notes on the mammals of Ontario. Boston Soc. Nat. Hist. Proc. 28 (1): 1-44; 44.

1899. Preliminary list of New York mammals. N. Y. State Mus. Bull. 6 (29): 271-390; 279, 340. October.

1900. Key to the land mammals of northeastern North America. New York State Mus. Bull. 8 (38): 59-160; 126. October.

1924. List of North American Recent mammals, 1923. U. S. Natl. Mus. Bull. 128: 1-673; 160.

1940. Bones of mammals collected by Baird in Pennsylvania caves. Jour. Mammal. 21 (3): 319-322; 320. August 14.

Miller, Gerrit S., Jr., and Remington Kellogg.
1955. List of North American Recent mammals. Bull. 205, U. S. Natl. Mus., xii+954; pp. 778-782.

Milton, G. F.
1893. Deer and wildcat shooting in southwest Georgia. Amer. Field 40 (1): 3.

Mohr, Carl O.
1943. Illinois furbearer distribution and income. Ill. Nat. Hist. Survey Bull. 22 (7): 505-537, illus.; 526. September.

Monson, Gale
1951. Great blue heron killed by bobcat. The Wilson Bull. 63 (4): 334. December.

Moody, George H.
1914. Bobcat killed by a wolf. Oregon Sportsman 2 (7): 9. July.

Moore, Joseph C.
1946. Mammals from Welaka, Putnam County, Florida. Jour. Mammal. 27 (1): 49-59; 55. February. (Bobcat depredations on turkeys.)

Morris, R. F.
1948. The land mammals of New Brunswick. Jour. Mammal. 29 (2): 165-175; 170. May. (Discusses occurrence of two races of bobcats: *L. rufus rufus* and *L. gigas* with thought that latter is a subspecies of *L. rufus*.)

Morris, Robert T.
1876. Animals of Connecticut. Forest and Stream 6: 214. May 11.

Morrison, Chas. F.
1886. Field notes on some birds of Colorado. Ornithologist and Oologist 10: 153-154.

Morton, Will
1918. Hunting the big cats. In the Open 8 (1): 5-9, illus. January.

Moseley, E. L.
1906. Notes on the former occurrence of certain mammals in northern Ohio. Ohio Nat. 6 (6): 504-505. April.

Mossman, Frank
1912. The lynx and his habits. Outdoor Life 29: 34-38. January.

Munro, J. A.
1947. Observations of birds and mammals in central British Columbia. Occas. Papers, British Columbia Provincial Museum 6: 1-165; 129. January. (On occurrence of bobcat, *Lynx fasciatus*, in this part of British Columbia.)

Munro, J. A., and Ian McT. Cowan
1944. Preliminary report on the birds and mammals of Kootenay National
Park, British Columbia. Canad. Field-Nat. 58 (2): 34-51; 48. March-
April.

Murie, Olaus J.
1951. The elk of North America. Stackpole Co., Harrisburg, Pa., and
Wildlife Management Institute, Washington, D. C. 376 pp., illus.;
147-149. (Bobcat as a predator on elk.)

Murrill, Wm. A.
1927. American wildcats. Forest and Stream 97: 476-478; 504.

Nagel, W. O.
1950. Table in the wilderness. Missouri Conservationist 11 (10): 4-5,
12-13, illus. October.
(Describes food habits studies in Missouri of bobcat among other
mammals.)

Nash, C. W.
1908. Wildcat (Lynx rufus). Manual of Vertebrates of Ontario. p. 96.

Neal, Dolores
1926. Fragments of the Old West. Forest and Stream 96: 583-586, 622-
623; 585, 623.

Necker, Walter L., and Donald M. Hatfield
1941. Mammals of Illinois. An annotated check list with keys and
bibliography. Chicago Acad. Sci. Bull. 6 (3): 17-60, illus.; 48. May 15.

Nelson, Bill
1942. Speaking of cats. Outsdoorsman 84 (1): 12-14; 12. January.

Nelson, E. W.
1916. The larger North American mammals. Natl. Geog. Mag. 30 (5):
385-472, illus.; 409, 412. (Distribution, life habits and economics of
bobcats.)
1921. Lower California and its natural resources. Mem. Nat. Acad. Sci.
16: 1-194, illus.; 132.
1924. Deer conditions in Refuge 1-D. [Trinity Forest, Inyo County, California.] Calif. Fish and Game 10: 94.
1925. Status of the pronghorned antelope. 1922-1924. U.S. Dept. Agr. Bull.
1346, 64 pp., illus.; 17. August (Bobcats in addition to coyotes
killed more than half the antelope herd on Wind Cave Game
Preserve in South Dakota.)
1930. Wild animals of North America. 254 pp.; 100-101. Natl. Geog. Soc.,
Washington, D. C.

Neubrech, Walter
1948. History of predator control in the State of Washington. Northwest Sportsman 3 (6): 10-12. Vancouver, British Columbia, Canada.
(Points out difficulties of controlling bobcat and other predators
by bounty system.)

Newsom, William M.
1930. The common bobcat a deer killer. American Game 19: 42, 50.

Norton, Arthur H.
  1930. The mammals of Portland, Maine, and vicinity. Portland Soc. Nat.
  Hist. Proc. 4 (pt. 1): 1-151; 52-54.

Oberholser, Harry C.
  1905. Mammals of western North Carolina. Pub. by the Biltmore Forest
  School, pp. 1-24; 7. September.

Orr, Robert T.
  1943. Mammals of the Clearwater Mountains, Idaho. Calif. Acad. Sci.
  Proc. (ser. 4) 23 (35): 511-536; 524, pls. 45-47. August 18.

Osgood, Frederick L., Jr.
  1938. The mammals of Vermont. Jour. Mammal. 19 (4): 435-441; 438.
  November 14. (On occurrence of bobcat, and payment of bounties.)

Over, Wm. H., and Edward P. Churchill
  1941. Mammals of South Dakota. Mus. and Dept. Zool., Univ. of S. Dak.,
  pp. 1-56 (mimeog.); 23.

Pack, Arthur N.
  1930. A sequel to a coyote story. Glacier Nat. Notes 3 (5): 42. May.

Page, Benjamin M.
  1896. Hunting the wildcat in southern California. Forest and Stream
  46: 96-97.

Parker, O. B.
  1916. Yamhill County notes. Oreg. Sportsman 4 (2): 142. April.

Parsons, Eugene
  1904. Colorado, past and present. Field and Stream 9 (7): 13-20; 17.

Patterson, J. N.
  1908. The magic mountain. Natl. Geog. Mag. 19 (7): 457-468; 468. July.

Patterson, Robert L.
  1952. The sage grouse in Wyoming. Sage Books, Inc., Denver, Colo. pp.
  xii + 341; 289-293. (Bobcat predation.)

Patton, Ben S.
  1916. Clackamas County notes. Oreg. Sportsman 4 (2): 147-148. April.

Pearce, John
  1947. Identifying injury by wildlife to trees and shrubs in northeastern
  forests. U. S. Dept. Interior, Fish and Wildlife Service Research
  Report 13, pp. 1-30; 20, illus.

Pearson, Leonard, and B. H. Warren
  1896. Diseases and enemies of poultry. Pa. Dept. Agr. Bull. 17: 95-124; 97.
  1897. Diseases and enemies of poultry. Pub. by Authority of Pa. State
  Legislature, Sp. Rept., pp. 1-749; 456.

Penner, Lawrence R., and Wesley N. Parke
  1954. Notoedric mange in the bobcat, Lynx rufus. Jour. Mammal. 35 (3):
  458.

Peterson, Randolph L., and Vincent Crichton
  1949. The fur resources of Chapleau District, Ontario. Canad. Jour. Research D 27: 68-84; 81-82. April. (Spread of bobcat to this area
  unknown previous to 1940's by Indian or white trappers.)

Peterson, R. L., and S. C. Downing
  1952. Notes on the bobcats (Lynx rufus) of eastern North America with

description of a new race. Contrib. Roy. Ontario Mus. Zool. and Palaeontology No. 33. April 8. Toronto, Ontario.

Phipps, Harold W.
  1915. Following the wolf tracks. The Outer's Book 30 (5): 457-467, illus. November. (Picture of bobcat.)

Pickens, A. L.
  1928. Mammals of upper South Carolina. Jour. Mammal. 9 (2): 155-157; 156. (Bobcat fairly common in the mountains.)

Pierce, James
  1820. Account of the geology, mineralogy, scenery, etc. of the secondary region of New York and New Jersey, and the adjacent regions. Amer. Jour. Sci. (ser. 1) 2: 181-199; 184.
  1823. A memoir on the Catskill Mountains with notices of their topography, scenery, mineralogy, zoology, economical resources, etc. Amer. Jour. Sci. (ser. 1) 6: 86-97; 93.

Pike, Zebulon M.
  1895. Expeditions of Z. M. Pike. Vol. 1. To headwaters of the Mississippi River, Aug. 9, 1805 to Apr. 30, 1806. Vol. 2, Arkansas journey and Mexican tour, July 15, 1806 to July 1, 1807. Coues. Ed. Vol. 2, pp. 373, 463.

"Pious Jeems"
  1907. Hunting in the Mississippi bottoms. Forest and Stream 69: 574. October 12.

Pittsburgh Press
  1943. [Photograph of bobcat, taken near Vandergrift, Pa.] Pa. Game News 14 (9): 7. December.

Plummer, John T.
  1844. Quadrupeds about Richmond, Wayne County, Indiana. Amer. Jour. Sci. (ser. 1) 46: 244-249; 246.

Pollack, E. Michael
  1949. The ecology of the bobcat (Lynx rufus rufus Schreber) in the New England states. Thesis submitted (unpublished), Master of Science degree, Univ. Mass., Amherst, pp. 1-120; 115, illus. August.
  1950. Breeding habits of the bobcat in northeastern United States. Jour. Mammal. 31 (3): 327-330. August.
  1951a. Food habits of the bobcat in the New England States. Jour. Wildlife Mgt. 15 (2): 209-213. April.
  1951b. Observations on New England bobcats. Jour. Mammal. 32 (3): 356-358. August.

Pollack, E. M., and W. G. Sheldon
  1951. The bobcat in Massachusetts. Div. of Fisheries and Game, Mass. Dept. Cons., pp. 1-23, illus.

Poole, C. G.
  1929. The economic status of the bobcat. Monthly Bull., Dept. of Agr. State of California 18: 458-464.

Popowski, Bert
  1952. Stub-tailed tabbies. S. Dak. Cons. Digest 19 (3): 2-3, 6, illus. March.

Presnall, C. C.
1933a. Wildlife notelets. Yosemite Nat. Notes 12 (3): 19. March.
1933b. A day on snowshoes. Yosemite Nat. Notes 12 (3): 22. March.
1933c. Taming a wildcat. Yosemite Nat. Notes 12 (6): 61. June.
1938. Mammals of Zion-Bryce and Cedar Breaks. Zion-Bryce Mus. Bull. 2: 1-20; 10, illus. January.

Price, Andrew
1904. A wildcat and a railroad rail. Forest and Stream 62: 209.

Progulske, Donald R.
1952. The bobcat and its relation to prey species in Virginia. (Thesis for M.S. in wildlife management, Va. Polytechnic Institute, Blacksburg, Va.)

Rafinesque, C. S.
1817a. Extracts from the Journal of Mr. Charles LeRaye, relating to some new quadrupeds of the Missouri region with notes by C. S. R. Amer. Monthly Mag. 1: 435-437; 437. October.
1817b. Lynx rufa. Amer. Monthly Mag. 2: 46.

Rand, A. L.
1933. Notes on the mammals of the interior of western Nova Scotia. Canad. Field-Nat. 47 (3): 41-50; 46. March. (Common occurrence of bobcat in Annapolis County.)
1944. The recent status of Nova Scotia fur bearers. Canad. Field-Nat. 58 (3): 85-96; 86, 94. May-June. (Status of bobcat, Lynx gigas, in Nova Scotia on value of pelt; distribution and killing of deer.)
1948. Mammals of the Eastern Rockies and Western Plains of Canada. Natl. Mus. Canada Bull. 108 (Biol. Ser. 35): vii + 237; 121-123, illus. September. Ottawa, Canada. (Occurrence of bobcat in Province of Alberta and value of its pelt.)

Randolph, E. F.
1904. A Colorado lion hunt. Forest and Stream 63: 468. December 3. "Ransacker."
1907. California wildcats and lynx. Forest and Stream 69 (6): 212. August 10.

Reagan, Albert B.
1909. Animals of the Olympic Peninsula, Washington. Indiana Acad. Sci. Proc. for 1908: 193-199; 197.

Rhoads, S. N.
1894. Ord's zoology of North America. Haddonfield, N. J., Abdg. Ed., p. 291.
1896. Contributions to the zoology of Tennessee. No. 3. Mammals. Acad. Nat. Sci. Phila. Proc., pp. 175-205; 201.
1897a. A contribution to the mammalogy of northern New Jersey. Acad. Nat. Sci. Phila. Proc., pt. 1, pp. 23-33; 32.
1897b. A contribution to the mammalogy of central Pennsylvania. Acad. Nat. Sci. Phila. Proc., pp. 204-226; 221.
1903. Mammals of Pennsylvania and New Jersey. Privately published, Philadelphia, pp. 1-266; 141.

Rhoads, Samuel N., and Robert T. Young
1897. Notes on a collection of small mammals from notheastern North Carolina. Acad. Nat. Sci. Phila. Proc., pp. 303-312; 312.

Richard, E. D.
1949. Ohio trapper makes rare catch. Ohio Conservation Bull. 13 (4): 30. April. (Reported take of 53-lb. bobcat in Lake County.)

Richards, George
1908. An unusual nesting locality for the Rocky Mountain nuthatch. Condor 10 (5): 194-195; 195. September-October.

Riney, Thane
1951. Relationships between birds and deer. The Condor 53 (4): 178-185; 182. July-August. (A doe deer chases a bobcat after deer was alerted by calling of Steller jays.)

Robertson, O. D.
1909. Trapping beaver in the Rocky Mountains. Outdoor Life 23: 339-342; 342. April.

Robinson, Weldon B., and Eugene F. Grand
1958. Comparative movements of bobcats and coyotes as disclosed by tagging. Jour. Wildlife Mgt. 22 (2): 117-122, April.

Roemer, F.
1849. Texas. Pp. 462-464; 464. Bonn, Germany.

Rollings, Clair T.
1945. Habits, foods, and parasites of the bobcat in Minnesota. Jour. Wildlife Mgt. 9 (2): 131-145, illus. April.

Roosevelt, Theodore
1885. Hunting trips of a ranchman. Medora Edition, N. Y. Pp. 21-25. (On the destruction of poultry.)
1901. With the cougar hounds. Scribner's Mag. 30: 417-435, 545-564; 428, illus. October.

Roslund, Harry R.
1951. Mammal survey of north-central Pennsylvania. Pa. Game Comm., Harrisburg, Pa. Pp. 1-55; 31-32, illus.

Ross, Roland Case
1928. Dogs dislike fox flesh but relish that of wildcats. Jour. Mammal. 9 (3): 250.

Rowley, John
1902. The mammals of Westchester County, New York. Abst. Proc. Linn. Soc. New York, Nos. 13-14, pp. 31-60; 47.

Rust, Henry Judson
1946. Mammals of northern Idaho. Jour. Mammal. 27 (4): 317. (Distribution of bobcats and its occurrence in Canadian Zone, but severe winter drives it to lower elevations in Transition Zone in search of food.)

S———, D. S.
1868. The Prairie dog. Amer. Nat. 2: 217. June.

S———, G.
1905. Moose hunting in Nova Scotia. Forest and Stream 65; 395. November 11.

Safely, Grant
1908. After sheep and elk in Wyoming. Outdoor Life 21: 341-343; 343. April.

Safford, W. E.
1919.  Natural history of Paradise Key and the nearby Everglades of Florida. Ann. Rept. Smithsn. Inst. 1917: 377-434; 424, 64 pls., map.

Sage, John H.
1895.  A Connecticut wildcat. Forest and Stream 44: 25. January 12.

Sampson, Alden
1906.  Wild animals of the Mt. Rainier National Park. Sierra Club Bull. 6 (1): 32-42: 36.

Sampson, Frank W., and Rudolf Bennitt
1947-48.  Ways and means in wolf-coyote-bobcat control. Missouri Conservationist 8 (12): 4-6, illus., December; 9 (1): 4-5; 5, illus. January.

Sargood, W. W.
1914.  King of the wilderness—October Mountain, Whitney Game Preserve. Forest and Stream 82: 614, 627. May.

Saunders, Wm. E.
1932.  Notes on the mammals of Ontario. Roy. Canada. Inst. Trans. 18 (pt. 2) (40): 271-309: 287. July.

Sawyer, Edmund J.
1941.  Bobcat at bay. Western Sportsman 7 (5): 3-4. October. (A fine illustration bringing out bobcat's various attitudes when confronted by man.)

Say, Thomas [in James]
1823.  Account of Long's expedition to the Rocky Mountains. 2 vols. Vol. 1, pp. 1-503; 369.

Schantz, Viola S.
1939.  A white-footed bobcat. Jour. Mammal. 20 (1): 106.

Schmoe, Floyd W.
1927.  The wild life "ceiling." Mt. Rainier Nat. Notes 5 (9): 2-3. August 29.

Schoonmaker, W. J.
1929a.  Weights of some New York mammals. Jour. Mammal. 10 (2): 149-152; 150. (Weights of 5 bobcats.)

1929b.  Notes on some mammals of Allegheny State Park. Jour. Mammal. 10 (3): 246-249; 247.

1936.  How heavy is your game? Field and Stream 41 (4): 72. August.

Schultz, C. Bertrand, and Edgar B. Howard
1936.  The fauna of Burnet Cave, Guadalupe Mountains, New Mexico. Acad. Nat. Sci. Phila. Proc. (1935) 57: 273-298; 285.

Schultz, Vincent
1954.  Status of the bobcat in Tennessee. Jour. Tenn. Acad. Sci. 29 (1): 66-72. January.

Schwarz, Frank
1920.  Mammals of Missouri. St. Louis Nat. Hist. Mus. Assn. Bull. 1 (3): 38-44; 42. June.

Scoville, S. S.
1892.  Remarks concerning the Texas wildcat lately presented to the society. Ornithologist & Oologist 17 (4): 60. April.

Seagears, Clayt
1948-49.  The cat nobody knows. N. Y. State Conservationist 3 (3): 32-33,

illus. December-January. (A brief, but good general account of bobcat in wooded sections of New York State.)

Sellards, E. H.
1916. On the discovery of fossil human remains in Florida in association with extinct vetebrates. Amer. Jour. Sci. (ser. 4) 42: 1-18; 15.

Seton, E. T.
1913. Wild animals at home. Doubleday Page & Co., New York. 226 pp.; 224, illus.
1920. Bobcats and wild turkeys. Jour. Mammal. 1 (3): 140.
1929. Lives of game animals. 4 vols. Vol. 1, Part 1, pp. 183-185.

Shaw, J. N.
1947. Some parasites of Oregon wildlife. Oreg. Agr. Exp. Sta., Tech. Bull. 11, Corvallis, Oreg. May.

Shelby, Evan, et al.
1954. The Shelby family papers. Library of Congress Quarterly Journal of Current Acquisitions 11 (3): 140-153; 142. May.
(Early colonial sale of bobcat skins.)

Sheldon, Carolyn
1936. The mammals of Lake Kedgemakooge and vicinity, Nova Scotia. Jour. Mammal. 17 (3): 207-215; 211. August 14.

Sheldon, H. H.
1933. The deer of California. Santa Barbara Mus. Nat. Hist., Occas. Pap. No. 3, pp. 1-71; 57, illus. November 1.

Shelton, Alfred C.
1915. Weights of fur-bearing animals. Oregon Sportsman 3 (7): 151. July.

Sherman, H. B.
1936. A list of the Recent land mammals of Florida. Fla. Acad. Sci. Proc. (1936) 1: 102-128; 113.

Shinn, Chas. H.
1889. Rod and gun in Siskiyou. Forest and Stream 33: 404. December 12.

Shipley, Mrs. George
1925. Deer and bear in northern Maine. Forest and Stream 95: 10, 56-57; 57.

Shobe, Harrison
1948. Wildcats in deer yards. West Virginia Conservation 12 (1): 17, 21. April. Charleston. (Bobcat living with and on deer; bobcats preyed on a trapped bobcat, and dragged it to the den.)

"Shongo" (Davis, S. T.)
1892. A hunt in the Rockies. Forest and Stream 39: 115, 137, 159; 159.

Sickels, Robert
1949. Record bobcat. New York State Conservationist 4 (2): 36. October-November. (A bobcat poor in flesh, killed in 1946 on East Hill, Keene, N. Y., weighed 37 lbs.)

Simpich, Frederick
1919. A Mexican land of Canaan. Marvelous riches of the wonderful west coast of our neighbor Republic. Natl. Geog. Mag. 36 (4): 307-330; 319.

Simpson, R. B.
    1891. Correspondence. Ornithologist & Oologist 16 (7): 111. July.

Sisseton Courier
    1944. Kills bobcat with slingshot. S. Dak. Conserv. Digest 11 (2): 3.
    February.

Skinner, Milton P.
    1927. The predatory and fur-bearing animals of the Yellowstone National
    Park. Roosevelt Wild Life Forest Exp. Sta. Bull. 4 (2): 156-281;
    203. June.

Sloan, Samuel J.
    1903. Boy and cat. Forest and Stream 60: 110.

Smith, Edwin Dudley
    1890. New Mexico game galore. Forest and Stream 35: 309.

Smith, Joe Heflin
    1951. Calling all coyotes. Field and Stream 56 (5): 34, 35, 123-125.
    (Successful calling up of bobcat and coyotes by imitating squeal
    of a rabbit, to within gunshot range.—Tex.)

Smith, Capt. John
    1612. Travels and works of Capt. John Smith. Pp. 59-60. (Mentions the
    wildcat [retchu-mguoyes] among Virginia's mammals in describ-
    ing what he knew of a total of 17.)

Smith, Lou
    1927. John's wildcat. Forest and Stream 97: 440.

Smith, O. W.
    1910. Young wildcats. Forest and Stream 75: 331.

Smith, Roland W.
    1940. The land mammals of Nova Scotia. Amer. Midland Nat. 24 (1):
    213-241; 229. (On the abundance of bobcats in this province.)

Snyder, W. E.
    1902. A list with brief notes of the mammals of Dodge County, Wis-
    consin. Wis. Nat. Hist. Soc. Bull. 2: 114-126; 123.

Soper, J. Dewey
    1923. The mammals of Wellington and Waterloo Counties, Ontario. Jour.
    Mammal. 4 (4): 244-252; 252. November. (Bobcat occurs rarely in
    northern districts of these counties.)
    1946. Mammals of the northern Great Plains along the international
    boundary in Canada. Jour. Mammal. 27 (2): 139-140. (Distribution
    of bobcat in Manitoba-Saskatchewan, Canada.)

Spurrell, John A.
    1917. An annotated list of the mammals of Sac County, Iowa. Iowa Acad.
    Sci. Proc. 24: 273-284; 280.

Stalnaker, Wayne
    1952. Wildcats kill deer. West Virginia Conservation 15 (10): 42. January.

"Stanstead"
    1903. Vermont notes. Forest and Stream 61: 87. August 1.

Stebler, A. M.
   1939. An ecological study of the mammals of the Badlands and the Black Hills of South Dakota and Wyoming. Ecology 20 (3): 382-393; 389. July.

Steiger, H. R.
   1902. Pacific coast items. Forest and Stream 59: 344. November 1.

Stephens, Frank
   1906. California mammals. 351 pp., illus.; 210. (Bobcat distribution in California.)
   1914. Arid California and its animal life. Rept. Calif. Fish & Game Comn., pp. 1-5; 4.
   1921. An annotated list of the mammals of San Diego County, California. San Diego Soc. Nat. Hist. Trans. 3 (3): 41-56; 50. April 20.

Stephens, T. C.
   1922. Mammals of the lake region of Iowa. Okoboji Prot. Assn. Bull., pp. 47-64; 58. June.

Stevens, M. R.
   1912. Trapping in the Santa Ritas. Forest and Stream 79: 101-102. July 27.

Stevenson, Wm.
   1944. A frustrated bobcat. Yosemite Nat. Notes 23 (4): 43-44. April.

Stiles, C. W., and Clara Edith Baker
   1935. Key catalogue of parasites for Carnivora (cats, dogs, bears, etc.) with their possible Public Health importance. Nat. Inst. Health Bull. 163: 949, 1047. U. S. Treasury Dept. (Parasites found in and on the bobcat.)

Stone, Witmer
   1904. Notes on a collection of Californian mammals. Acad. Nat. Sci. Philadelphia Proc., pp. 586-591; 588.
   1908. The mammals of New Jersey. Ann. Rept. N. J. State Mus. for 1907, pt. 2. pp. 33-110, illus.; 110.

Stone, Witmer, and W. E. Cram
   1905. American mammals. Pp. 284-286. Doubleday, Page & Co., Garden City, N. Y.

Strecker, J. K., Jr.
   1910. Notes on the fauna of northwestern Texas. Annotated list of the mammals of Armstrong County. Baylor Univ. Bull. 13 (4-5): 21-26; 25. July-September.
   1924. The mammals of McLennan County, Texas. Baylor Univ. Bull. 27 (3): 3-20; 16. September.
   1926a. A check-list of the mammals of Texas, exclusive of the Sirenia and Cetacea. The Baylor Bull. 29 (3): 1-48; 17. August.
   1926b. The mammals of McLennan County, Texas. (Supplementary notes.) Contrib. Baylor Univ. Mus. No. 9, pp. 1-15; 7. October 15.
   1928. A preliminary list of the mammals of Caddo and DeSoto Parishes, Louisiana. Contrib. Baylor Univ. Mus. No. 15, pp. 10-15; 14. July.

Sturgis, Robert S.
   1939. The Wichita Mountains Wildlife Refuge. Chicago Naturalist 2 (1): 9-20; 12. March.

Suckley, Geo. A.
  1860.  Reports [on mammals]. Pac. R. R. Repts. 12 (book 2): 89-139; 90.
Sumner, E. L., Jr.
  1931.  An outline of the habits of the bobcat with some directions for
         trapping. Calif. Fish and Game 17 (3): 251-254, illus. July.
Surber, Thaddeus
  1932.  The mammals of Minnesota. Minnesota Game and Fish Dept.,
         St. Paul. 84 pp.; 56.
Surface, H. A.
  1901.  A thrilling experience. Forest and Stream 56: 244. March 30.
Sutton, George M.
  1928.  The mammals of Cook Forest. The Cardinal 2 (3): 76-81; 80.
         January.
Svihla, Arthur, and Ruth D. Svihla
  1933.  Mammals of Clallam County, Washington. The Murrelet 14 (2):
         37-41; 39. May.
Svihla, Arthur, and Ruth D. Svihla
  1940.  Annotated list of the mammals of Whitman County, Washington.
         The Murrelet 21 (3): 53-58; 55. September-December.
Svihla, Ruth D.
  1931.  Mammals of the Unita Mountain region. Jour. Mammal. 12 (3):
         256-265; 260. August.
Swan, James G.
  1857.  Three years residence in Washington Territory. 409 pp.; 28.
Swaney, O. N.
  1921.  Game in Indiana. Forest and Stream 91 (12): 554.
Swenk, Myron
  1920.  The birds and mammals of Nebraska. Nebraska Blue Book, pp.
         464-483; 482.
Swenson, Sidel B.
  1931.  The mammals of Minnesota. Fins, Feathers, and Fur, No. 94, pp.
         3-10; 8. February.
Taylor, W. P.
  1911.  Mammals of the Alexander Nevada Expedition of 1909. Univ.
         Calif. Pub. Zool. 7 (7): 205-307; 293. June 24.
  1919.  Notes on mammals collected principally in Washington and Cali-
         fornia between the years 1853 and 1874 by Dr. James Graham
         Cooper. Calif. Acad. Sci. Proc. (ser. 4) 9 (3): 69-121; 89.
  1922.  A distributional and ecological study of Mount Rainier, Washington.
         Ecology 3 (3): 214-236; 217. July.
  1943.  Food habits of Texas fur animals (except the gray fox). Texas
         Coop. Wildlife Research Unit, Quart. Rept. 3 (3): 23-27; 24.
         January-March.
Taylor, W. P., and W. T. Shaw
  1927.  Mammals and birds of Mt. Rainier National Park. U. S. Dept.
         Interior, Natl. Park Service, Washington. Mammals, pp. 1-249; 59.
  1929.  Provisional list of land mammals of the State of Washington. Chas.
         R. Conner Mus., Occas. Pap. No. 2, pp. 1-32; 14. December.

Thomas, Oldfield
1898. On new mammals from western Mexico and Lower California. Ann. & Mag. Nat. Hist. (ser. 7) 1 (1): 40-46; 42.

Thompson, Ben H.
1933. Toroweap the new Grand Canyon National Monument. Grand Canyon Nat. Notes 8 (4): 162-169; 168. July.

Thompson, Ernest Seton
1898. Mammals of the Yellowstone National Park. Recreation 8: 365-371; 371. May.

Thompson, Zadock
1842. Natural history of Vermont. P. 37.

Tibbits, J. S.
1900. Wild animals of Wayne County, Michigan. Mich. Pioneer & Hist. Coll. (1874-76) 1: 403-406.

Tonkin, George
1917. Little tiger. Oreg. Sportsman 5 (4): 273-274. October.

Townsend, Chas. H.
1888. Field notes on the mammals, birds, and reptiles of northern California. U. S. Natl. Mus. Proc. 10: 159-241; 189, 1887.

1912. Mammals collected by the "Albatross" Expedition in Lower California in 1911, with description of a new species. Amer. Mus. Nat. Hist. Bull. 31: 117-130; 130, illus. June. (On occurrence of bobcat.)

Travis, Chas. E., Jr.
1952. .22 wildcats and woodchucks. Pa. Game News 23 (4): 25. July.

"Tripod"
1911. Fight with a wildcat. Forest and Stream 76: 377.

Triska, F. W.
1916. Bounties paid in Harney County for predatory animals. Oreg. Sportsman 4 (2): 155-156. April.

True, Frederick W.
1891. The puma, or American lion: Felis concolor of Linnaeus. Ann. Rept. U. S. Natl. Mus. 1889: 591-608; 591.

Tucker, Wm. J.
1930. Texas yearbook on conservation of wildlife, 1929-30. Texas Game, Fish and Oyster Comn., pp. 21-42; 28, illus.

Turner, J. H.
1897. Noxious animals and animal pests. Fifth Rept. Dept. Agr., B.C. for 1895-96, pp. 1168, 1169.

"Typo"
1885. The game of Ventura. Forest and Stream 25: 147.

Tyrrell, J. B.
1889. Catalogue of the Mammalia of Canada exclusive of the Cetacea. Canad. Inst. Proc. (ser. 3) 6: 68-91; 72.

Ulmer, Fred A., Jr.
1941. Melanism in the Felidae, with special reference to the genus Lynx. Jour. Mammal. 22 (3): 285-288. (On the occurrence of two cases in Florida bobcats.)

U. S. Biological Survey
1924. [Bobcat attacked by coyote.] The Survey, Biol. Survey, U. S. Dept. Agr. 5 (3): 4. March 25.

Van Cleave, Harley J.
1953. Acanthocephala of North American mammals. Illinois Biological Monographs 23 (1, 2): 119, 122. Univ. Ill. Press, Urbana. (Occurrence of thorny-headed worms in bobcat.)

Van Hyning, T., and Frank C. Pellett
1911. An annotated catalogue of the Recent mammals of Iowa. Iowa Acad. Sci. Proc. 17: 211-218; 218.

"Vermonter"
1906. Vermont notes. Forest and Stream 66: 265. February 17.

Vestal, Elden H.
1938. Biotic relations of the wood rat (Neotoma fuscipes) in the Berkeley Hills [California]. Jour. Mammal. 19 (1): 1-36; 32. (Bobcat as an enemy of the woodrat.)

Visher, Stephen S.
1914. A preliminary report on the biology of Harding County, north-western South Dakota. S. Dak. Geol. Survey, Bull. No. 6, pp. 1-126; 90.

Voge, Marietta
1953. New host records for Mesocestoides (Cestoda: Cyclopes hylheden) in California. Amer. Midland Nat. 49 (1): 249-251.

Wack, Henry Wellington
1901. The sportsman's elysium of the south. Field and Stream 5 (12): 731-737; 734.

Wailes, B. L. C.
1854. Report on the agriculture and geology of Mississippi. Pub. by order of the Legislature, pp. 310-317; 315.

Walmsley, Harry R.
1915. Will the bobcat fight? Recreation and Outdoor World 52 (3): 135-136. March.

Warden, D. B.
1819. A statistical, political and historical account of the United States of America, from the period of their first colonization to the present day. 3 vols. Vol. 2, p. 411.

Warren, E. R.
1906. Mammals of Colorado. Colo. College Pub., Gen. Ser. No. 19, Sci. Ser. No. 46, vol. 11, pp. 225-274; 258.
1908. Further notes on the mammals of Colorado. Colo. Coll. Pub., Gen. Ser. No. 33, Eng. Ser. 1 (4): 59-90; 81.
1942. The mammals of Colorado: Their habits and distribution. Univ. Okla. Press, Norman. 330 pp.; 107-109 (Account of occurrence of two races of bobcats in Colorado: L. r. baileyi and L. r. uinta.)

Weaver, Richard Lee
1939. Attacks on porcupine by gray fox and wild cats. Jour. Mammal. 20 (3): 379. (In which two bobcats survive attacking porcupine.)

Webster, E. B.
1920. The king of the Olympics. Pub. by The Port Angeles Evening News, pp. 1-227; 143.

Welter, Wilfred A., and Dwight E. Sollberger
1939. Notes on the mammals of Rowan and adjacent counties in eastern Kentucky. Jour. Mammal. 20 (1): 77-81; 79.

Wentworth, Edward Norris.
1948. America's sheep trails, history personalities. Iowa State College Press, Ames, Iowa, Pp. 480-481. (Effects of bobcats and other predators on American sheep industry.)

Wenzel, Orrin J.
1911. Observation on the mammals of the Douglas Lake region, Cheboygan County, Michigan. 13th Rept. Mich. Acad. Sci., pp. 136-143; 142.

1912. A collection of mammals from Osceola County, Michigan. 14th Rept. Mich. Acad. Sci., pp. 198-205; 204.

Whitaker, Herman
1915. The wonderland of California. Natl. Geog. Mag. 28 (1): 57-104; 63.

Whitlow, Wayne B., and E. Raymond Hall
1933. Mammals of the Pocatello region of southeastern Idaho. Univ. Calif. Pub. Zool. 40 (3): 235-276; 250. September 30.

Wied, Maximilian Prinz zu
1841. Travels in the interior of North America 1832-1834. Coblenz, 2 vols. Vol. 1, p. 431; vol. 2, p. 87. (Notes regarding mammals about New Harmony, Indiana wherein bobcats are quite common 1832-33.)

1862. Verzeichniss der auf seiner Reise in Nord-Amerika beobachteten Saugethiere. Berlin, pp. 1-240, 4 pls. Reprinted from Arch. f. Naturg., vol. 27, pt. 1, pp. 181-288 [equals pp. 5-112 of reprint.] 1861; and Arch. f. Naturg., vol. 28, pt. 1, pp. 66-190 [equals pp. 113-237 of reprint.] 1862. Plates 1-3 in vol. 27, and 4 in vol. 28.

Williams, Samuel Cole
1928. Early travels in the Tennessee country 1540-1800 with introductions, annotations and index, pp. xi + 540; 519, illus. Johnson City, Tenn. (Probably first mention of bobcat in Tennessee December 12, 1799.)

1930. Beginnings of west Tennessee: In the land of the Chickasaws, 1541-1841 pp. xii + 331; 96, 180. Johnson City, Tennessee. (Occurrence of bobcat 1819 in western Tennessee.)

Williams, Samuel Howard
1928. Mammals of Pennsylvania. Univ. Pittsburgh, 163 pp.; 108.

Wilson, Gordon
1923. Birds of Calloway County, Kentucky. The Wilson Bull. 35 (3): 129-136; 129. September.

Winslow, R. H.
1906. A bear hunt in the El Capitan Mountains. Field & Stream 11 (7): 635-636.

Wolkenhauer, Hazel E.
1949a. Living with lynxes. Nature Magazine 42 (4): 176-177. April. (Bobcats as pets.)

1949b. Bobcat borders. Nat. Humane Review 37 (5): 11, 30, illus. May. (Bobcats in captivity, as pets, raised after 4 months old.)

Wood, Frank Elmer
   1910.  A study of the mammals of Champaign County, Illinois. Ill. State
          Lab. Nat. Hist. Bull. 8: 501-613; 567.
Wood, N. A.
   1911.  A biological survey of the Sand Dune region on the south shore
          of Saginaw Bay, Michigan. Mich. Geol. & Biol. Survey Pub. 4;
          309-312; 311.
   1914a. An annotated check-list of Michigan mammals. Univ. Mich. Mus.
          Zool., Occas. Pap. No. 4, pp. 1-13; 8.
   1914b. Results of the Shiras Expedition to Whitefish Point, Michigan.
          Mich. Acad. Sci., Rept. 16: 92-98; 96.
   1917.  Notes on the mammals of Alger County, Michigan. Univ. Mich.
          Mus. Zool., Occas. Pap. No. 36, pp. 1-8; 6.
   1922.  The mammals of Washtenaw County, Michigan. Univ. Mich. Mus.
          Zool., Occas. Pap. No. 123: 1-23; 14. July 10.
Wood, Norman A., and L. R. Dice
   1924.  Records of the distribution of Michigan mammals. Papers Mich.
          Acad. Sci., Arts, and Letters 3: 425-469; 446-447.
Woodbury, John L.
   1925.  Maine deer change habitat. Forest and Stream 95: 350.
Wright, A. H.
   1920.  The mammals of Otter Lake Region, Dorset, Ontario. Canadian
          Field Naturalist 34: 167.
Wright, Bruce S.
   1948.  Survival of the northeastern panther (Felis concolor) in New
          Brunswick. Jour. Mammal. 29 (3): 235-246; 240, illus. August.
          (Puma as enemy of bobcat.)
Young, Andrew W.
   1872.  History of Wayne County, Indiana. (Contains record of bobcats).
Young, C. J.
   1892.  Notes on the natural history of the Blue Mountain, County of
          Leeds, Ontario. Ottawa Nat. 6: 45-51; 47.
Young, Stanley P.
   1928.  Bobcat kills deer. Jour. Mammal. 9 (1): 64-65.
   1930.  Conquering wolfdom and catdom. Southwest Wilds and Waters
          2 (1): 6-7, 47, illus. January. Oklahoma City, Okla. (The wolf and
          bobcat in Oklahoma.)
   1931.  Hints on bobcat trapping. U. S. Dept. Agr., Bur. Biological Survey
          Leaflet 78: 1-6, illus. June.
   1940.  "Catnipping" our big cats. Western Sportsman 4 (6): 4-8, 4, illus.,
          May.
   1941.  Hints on bobcat trapping. U. S. Dept. Int., Fish and Wildlife
          Service Circ. 1: 1-6, illus.
   1946.  Sketches of American wildlife. Pp. xii + 143; 50, illus. Caxton
          Printers, Caldwell, Idaho.
   1950.  Rabies in the wild. Amer. Forests 56 (8): 26, 30, 42, illus.
Youngblood, C. Dewey
   1950.  Tracking the cat family in lower Tenaya Canyon. Yosemite Nature
          Notes 29 (11): 109-111, illus. November.

# INDEX

189